A Voice From The Ranks
of the Scots Guards

Norry Hughes

AuthorHouse™ UK Ltd.
500 Avebury Boulevard
Central Milton Keynes, MK9 2BE
www.authorhouse.co.uk
Phone: 08001974150

© 2009 Norry Hughes. All rights reserved.

No part of this book may be reproduced, stored in a retrieval system, or transmitted by any means without the written permission of the author.

First published by AuthorHouse 9/10/2009

ISBN: 978-1-4389-9259-4 (e)
ISBN: 978-1-4389-9258-7 (sc)

This book is printed on acid-free paper.

A Voice From The Ranks of the Scots Guards

"…it is man, creative, mysterious, and unpredictable, who is the proper subject of the historian, not the subterranean collective urges of the spirit of the age or of the 'needs' of an as yet non-existent society."

- *David Watkin, Morality and Architecture*

There has not been a single day since before the birth of Christ that the Island of Britain has been at peace with itself, or its neighbours, and as the World developed and diversified so did the hostilities. So war becomes the eternal British legacy to its peoples.

- *Norry Hughes Sevastopol*

Dedications

Oleg Smirnov, A Journalist and friend reporting for the HTC TV Network Sevastopol, who from 2001 has supported my personal campaign up at Cathcart Hill.

Maria Ivanova, Guide and official worker for the German 2nd WW Cemetery, Sevastopol. A dignified place of remembrance for the German nationals who come here looking for the graves of their fallen from the 2nd World War.

The neglected British Monument at Cathcart Hill, and now to be denied, and forgotten, by the British Embassy in Kiev.

This publication will keep it remembered as the official British Monument opened in September 1993.

About the Author

Norman Walter Hughes was born, July 1939 in Walthamstow, East London. He had arrived in time to join yet another World War, just a short generation after the carnage of the first one. Young Norman survived that 2nd war however, and went on to pass the 11plus examination. Sometime after finishing his secondary education he went on to join the Scots Guards as a 'Boy entrant'.

The idea of joining the 'Guards' was all about the physical challenge, for he was quite satisfied with his academic standard at that time. Plus the fact that as even as a born 'Cockney' he was joining the 'Scots Guards' rather than the 'Grenadier's'. This ethnic peculiarity break was of no consequence neither, for Norman has neither concerned himself with any feelings one way or another with ethnic beliefs, nor difference's in appearances. He was then to experience service life with the Scots Guards between 1956-1976, at the time when the Empire was breaking up and down, and is currently completing his memoirs which covers those two decades of army service.

In 1978 Norry returned to the classroom at Moray House College of Further Education in Edinburgh for two years in order to qualify as a Community Education Worker. Having qualified, he served on the management staff of Community Education Centres in and around Edinburgh throughout the next four years. In 1984 he resigned from the Community Education Service to become a self employed property developer.

By 1989, just five years after quitting local government, Norry owned and managed his own Guest House and a Hotel in Edinburgh. He sold his business in 1999 at the age of sixty, having decided to take early retirement.

Norry initially retired to Cyprus in 2000, but then moved to take up permanent residence in Sevastopol in 2002, where he now lives 'happy ever after', making himself useful as a Crimea War researcher, writer, and sometimes guide around Sevastopol and onto the battlefields. He also spends time at local Schools and Universities where he supports English speaking tutorial groups.

Norry is now completing his next two books;

'What a Way to Carry On Ambassador'

A caustic black humoured voyage through his negative relationship with both the British Embassy in Kiev, and the British government in London during his 8 years of life in Sevastopol. This book will also cover the complete story of the neglect at the British Monument on Cathcart Hill by those responsible for its upkeep

'20 years with the Scots Guards'

Covering the period from August 1956 to August 1976, when Norry served with the Scots Guards, and No1 Guards Independent Parachute Company.

Acknowledgements

Acknowledgements will be signified throughout the book's length. They include those who have supported this publication and what it sets out to achieve, and also to those who have helped, (and hindered), my evolutionary and revolutionary progress since I came to live in Sevastopol, and then set about putting this updated journal together.

With this assertion in mind I shall draw the reader's attention to the two most encyclopedic modern publications on the researched detailed history of the Crimea War so far published. I feel I should draw people's attention to these works for they comprise writings of skilled and professional writers, individuals well versed in the art of writing for the status quo, which has always been the engineer for more of the same please, and it is in that manner that they do their work well rather than to advocate any form of much needed change in the present day government of the 'United Kingdom',

CRIMEA

The Great Crimean War 1854-1856

Author Trevor Royle Published 1999

And

THE CRIMEAN WAR

A CLASH OF EMPIRES

IAN FLETCHER AND NATALIA ISHCHENKO

Published 2004

A main acknowledgement is to explain the method in which I have decided to amend and update the original Sir Frederick Maurice documented and published history of the Scots Fusilier Guards unfortunate adventures during the invasion of the Crimea 1854-1856. The original regimental documented history, has been a closed book after its publication in London,1934. Perhaps it was read by the self interested few of the Scots Guards establishment at that time, but then to be gently laid to rest. It has now been not so gently reincarnated by myself.

I decided to fuse the original regimental history with the updates by taking a leaf from the *Times* Newspaper precedent as it openly, and continually, chided Kinglake after the Crimea War had concluded and the newspaper had used hindsight, and the Kinglake history, to make further sense, or perhaps sidetracking the Kinglake journal into another lateral perspective from the historian's documented work of the Crimea campaign. The *Times* had reviewed the Victorian historian's writings during the invasion of the Crimea, to the death of Lord Raglan in June 1855

I have also taken excerpts from the battle of the Alma, from Colonel E I Totleben's publication of 1864, which was also reviewed by the *Times* which takes to task the Russian perspective of the Crimea Campaign. The Totleben book was first published in France, and in the French Language. Apparently, and according to the *Times*, it was to become a scarce and expensive publication.

One piece of modern good news however was the single generous and time consuming gesture from Major (Retd) Ron Clemison MBE, the Social and Welfare Officer at RHQ, Scots Guards at that time during 2000. He was kind enough to send me an A4 Photostat copy of the relevant chapters of the Scots Guards History by Sir F Maurice at my request, This gesture which began the battles rolling towards my corner in Cyprus, enabled me to plan my next retirement adventure to the City of Sevastopol. Unfortunately however this spirit of consensus between myself and the RHQ of the Scots Guards was not to continue once I found the British Monument at Cathcart Hill lying in forgotten neglect, and my former regiment's part to play in its downfall.

There was also the matter in which the Scots Guards RHQ, and senior ranks of the Scots Guards Association, did not seem able, nor particularly interested in rallying the members around the colours for a commemorative re-run of the story of the Alma battle in time for the 150th commemoration of 2004, in which the regiment claims to have won four Victoria Crosses. The idea being to hold a regimental 'Alma Gathering' up on the 'Great Redoubt', the scene of the Scots Fusilier Guards misfortune during that first battle against the Russian's at the River Alma.

The regimental history sent to me in Cyprus was to also serve the purpose of supporting the intention of my initial visit to Sevastopol, as I wished to view the war not only from the larger picture scenario, but also from the Scots Fusilier Guards perspective. This regimental history was then to become very important to my early endeavours to not only research the Crimea War, but also to answer some of the questions that were to arise as I made my way around the sites of the Allied Invasion of the Crimea in 1854, with the Regimental History in hand, and the Scots Guards Regiment in close heart and mind. However the situation soon arose that the regimental history had information gaps, causing this researcher some confusion and disappointment. The shortcoming was to leave me with a sense of frustration, for during my initial research, the Scots Guards history seemed unable to fit into the larger picture of the Crimea War, almost as if the Scots Fusilier Guards were fighting a war within a war, turning their part to play from the main event into a shortened regimental sideshow?

Another sideline acknowledgement could be helpful to the prospective Crimea War tourer who arrives in Sevastopol for the business of researching and visiting the Crimea War sites. For when the sun is shining, and the air conditioned bus journey in and around the sunny Sevastopol District is comfortable, and very sociable, a large piece of the Crimea War jigsaw may well disappear. That disappearing act may well be the ground that the bus travels over, and where the war was fought, for a crucial element that the opposing armies had to contend with, namely the ground, then becomes lost to the visitor sat relaxed in their well heeled coach. If anyone is serious about researching the complete saga of the invasion of the Crimea, then seeing, and trying to understand the ground it was fought over is a fundamental beginning, and must be continued throughout the visit. Anything less is just not on, for the ground was to provide the stage for the many actors in the larger theatre of the Crimea War saga.

There was however one very special book which was very kindly sent to me by a Welsh lady named Bridget Geoghegan, whose ancestor actually rode in the Charge of the Light Brigade. The book's is titled, *Thomas Brassey, Railway Builder & Canada Works, Birkenhead,* by John Brassey, published by John Miller (UK) Ltd, Wirral Cheshire in 1993, tells the full story of the major achievement of the Building of the Crimea Railway, and built at cost price to the British Government. Though it is an interesting fact that to tell the story of the building of the Crimea Railway, the company had to write and publish the book themselves, who along with Timothy Gowing should now be acknowledged as having made this effort.

But most of all I acknowledge my own tenuous, and detailed search for the plentiful supply of useful information over the ground, through the many books, and into the internet. My wanderings over the ground the war was fought normally in the company of those good people who had taken the time and trouble to be in touch so that I may support their visits to the main places where the conflict took place. I may now thank those good people who have facilitated my many interesting forays into Sevastopol, and its hinterland, in my personal learning curve. In that respect I mention two former comrades from the Scots Guards who came to visit. Alan Ward and Allan Hendry, both visited here in Sevastopol during the early days of my residency in this fine city, both of whom were appalled up at Cathcart Hill, but when returned to Britain and asked the relevant questions of the RHQ and the Association, were to be quickly silenced.

Perhaps the main acknowledgement however could be to the intellectual advantage to be gained over many of the sinews of British government intolerance by the advent of the Internet. A facility which provides a quality and depth of information, and where the most humble of citizens may take on the arrogant and stupid mindsets of the ancient form of British government. A governmental process which no longer may pass the test of time, but should gently go to rest in exchange for something better that works within the new rule book which has been created by the emerging Globalisation, multi ethnic culture revolution which is happening all around the World at this time. The technical resource of the Internet now in place is to also be deserving of another acknowledgement, for it is now providing and proving the communication technology not only for researchers and whatever may turn them on, but also for the awakening of the true path of Global Democracy, and where every little input will find its place and its part, therefore ensuring that every person has a part to play, and just to leave it to any form of archaic government is surely a present crime against the progress of humanity, for perhaps the time has really arrived when politicians may not be trusted with the mission of leading and managing constituents without some further guidance?

I may also take this opportunity to pass onto the reader the bad feeling which still exists between the Local government here in Sevastopol and the British Embassy in Kiev. But that is another story for another sad day of British imperialism and its legacy. Which Includes the contribution this book attempts to make, along with the many e-mails which have gone before, and which receive very few replies, for anything the British Government, or their Embassy in Kiev may offer is but evidence against them, so it is they who now offer silence as the governing option. That is the best they may do for all other patronizing options they tried to offer have long been silenced.

Perhaps another acknowledgement that I should place on record. In his 2000 publication *'The Great Crimea War'* in which the respected Edinburgh Author, and Journalist, Trevor Royle, takes an interesting, and very plausible written path from the Crimea War being a main causal of the 1st Great War 1914-1918, then through the vengeful evils of the *'Versailles Treaty'* which had disadvantaged Germany and its peoples, who then through little fault of their's had to suffer, and continue to endure post 1st WW, and thus ever onwards towards the inevitable rise of Hitler and the Nazi doctrine.

Next on the agenda, came the 2nd World War, which was then to lead directly to the Soviet Iron Curtain, and thus the 'Cold War'.

All this providing and acknowledging evidence that the British Government's folly in taking on the futility of the Invasion of the Crimea was to stretch even unto or own times, and no doubt beyond, for we must remember that the troubles and difficulties in the Balkans, elsewhere and further to the East still rumbles on. However I trust that this update may show the way through history to the present, and into the future, for that is another sacrosanct aim of this publication.

That is if you look for it?

I also say thanks to the Irex Centre, and the Tolstoy Library in Sevastopol who have both tried to understand what I am about with interest and support, whilst not quite understanding what this update is all about. Perhaps they may, given time and conversion of this publication from the English to the Russian language. They may then realise that this update legacy may also serve some of their present and future interests and purposes.

I may also take this opportunity to again thank all those who have stimulated my research by being led around the sites by myself, whilst they have asked probing questions, and then entered into debate around the subject matter, plus all of the lateral thinking that should go along with it.

A further acknowledgement to myself is that I do this thing for purely altruistic reasons stemming from the 'noble savage' mentality and philosophy of neighbourly Public Relations reasoning's, and should there be any financial net profit from the sale of this publication, then I will seek the support of the British Embassy, Kiev, and the Sevastopol Authority in spending that money on an equal share agreement. An arrangement with these other two Government agencies in providing improvement and long term maintenance and security to the shared history of the Crimea War Battle Sites in and around Sevastopol.

Especially at Inkerman which is now being used by private contractors for a rubbish dump, and where some of the important areas of the Inkerman battle are now covered by secondary 'jungle'!

Contents

About the Author. vii

Acknowledgements ix

Introduction xviii

A Personal Tribute to Timothy Gowing the First Voice from the Ranks. 1

The Complex Relationship of the British 'Three Estates' . 8

An Introduction to the Scots Guards Regimental History 14

Profile; Major-General Sir Frederick Barton Maurice . . . 18

Advancing into the Crimea Regimental Campaign History 22

Purchase of Commissions 27

Crimea War, Beginnings and the Endings 31

Sir F Maurice Regimental History begins. 37

The Journey of the Scots Fusilier Guards to the East . . 41

Ravages of the Cholera and of Politics 55

His Royal Highness Prince George, Duke of Cambridge 72

A Very Special Cabinet Meeting. 83

A *'Dormant Commission'* 89

The Dog 'Bob' 95

Sir Colin Campbell, of the Highland Brigade 110

The Highland Brigade in the Crimea 117

The Minie Rifle 125

The French participation in the invasion of the Crimea 134

The Landing at Calamity Bay and the advance to the Alma 137

The Battle for the Alma Continues 148

Lieut-Colonel F. Haygarth 163

Captain R. Gipps. Account of the Alma Battle. 165

Lord Wantage's account of the Battle of the Alma 169

Battle of the Alma, a Russian Chronicle. 174

Inkerman and Sebastopol. 187

The Battle of Inkerman 193

Florence Nightingale arrives at Scutari 209

William Howard Russell 216

Inkerman and Sevastopol Continued 219

Richard Cobden MP 224

Outside Sebastopol 250

Building the Balaclava Railway 254

The Spring Offensive 265

The Final Battle of the Tchernaya, Retchka 268

The Final Hours 280

The Warriors Final Parade 286

The British Scandal at Cathcart Hill 292

Conclusions, Considerations. and Consequences . . . 295

Introduction

The publishing of this updated journal has opened a long awaited window of opportunity for myself to question a certain important part of British history, and a British Guards regiment's part to play within it.

But first let us begin from an understanding of a Historical point to note;

The Great Storm of November 14th, followed by the worst winter ever recorded in the area of the Southern Crimea took place in 1854. Therefore the problems besetting the Allied forces, and especially the British contingent, were to be made even worse by the extreme and harsh conditions of that particular winter, setting many more challenges to an invasion that was only 'half cocked' from its conception to its implementation, and then on throughout the campaign itself.

Then there is the question of who won the Crimea War?

Many writers have given the false impression that somehow Britain was the winner of the Crimea War?

Whereas the research I have carried out during the last 8 years confirms that the British army was to emerge from that war as very much the losers, and with a bloody nose militarily and politically. The army did however learn some hard fought, though superficial lessons for the future, which I do not think they were ever to put into practice fully, though some superficialities were to be put into place.

The abolishment of the purchasing of commissions as one example. And I deal with this act of privilege later in the book. Plus the advancement of the Military Academy as initiating 'excellence' is another. However the main and hard lessons to be learned were to be found much closer to England than to the armies ability, or lack of it in the Crimea or any seat of academic learning, and sadly have still not been learned to present times

To make this point clear I have selected recorded information which serves to provide some of the updates. This information which I have added to the history reveals that the appalling administration and incompetence that the Crimea War has become noted for, was not all the fault of the British Army of the East, nor even governmental neglect and casual management back in Britain, but actually arose from the inability of the 'complex relationship' of the 'three estate' systems, and process of the British form of State administration to govern within a natural public arena and environment, failings which went onto produce;

A Cause and Effect syndrome

Some of the main facts of this common syndrome of past and present British government's are further bought to light as the history is updated. Though only as they attach themselves directly, and politically indirectly, adding to the many troubles of the Scots Fusilier Guards experiences in the Crimea.

Another point to note is the anomaly of the Naval Brigade who were to suffer far less than its army partners during the harsh campaign in the Crimea, and whether on ship, or land, seemed to be able to organize themselves on a higher level than their soldier counterparts?

One well known example of the 'three estate', administration is that of the infamous 'Charge of the Light Brigade', where the two Cavalry commanders, Lord's Lucan and Cardigan, had bred such contempt in the mind of Capt. Edward Nolan that the chain of events which led to the action begun from his handing over of the 4th order to Lord Lucan without giving due explanation, and Lucan not demanding it? Captain Nolan was an experienced and professional soldier, who had seen active service in India, whereas the two Lords were from the titled ranks of the British aristocracy where the 'purchase of commissions' had brought them their ranks, leading to their commands in the field. Once there in command positions the army commander Lord Raglan could do very little about the problem of the two Lords and their self induced personal acrimony, one with the other. Mainly because of their personal, and family connections to the Monarchy and all that went with it.

Another circumstance which caused disquiet amongst the line regiments was the situation where a NCO from the Guards being offered a commission which was never to be offered or served in their own ranks of the guards, but always in a line regiment giving the impression that this new officer is good for the regiment he has been passed onto, but not good enough for his own guards regiment?!

Therefore this situation of the crisis management followed by incompetence displays itself for all to see and wonder at the charge to the Russian guns, buying and selling of commissions, and the handing out of certain commissions, and all as the direct result of the complex relationship of the three estate model of British governance. This ancient fault which in its working of 'just being there', was to seriously weaken the workings of the British Army at the Crimea war rather more than support it.

Many of the same inherent problems in the British administration are still with us to this day, producing similarities which are still part of the makeup of the ever ongoing process of crisis management, and then incompetence, of the British government. The book makes the point that this poor state of affairs will continue until the British unconstitutional form of archaic government is modified for an up to date and simplified form that is transparent, and seen to work in the modern era of continuing globalization, for without doubt a written British Constitution will bring a fresh form of administration and management that can work for the people by the people, all moving towards the pursuit of happiness, and with the written British Constitution to show them the way.

Whilst updating the regimental history at salient points, the journal also takes you on a voyage of discovery finding answers to known mysteries from the Crimea War, such as the hidden reason for the 'Dormant Commission' being handed to General Sir George Cathcart, though it will be forever denied by those closest to the affair.

The journal also now includes mysteries and State secrets that have been glossed over by generations of 'establishment' writers, for the very reasons that the history updates within the pages that follow considers these mysteries as part and parcel of the misshapen, and present British State which the establishment writers have taken care to stay clear of criticising.

It has also been quoted 'that history has been written by the winners'. However I dispute that claim when it comes to the many books which base themselves on the history written from the Invasion of the Crimea, 1854-1856. In my opinion and reading experience, Crimea war testimonials tend to strongly reflect the misery that stemmed from the many dreadful problems which arose, and always from the soldiers point of view, and normally from the officers close to their 'Fortnum and Mason' hampers making play in their letters on the hardships suffered by the rank and file, though were in essence making it sound as if it was they who were also suffering, but could still send sympathetic signals back to Britain of how they were also in dire straits, but were holding on and not giving up. Therefore by using the myth 'that from adversity, comes victory' line, to protect the inherent weakness of the crisis management and incompetence by adding it to a brief summing up of 'great effort through adversity to victory', and similar distractions, and so confuse the researcher and reader who the winners and losers actually were.

Therefore all adding to the 'Cause and Effect' syndrome which disputes history when it comes to the selection of the winners from the losers, for Instead of making sound judgements around the essential lessons to be learned, and then passed on by the true historian rather more than the 'novelist' historian, who is writing for the profit motive and needs to sensationalise the history to satisfy the prevailing needs of the readership, rather more than those of the true researcher or historian who is seriously looking for lessons to be learned and for truth to be the serious winner..

The Crimea War was in factual terms to become another lost cause in a string of British colonial adventures, and history confirms that fact, furthermore Britain became all time losers in the Crimea from that time to this.

No doubt in time to come regimental histories will also talk in glowing terms of their present time invasions of Iraq and Afghanistan and turn those miserable affairs into a winners job lot as well?

Neither does the Scots Guards written history of the Crimea War contribute any credit for skills and lessons learned by the regiment during the time of the short but terrible conflict, when in fact there were lessons to be learned and skills developed, though only to be lost as the Battalion returned to its sentry boxes and ceremonial parades, and forget the soldiering lessons learned in the Crimea.

It has also come to sadly pass that this Crimea War history, (which also belongs to all the other countries and military forces and governments' involved as a shared history), had then been passed on to those with a financial or family self interest, and then passed on yet again to provide for further self interest, in all terms., but especially, political, militarily and financial profit.

In effect this prolonged manipulative subjectivity taken from many of the writings, films, TV documentaries manifested since has guaranteed that these past 'records' have been able to persuade the people of Britain, and the past British Empire, to believe in a continuous self fulfilling set of historical victorious prophesies. These past 'truths' that now need to be seriously questioned.

I also question those many others who have no time for the true historical records and how it may reflect into their own times, but instead write for financial gain, parochial comfort, and little else. But in so doing conform, and confirm the basic form of the British establishment writer. Thus maintaining the false status quo of 'Great Britain', the winner in all wars, and gloss over the majority that have been lost with disastrous effect for the families of Britain through the ages of empire building.

In conclusion, I now need to know and understand the reasons why the great efforts made by those unfortunate enough to be serving in the ranks of the Scots Fusilier Guards during the Invasion of the Crimea, 1854-1856, were to be let down by the privileged few responsible for the publishing of their very simplistic regimental history covering the invasion of the Crimea in 1854.

And then there is the present time question of the total neglect of the British Monument at Cathcart Hill to be answered for by the Scots Guards RHQ.

Questions which reach back to the monuments beginnings in 1991, in liaison with the British Foreign and Commonwealth Office, Crimea War Research Society, and others of the British establishment, all working in unison with the Russian builders. These 'officials' from the 'Great and the Good' of British Hierarchy, including members of the British Royal family.

These serve as perhaps the best demonstration of how the complete British Administration cannot even be bothered, and certainly not trusted, to raise a Memorial Monument to their own 'regimental family' outside of their homeland of Britain.

Though sadly this monument at Cathcart Hill is a mainly British forces affair, and yet not any of the many RHQs will question the British Foreign and Commonwealth office on the issue?

Let me now shift my gaze from the profiteers, charlatans, monarchists, politicians and many others who have been personally enriched, or perchance put at their ease by history written by the 'winners', to the many who suffered as a result, and Timothy Gowing was one of these unfortunates. However he was man enough to leave his own record of events.Therefore ensuring that the the Timothy Gowing Legacy is strongly engrained within this updated historical record. Timothy Gowing was a good man, a good soldier and a good Christian. He suffered throughout his life like so many others of his times from the effects of bad British government. He was to suffer in England, then as a soldier during the Crimea War, and then to India, and when he finally returned to live in England he continued to suffer. He suffered in silence and in dignity all of his 74 years as a direct result of bad and non-caring British Government.

In life Timothy was to demonstrate in full the ethics of the stoic. However these days we no longer have to suffer in silence and with dignity, but may speak out in an effort to change that which stems from bad and uncaring government to that which it should be. For by staying silent along with the dignified ingredients and supplements suits the ineptitude of continuing British government's, whilst doing the individual, nor serving the people any more democratic rights.

I too have suffered throughout my life from the same badly managed British government,.

I was fated to be born just two months before the beginning of the 2nd WW. My parents families were both to suffer in the 1st WW, and I was to go through my young life feeling the effects of the Blitz, a broken up family life during the war, evacuation, and then onto a broken home as a post war bonus, and I was just six years old.

Later on in my young life joining the army was an option that was to settle me down to begin to live my life in an orderly manner. But it was not to be as easy as that, for the parochial 'social contract' demanded of a 'Guardsman' carries much responsibility, an inborn courage and unpleasantness from the complications and pretence that the military life brings along with it. The 'Much Ado About Nothing' mentality and process of the making of a Guardsman, as I now label the experience of my Army life with the Scots Guards.

The books title, and the introduction may then prepare the reader for what is to be found in its contents. For within the title and the book, I pay a silent tribute to a very distinctive Crimea War soldier who in my estimation emerges from the terrible human tragedy of the Crimea War still in Christian faith, and remaining loyal to the British establishment at that time. But then again he had very little choice but to conform.

Once upon a time, both as a serving Scots Guardsmen, and then when discharged, I tried to uphold the same inner core values on myself as Timothy Gowing, and even at this time of 2009 and in my 70th year, I still continue my Crimea War research, and by maintaining the crusade at Cathcart Hill will uphold my Christian Values,

Unfortunately the British Government have no Christian thoughts on their very own form of the 'Christian' folly crumbling away outside Sevastopol. A folly of their making which at some time they will have to answer for.

However I now have a personal let out clause, for now happily settled in Sevastopol, I see myself as European, and greater Europe is where my hopes and ambitions for future good government may well come from. Unfortunately, and like Timothy Gowing I shall not be around to appreciate its coming. However unlike Timothy Gowing I may well help good government along the road.

And that is what this book also sets out to achieve

Timothy Gowing continued to stand by his sense of character values by being proud to be born British and Christian, but then again is this not a praise worthy trait of many generations of British people? Or is it because they know no better than to just stay the course and suffer in silence and dignity, and therefore have been taken for granted by many successive British Governments.

Well, this particular voice from the ranks will now tell the story of the Crimea War as it fits into my scheme of things past, rather than just staying still and saying nothing about the cheapskate job by the Regiment as it has prepared its own version of the Crimea War as applied to itself, with no real thought or consideration given to those who fought and died during its time hard fought. Neither has the writing of this book been an easy task for myself, for the information now available reference the Crimea War is bountiful. Plus there is indeed a difficult situation of choice, flavour and sense of distinction and importance in the material to choose from to bring the regimental history up to parr. Making it compatible with the subjective selection of the vast amount of information now available, especially via the Internet.

My approach therefore has been to select the information which I believe would be relevant to the present day Scots Guards family readership, but based upon the experiences of the British Army investing Sevastopol. Neither have I inserted some regimental movements and other statistics of the period covered, for those items do not change, nor update, and will always remain as they were at that time, and therefore I have left them in the original F Maurice History. I have however included some important statistics from the regimental history as part of this update

I also believe that I have given the reader access to information which has never before been put together in this very unique fashion. But which in form adheres closely to the connection between the Regiment, its serving and former members, its relationships with monarchy, military and government, and the history of the invasion of the Crimea as it now stands, and is perhaps understood in present day political and military environments. If the reader then understands the movement of their personal use of history as a means of changing the present, and then challenging the future, then this publication may also serve to bring fresh thinking to the constitutional role of the British Government and its many Departments and Offices, and by the people these authorities govern.

I have also tried to keep the contents simple, for like most of the 'smaller' British imperialist and colonial fought wars of the 19th century, and then viewed with long term hindsight, its ingredients become easier to comprehend, place in context, and then pass onto the many interested readers and historical activists of these present times, so that may join the quest for historical truth leading to an enlightened future.

There are other explanations as to why I believe it is necessary to publish this book, and I cover most of these within its pages.

There is however one other focused crucial element in the making of this publication. It is an attempt to bring some Democratic light to the darkened corridors of the British Imperialist Embassy in Kiev, and to the local authority in Sevastopol around the issues of maintaining the Crimea War Sites, and also to finally solving the problems of the British Monument at Cathcart Hill.

A mutual issue of interest between the two authorities which has been ongoing since 1991.

If that mission at Cathcart Hill could then be accomplished, I along with this publication may be said to have contributed something worthwhile in breaking a deadlock between the Russian builders of the British Monument and the British paymasters. A disagreement which has now been going the rounds at the British Embassy in Kiev, the Scots Guards

RHQ, Crimea War Research Society, and the Sevastopol local authority since 1992.

Another of the sideline nasties that has raised its ugly head has been the fact that the Sevastopol local authority have been trying to sell the crumbling ruins of the Cathcart Hill memorial monument for some years past as a 'Tourist Attraction'. They have construed this aim in order to retrieve some of their financial losses incurred during the building of the Monument and then the attached debate which has gone on since?

It would seem to me however that the British Embassy in Kiev welcomes this sideshow, for if it succeeds the British Foreign and Commonwealth Office in London and other privileged bystanders will smile gratefully, and then continue to walk by on the other side. Adding yet another unholy chapter to the opening of the 'Kuchma' monument of 2004 to commemorate the 150th year of the beginning of the invasion of the Crimea. The opening of the new monument which led to an attempt by the British Embassy in Kiev to lose the British monument at Cathcart Hill in preference to the new one built by the Ukraine administration, and in close discussion with the local authority in Sevastopol.

Added to this 'showing the flag' misplaced effort of the British Ambassador at that time, was the theatrical display of the British warship HMS York, docked in the harbour close by to remind the Russian's that this was a peaceful mission. Such is the manner in which the British government do their business in Sevastopol.

In conclusion to the introduction; it will be very quickly noted that I have tried to merge the updates in with the original manuscript to allow the reader, or researcher, to continue on as with one continual work, thus alleviating the business of jumping around between the original work and the updates.

Just as the 'Times' would have liked Kinglake's later editions to his original volume to appear

And my thoughts on the ruins of the British Monument to suit this introduction;

The British Memorial Monument up at Cathcart Hill is a British Monument, which then makes it a total British responsibility.
Norry Hughes Sevastopol Summer 2009.

A Personal Tribute to Timothy Gowing the First Voice from the Ranks

How many more are there?

This personal Update is a tribute to the Memory of Timothy Gowing 7th Fusiliers in whose footsteps I now follow.

Timothy Gowing his life and times: A Brief History of A Hard Fought Christian Life 1834-1908

No collection of Crimea War records made up from any private, public or personal library would be complete without a copy of Timothy Gowing's book, *'A Voice from the Ranks'*. Or at least a print out from the World Wide Web from the original publication. As far as I am aware Timothy Gowing was the only soldier from the ranks that wrote fully of his entire experiences directly from the Crimea campaign. He wrote honestly and well, and as if he was speaking to his listeners or readers. He would write his notes as soon after the event, or situation, as possible whilst they were from fresh from experienced knowledge. Timothy also continued on doing his utmost to remain balanced between loyalty to both his Regiment, and the wider British public interest at that time. He was also to bring to light some of the darker human tragedies of that ill thought out spectre of Victorian Gunboat Diplomacy.

He was a lifelong practicing Christian in manner and deed, born in Halesworth, Suffolk on the 5th April 1834. His Father was the local Baptist Minister. The family later moved to Norwich in 1839 and the young Timothy was there educated. His Father was to remain as the Minister of Pitt Street Baptist Church for the next 24 years. Meanwhile the young and fast maturing Timothy developed an interest in a military career, and was determined to become a soldier. Early in 1854 he enlisted in the Royal Fusiliers as a Private soldier. He was then 20 years of age.

His recruit training took him to Manchester, and then on to Winchester. Having completed his training he was immediately posted to the Crimea. During his time in the Crimea Timothy was to be engaged in the major conflicts of the Alma, Inkerman, and the investment of Sevastopol. After Inkerman he was to write of the supreme efforts of the Guards at the Sandbag battery. He also served at both of the major assaults of the Redan during the campaign.

Whilst serving in the Crimea campaign he was promoted through the junior NCO ranks and finally to Sergeant. Wounded on several occasions he was always to return to his parent unit and continue the fight against the Russians in Sevastopol. He was to rise to the rank of acting RSM by 1859 and then offered the opportunity of a commission in one of the Sepoy regiments whilst in India but declined the offer, preferring to remain with the Royal Fusiliers. In 1862 he was offered a commission in the Royal Fusiliers but once more he declined, this time on financial grounds. He did not think that he would be able to support his growing family (of five children in four years of marriage) on an officer's pay. In 1864, having completed a ten-year enlistment, he re-enlisted for a further term, to give himself a full twenty-one years' service and thus qualify for a pension. He remained in India during this time.

A Personal Tribute to Timothy Gowing the First Voice from the Ranks

His family was all but wiped out by cholera in 1869: only one child of the eight survived. The other seven died on the same day. His wife also died in India and when Gowing returned to England in 1876, at the age of 42, he took only two of the children born to him in India. Gowing went to live in Southport and re-married, fathering another seven children; his second wife died in 1890. His third wife, Elizabeth, survived her husband.

Between returning to England and his death, Gowing lived in a number of different towns in Lancashire and Yorkshire. He had his account of the Crimean War and his service in India during the Mutiny published privately and sold them to office and factory workers in Lancashire: other than his army pension of 2/6d a day, this was his only income.

Timothy Gowing died on 3 February 1908 at the age of 74.

I now point out a personal case of history updated to show just how close history may remain to us, though we feel and see nothing, but this does not stop the understanding that those days past still reflect onto our own times and conditions.

Private Edwin Hughes, 13th light dragoons died May 1927 aged 96. he was buried in Blackpool with full military honours

Timothy and Edwin served in different arms, one an infantryman, the other a cavalryman, but both on the strength of the British Army in the Crimea, and now both returned to take up their legacies in this publication

Trooper Edwin Hughes was the last surviving member of the 673? unfortunates, who rode in the charge of the

A Personal Tribute to Timothy Gowing the First Voice from the Ranks

Light Brigade at Balaclava in 1854. He died in 1927. I then came on the scene with my birth in 1939, so just 12 years had past between us.

This point demonstrates to me how close generations may be to each other as history and wars pass us by, from this one example from the Crimea War to the 2nd World War, and now to my life here in Sevastopol, so history turns a full circle from one unrelated 'Hughes' to another, and from, and now returned to Sevastopol.

It is also just possible that there are persons alive today who actually knew of someone who had fought in the Crimea Campaign at that time? Another example from my family archives. My son Brian followed after me as part of Britain's overstretched armed forces to take an unprepared role in active service in the Falklands with the Royal Fleet Auxiliary. Then there was my own father who had been in the forefront of military service throughout the 2nd WW with the Royal Artillery, along with his 4 brothers and one sister who all came back from the war sound in body, though I am never sure of the 'mind'.

Then there was my names sake Grandfather, Norman Walter Hughes, a sergeant in the Middx Regt, (one of Cathcart's regiments of the 4th Division if I remember correctly (57th regiment)) who died in April 1918 and was awarded the Military Medal as a consolation prize for my grandmother who then had 5 sons and one daughter to care for in 'A land fit for heroes'. And then for twenty years granny reared them only to wave them farewell as she saw them all off to the replay war with Hitler in 1939.

Myself having been discharged from the 1st Bn Scots Guards in August 1976 I had decided that one of the first things I had to do was to find out how Grandfather had lost his life in World War I, and as a token of his service been awarded the Military Medal. I therefore penned a letter to the appropriate Government agency and received a very short official reply as the resulting answer. Somehow its contents did not fit Grandfathers efforts and sacrifice, and anyway how could it have been when we were to start the scene all over just a short generation after his untimely death?

The following citation is recorded;

His Majesty the King has been graciously pleased to approve the award of the Military Medal for bravery in the field to the under mentioned

LIST OF NAMES INCLUDING G41538 SGT N W HUGHES MIDDX REGT

ALSO AWARDED WAR AND VICTORY MEDALS

IT IS REGRETTED THAT THIS IS THE ONLY INFORMATION AVAILABLE FROM THE SERVICE DOCUMENTS NOW HELD

YOURS FAITHFULLY

J S PARKER (MRS)

3 MARCH 1977   MINISTRY OF DEFENCE

In my opinion we read above of yet another example of how the British government tends to run parallel with their people rather more than amongst them as we note the short and sharp ending of Grandfathers documented life. We may also note that he was to die a Military Medal hero, though the brief official testimony above certainly makes no hallmark of this fact and without a citation attached what is the medal?

A Personal Tribute to Timothy Gowing the First Voice from the Ranks

Therefore with Grandfather's example above it is not too difficult for me to believe that the Crimea Was yet another demonstration of this 'Cause and Effect' fact and fault line which has been handed down to the present times, passing through many wars and campaigns in the interim period. But now with a difference, for we are now fortunate in having the Internet at our disposal, so may do something about this terrible historic, social and political problem that being born British brings with it

I offer as further evidence for this personal conviction of being forever 'short changed' by a British establishment that runs parallel with its people, is that any Regimental History centred around the events of the Crimea War that fails to mention in any detail the three main items shown below fails dismally. These 3 crucial factors which led to the British Army surviving the Crimea War, (which I now believe was the best they could hope for,) displays yet again a shortfall demonstrated in full by the authorities, and shows just how little those in power, both in the Government and the military hierarchy, are willing to pay back in return for so much given and sacrificed.

Herewith below the 3 crucial elements omitted by the Scots Guards History of the Crimea War

The Minie Rifle

Florence Nightingale

The Crimea Railway

I have therefore duly updated the history with some detail of these three crucial component parts which enabled the British Army to survive this problematic phase of the Victorian Gunboat Diplomacy in action at the invasion of the Crimea.

A Personal Tribute to Timothy Gowing the First Voice from the Ranks

Neither am I taking advantage of the opportune nature of 'Hindsight', for the substance of the three major factors mentioned above was well noted at that time, though perhaps at Inkerman the fact that the French saved the British from defeat, and thus themselves, may not have been seen too clearly at that time. But the advantages of the Minie rifle certainly were! And Florence Nightingale had just arrived at the hospital in Scutari the previous evening, though without Mary Seacole.

The Complex Relationship of the British 'Three Estates' or of how many decided upon!?

Keep it simple, not in Britain they don't!

The unwritten format of the British Constitution does not work within the framework of functioning in close partnerships with other governments around the World. Neither has it ever worked for the best interests of the British people anyway, and was probably never meant to, or never really thought about in that democratic manner and method of governance, for let us remember that it all began in 1215 AD when a resident King John was bought to heel by some of his 'Barons', and 'Magna Carta' was heralded in. That is not a good place, nor time, to begin a present day British Constitution, with all the baggage and add-ons from 1215 to the present time. Though very much the opposing radical state of affairs were to be bought about when the 'Republic' was introduced by Oliver Cromwell, who had at least managed to write a primary secular constitution, for he saw this document as reinforcing his Republican Commonwealth, whilst getting rid of the rule of the Barons, Church of England autocracy, a parliament that rarely functioned with the interests of the country and people at the root of the debate, and finally ridding the country of a monarchy that had been very much responsible for the troubled history of Britain, which was now to be finally extinguished and a fresh beginning made.

Unfortunately Cromwell was not to live long enough to plant his ideas firmly on a national level. and after his death in 1658, self interest amongst the monarchists and lords was to return the monarchy in the shape of Charles 2nd, which was to once more bring about the religious problems that had beset Britain since Henry VIII, and remains to this day to stifle a written constitution in the 21st century, with the Queen head of the Church of England, in a land that is now supposed to have a secular administration. In fact it may now be known that the unwritten Constitution has been ineffective for many years, reaching back to the Crimea War, where it should have been seen as an obvious weakening of the British State through the top heavy management and privileged structure the unwritten constitution gave birth to, and so long ago.

The Invasion of the Crimea in September 1854, leading directly to the War in the Crimea region, was to throw into sharp relief many major flaws inherent in the process of the complex relationship between the leading factions of British governance, all working within the British format of government, and an unwritten constitution full of ancient conventions that had long since past their sell by dates. Nowadays, and In my experienced opinion of being born British and having to live with that fact for the past 70 years, I believe that the British 'three estates' form of administration has always been a destructive and delusionary force within the management of the British peoples (and once upon a time the Empire's) affairs. However there was one colonial country which has managed to escape many of the trials and tribulations of living under such a regime. That country is Australia, but I keep that ideal function of government until last, for I should like to finish this book on a happy note!

The truth of the matter quite simply is that the manner and methodology of the British administration has never gained the point where it reaches down to the masses of the greater population on an even keel, and at a personal level. It just cannot achieve this level of the democratic principle with its weighty and unwritten constitution which comes overloaded with historic, dynamic, legal and communication problems.

Thus the situation as at the time of the Crimea War shows this fraught relationship comprised of the State, of Monarchy, which also takes on the business of being head of the Anglican church, the Lords, along with Parliament, with the Military, and a newly fledgling Media, then reflected onto the World at large during that period of history. This particular 'Causal' was to be a mainstream reason for the crisis management caused by the war, both in the Crimea and the country, and continues on to this very day with countless examples and demonstrations to give facts to that cause and effect syndrome. Reaching evermore into these modern times with the underlying problems that come with this government form remaining in place and statute. And still continues on, in Iraq and Afghanistan for a modern demonstration.

The British Government in the meantime still refusing to change the constitution of the 'three estates', into a form of simple umbrella government that may manage Britain's affairs in a less complicated and more direct way. For having got rid of the baggage left over from a long history which has bought the British people so much misery, and during which times we have learned so little, and yet continues on still maintaining a form of government processes which has learned nothing, and forgotten even less.

If any imperialist conflict was to show that weakness of unbalanced management and the need for political reform then the Crimea War could have been a complete saving grace for the future, if anybody had been looking.

The Complex Relationship of the British 'Three Estates'

The point I am making now however, is that the British government and all of its works, may be seen and realized by an emerging new World order to require modification. But like the Danish King from the Hans Christian Anderson story who refuses to believe he is naked, may not realise that the British governmental awkwardness may now be seen throughout the Worlds governments, and their peoples. That is of course if it is looked for. But why should administrations overseas offer advice to encourage change in Britain, when many governments around the Globe look comfortably at Britain's perpetuating discomfort!

For another instance (and many more are easily found!) I am now aware that Sir F Maurice the author of the regimental history had problems with his loyalties between General Haig's Military leadership in the Field, and Lloyd George's Government in London during WW1. So yet again the communication problem arises between varying government self interests which makes one of the points reference the complex relationship between the Military and the British Governance clear enough. But continues to beg the question, what to do with the ever occurring eternal problem which is still never to be answered, nor ably and publicly questioned even to these present times?

Perhaps the American form of constitutional government has provided the answer with their open procedural Interviews and Select Committees acting in line with their 7000 word Constitution, and the Transparency which is demanded by the American Public at large.

These crucial elements of any Democratic Government are however denied to the British electorate. The critical problem being that the British people have no written Constitution to guide them in any affairs of State, and the Government holds sway on what is, or not, legitimate questions which the British People may ask of its Government, leaving lhe 'law statute' and adjoined 'conventions' becoming a tool wielded by successive governments under the heading of 'constitution', with absolutely no flexibility built in as time changes along with certain circumstances. But not for the British public at large!

For as long as this three estate model of government continues the British Public will be forever denied access to a fully Democratic relationship with the British administration. It will also continue to muddy the Military sphere of operations leading to the ongoing fact that the truth will always be held at arms length from the people in order to suit government self interests.

Certainly the relationship between the Media and the Military within the Field of Operations, both Political and Operational, should be wide open to both scrutiny and compromise, and the discussion consistently reviewed must be continued, for it is the people and their tax revenues which pay for the military upkeep and the wars. This public stake from the electorate must have a large and loud voice on how any war is conducted by their military forces, and government, along with the media standing by like vultures to uphold and ensure that right is right and in line with the democratic pulse of the greater majority of the British people.

The update which covers HRH the Duke of Cambridge yet again demonstrates another detailed fact of the flawed complex relationship which not only continually gets in the way of correct management but is also very dangerous, and from those days to these!

A relatively modern revelation might lie in the sad story of King Edward VIII, Mrs Simpson, Ribbentrop, and then the Hess affair, which lasted until his quiet passing away in Spandau prison, Berlin with the truth still not available to historians, nor the people of the World, whilst leaving another World War to take account of. I further believe that there is much mystery still remaining around relationships and diplomatic and political moves made by those with grace and favour which moved Britain closer to the 2nd World War rather more than peace moves and away from it?

An Introduction to the Scots Guards Regimental History

The History of the Scots Fusilier Guards during the Crimea War by Sir Frederick Maurice, was published in London in 1934. The book is now seriously out of date. It is also incorrect in certain definitive writings. Therefore requiring a present day make over by someone other than the Scots Guards RHQ Archives Dept. Which appears to be negligent in taking on this responsibility, or perhaps they do not see it as their job. So whose duty is it to at least monitor any regimental history?

Plus it is paid for from the public purse. A responsibility and accountability factor which has been around, and known of from the history's publication away back in 1934!?

In fact, and not just in my opinion, the Scots Guards Regimental History covering the period of the Crimea War fails in any manner, or form, to do justice to the part played by the Scots Fusilier Guards during the Crimea campaign. Whether this failing is by the author, or whether by senior Scots Guards Officers at that time of the book's writing who were negligent in thinking the campaign through. Or perhaps could not be bothered to reach for the full potential of the Regimental history from that time of the Crimea War, and the lessons learned. Of these points I will not comment, But I am of the opinion that any regimental history whilst recording the facts, should also comment on what the government, or military command should do to put these matters too rights in the future. Surely that is what a history in any form is all about!

In these present times, but lingering on from the Crimea War, there is also the financial RHQ embarrassment of money contributed by serving soldiers of the Household Division towards the raising of the British Monument at Cathcart Hill during the early 1990s. Soldiers money which was then allowed to be squandered, and thereby poses another set of unanswered questions which reach deep into the three estate form of British government, where all the main government elements are all involved, but together act more like the three wise monkeys than the three key parts of the British administration

Sadly the main regimental player acting for the Scots Guards (and the Guards Brigade) in the financing for the building of the Cathcart Hill Monument, Colonel Julian Lancaster MBE died sometime during the ongoing argument process, and RHQ will tell me nothing of the commitment to the Monument from the Scots Guards RHQ after his untimely death. Neither will the 'Freedom of Information Act' give me access to the answers from RHQ, These situations are all linked and joined, and should be dealt with by the Scots Guards Association working in close union with the Scots Guards RHQ to once and for all times sort the matter out in a sympathetic, interested and caring forum. But they will not for the magnetic hold of the three estates is more potent than gaining the truth to ex-Gdsn who think more of gaining favour with those who they still consider to be their Lords and Masters.

Certainly both the French, with their Crimea war memorial, and the 2nd W/W German Cemetery in Sevastopol, have managed their monument and cemetery on a firm long term basis. Working along with the Sevastopol district local authority to confirm that the ongoing management, maintenance and security are all well managed. So if the French and the German governments' may be trusted to look after their Monuments in and around Sevastopol, why can't the British administration. Or is this modern Monumental concern just to be another failing of the 'Three Estates', and those with an interest being held to silence by those that have caused this negligence?

Major General's Sir F Maurice publication of 1934 has also been further updated by myself to make the personal point, that as a tax paying British person, who served some twenty years in the ranks of the Scots Guards between 1956-1976, I therefore have as much claim to the inner sanctuary of the Regiment as any member of the British Royal Family.

Therefore ensuring that I also have as much right and concern to update the past history of the Regiment as any other person who wishes to do so. This democratic factor is yet another difficult proposition for the present administration in its archaic and elitist form to make sense of. I will also make the point that this is an updated history, and in no way have I set out to rewrite the previous publication by Sir F Maurice, but merely to update and modernise his original work of 1934

There are now some points I would make to the RHQ of the Scots Guards;

Why was it that someone who was not a Scots Guardsman was asked to write the history of the Regiment at that time. This is a question that I have every right to ask, and the Scots Guards RHQ have an obligation to give me a full reply?

Could it have been that there were no officers in the Regiment who were willing to commit themselves to writing the history, perhaps as a gesture of putting something back into the Regiment that gave them some taste of real life and form during their service in the Scots Guards. Was this the reason that it was thought necessary to call on a practiced writing professional to complete the history?

The writing of the history itself could not then have been well, nor closely researched. But rather patched together with the information laid before the author by the staff at the Regimental Headquarters of the Scots Guards. Then insufficiently proof read, nor fully edited before publication.

The regimental history of the Scots Fusilier Guards sent to my home in Cyprus in 2000 by Major Ron Clemison MBE, covered the period of the regiment's completed involvement in the invasion of the Crimea. This period covered the beginning of the affair in February 1854, from their stations in London and Windsor throughout the campaign, 1854-1856, and their return to England in July 1856. This epic experience was covered in the regimental history in 66 pages, which is no more, nor less, than the first three stories to be read in the edition of the 'Complete Sherlock Holmes short stories'.

Does that futile effort from a British Guards Regiment really cover the human sacrifices made, and then when the British Monument at Cathcart Hill is added to the sum total all adding up to a less than a fair game of cricket.

Nor a war won, nor a monument built, on the playing fields of Eton, Winchestor, or Harrow, WHAT!?

Profile; Major-General Sir Frederick Barton Maurice 1st Baronet GCB GCMG GCVO DSO

The Major General was a British General, Military Correspondent, Writer and Academic. He was famously forced to resign his commission in May 1918 after writing a letter to *The Times* criticising Prime Minister David Lloyd George for making misleading statements about the strength of British forces in France. He also founded the British Legion in 1920, and served as its president from 1932 to 1947.

(Reminiscent of a great Scots Guardsman, Major General Sir John Acland and his letter to *the Times* Newspaper around the unfairness of the 2nd Bn Scots Guards being made redundant in 1971. This redundancy was only to last for some 9 months before the 2nd Bn. was reformed for service in Northern Ireland. At least Colonel Acland had the guts to make his point whilst the remainder of the senior staff of the Scots Guards establishment stayed silent. Why is it that these 'gentlemen' are very good at keeping control of their Guardsmen, but not so good at dealing with their seniors?)

Early life and military career

Maurice was born in Dublin, the son of John Frederick Maurice, a British Army officer and military historian. He attended St. Paul's School and Sandhurst before joining the Derbyshire Regiment in 1892. His first overseas posting was to India in 1897-98 during the Tirah Campaign. During this time, he served as aide-de-camp to his father, Major-General John Frederick Maurice. After a promotion to captain in 1899, he fought in the Second Boer War. After returning from South Africa, he entered the Staff College in 1902. Later that year, he was posted to the War Office and, in 1911, promoted to major. Two years later, he was promoted to lieutenant colonel in 1913 and transferred to the Staff College as an instructor.

World War I

On the outbreak of war in 1914, Maurice was posted to France and assigned to 3rd Infantry Division as a staff officer. He saw action at the Battle of Mons in August 1914. In early 1915, following the appointment of William Robertson as Chief of the Imperial General Staff, Maurice was posted to London as Director of Military Operations for the Imperial General Staff, and in 1916 he was promoted to major general.

Resignation

Following the dismissal of Field Marshal Sir William Robert Robertson, in February 1918, 1st Baronet, GCB, GCMG, GCVO, DSO (29 January 1860 – 12 February 1933) a British officer who served as Chief of the Imperial General Staff (CIGS) from 1916 to 1918 during the First World War. He was the first British Army soldier to rise from private soldier to Field Marshall) Maurice became convinced that troops were being withheld from the Western Front in order to undermine the position of Douglas Haig. When David Lloyd George announced in the House of Commons that British troop levels on the Western Front were at all-time highs, Maurice believed that he was deceiving both Parliament and the British public. In his capacity as Director of Military Operations, Maurice knew that the troop statistics available to his office did not bear out Lloyd George's claims, and he wrote to Robertson's successor, Henry Wilson, to outline his position. After Wilson failed to respond, Maurice wrote a letter to the *The Times*, criticizing Lloyd George for misleading the public about the state of the British Expeditionary Force during the German Spring Offensive. The publication of this letter on 7 May caused a minor political storm, and members of the Conservative opposition called for a debate. This subsequently occurred on 9 May, and Lloyd George was able to imply that the source of confusion was, in fact, Maurice's office, rather than the Prime Minister's. Maurice was initially suspended, and ultimately forced to retire; he was also denied a court martial.

Postwar life

Following his forced resignation, Maurice served as a military correspondent, initially for the *Daily Chronicle*, and later for the *Daily News*. In 1921, he was one of the founders of the British Legion, and although he was not initially very active in the organization, he would later serve as the president from 1932 to 1947. The following year, he was appointed principal of the Working Men's College in London, a position he held until 1933, when he left to take a similar post at East London College. He was also appointed as a professor of military studies at the University of London in 1926, and taught both there and at Trinity College until the end of his life.

Maurice died on 19 May 1951, in Cambridge.

Publications

The Russo-Turkish War, 1877-1878 (Special Campaign Series, 1905)

Sir Frederick Maurice: a record of his work and opinions (Edward Arnold, London, 1913)

Forty Days in 1914 (Constable and Co, London, 1919)

The Last Four Months (Cassell and Co, London, 1919)

The Life of Lord Wolseley (William Heinemann, London, 1924)

Robert E. Lee, the soldier (Constable and Co, London, 1925)

Governments and War (William Heinemann, London, 1926)

An aide-de-camp of Lee (Little, Brown and Co, London, 1927)

The Life of General Lord Rawlinson of Trent (Cassell and Co, London, 1928)

British Strategy (Constable and Co, London, 1929)

The 16th Foot (Constable and Co, London, 1931)

The History of the Scots Guards (Chatto and Windus, London, 1934)

Haldane (Faber and Faber, London, 1937, 1939)

The Armistices of 1918 (Oxford University Press, London, 1943)

The Adventures of Edward Wogan (G Routledge and Sons, London, 1945)

Advancing into the Crimea Regimental Campaign History

We begin the main narrative with a quote from a well respected and authoritive Edinburgh author and journalist,

Trevor Royle

Author of '*The Great Crimean War*'. **Published 2000**

On page 231 he makes an interesting comment about paintings which were commissioned as a result of actions fought in the Crimea War;

'Also the battle itself spawned many well known examples of Victorian military art such as the stirring though fanciful, depiction of the Scots Fusilier Guards advancing under fire with their Colours flying proudly'

Alma Battle

I add as a footnote to the comment above that as a Crimea War historian it is my job to seek out the truth and to pass it on to those interested. This history may also include those paintings which are still shown to the 'Great and the Good', in order that they shall enable the images of ' Regimental Glory' to live on in young men's minds, and then stay put. And for the remainder of their lives!

Some more on the Lady Butler painting,

Scots Guards saving the Colours at Alma

The Scots Guards RHQ have made this painting appear as the truth. However it may now be shown up for the dishonorable half truths it tells. Unfortunately the time line is too late to curb the mindsets it has helped produce since its probable first showing at Scots Guards RHQ as part of the ceremony in which the Scots Fusilier Guards became the Scots Guards sometime in 1877.

Also present would have been the affable fatherly figure of HRH the Duke of Cambridge, then Commander in Chief of the British Army, looking on with a happy smile on his face. Being content that now the ghosts of his, and the Regiments failings at the Alma could be finally laid to rest, and his part to play in the larger real picture of his overall performance as Commander of the 1st Division in the Crimea could be forgotten.

I am however fortunate in that the information that is now readily available in which to study the politics and reasons for the Crimea War is now so much more available than when Major General Sir F Maurice took up the commissioning of the Scots Guards Regimental History in the early 1930s. However much of this update is not with the use of any hindsight, nor added knowledge, but more to do with inadequacies in the Scots Guards RHQ systems and thought processes at that time of the books publication. That failing however provides no excuse, nor reason, for the original regimental history, nor its negative after affects here in Sevastopol more than 150 years on from the war and now nearing some 80 years from the Maurice publication. Though be warned that such is the manner and method by which past conflicts and deeds may be written by those that have the privilege and power to rewrite history, though may now be overturned and the truth switched on with the innovation of the Internet.

If I am now to set the scene for an understanding of the British point of view, or perceptions, of what the conflict in the Crimea was all about at that time in 1854, then perhaps a natural starting point is to gage the mindset of the British Nation at that time in 1854. Whilst at the same instant recognising my mindset which continues to show itself throughout this updated journal. As the reader may realize as they read their way through this update in which I have strived to demonstrate my personal interest in the subject matter selected, in a varied, and what I personally regard as an important share of the Scots Guards Regiments history interacting with my life here in Sevastopol.

The twenty years I served with the Scots Guards between 1956-1976, were to provide the meaning and substance of my life from 1956 until the present time of my retirement life in Sevastopol, where history now offers the fruits and awards of my self inflicted interest. I further argue that my update in the pages of the Scots Guards regimental history was from genuine concern for the truth, which I am now being punished for by senior members of the regiment and the Scots Guards Association. Yes, for official Mindsets may cause confusion and paradoxes, and go on to cheapen and undermine the truth, and for the last thousand years, at least!

Furthermore I now believe that the retirement phase of ones own evolutionary life span is a natural phase of reflection, plus the promotion of self learned lessons that life has moulded with, and into, now interacting with the past and its still living history. Old age also serves to provide information, and perhaps also advocating some advice that could save the unwary the time consuming, and effort, of the re-learning of some lessons from life, for others could better make use of my mistakes rather than making their own.

In my opinion, now framed on seventy years of having experienced living history, how little has changed of the British Governments usage of certain groups of British people since those times of the Invasion of the Crimea in 1854, even until present times with the invasions of Iraq and Afghanistan. For what good were any of these invasions on behalf of the general interest's of the people of Britain, or the British Military and Security Forces which are in place as basic requirements for the safety and security of the Mother country, rather more than in continuing British past revisits of Gunboat Diplomacy around the Globe. Especially so when the established, and successive governmental order is asked to cooperate and return these sacrifices made by the people, to the people, and they never do, nor have ever reciprocated any of this devotion or loyalty of the people been returned to those who were so willing to contribute.

This update provides examples of exactly what I am saying reference loyalty working at both ends, from the bottom up, and then the top down, which is rarely demonstrated by successive 'Oil Change' British Governments which in modern day terms treat the British people as little more than idiots. Whilst if the truth be known, perhaps the Government is right, for whilst it is said that any country and its peoples receives the Government it deserves, then perhaps it could be well said that the Government receive in turn the constituency it deserves. In which case Britain and its people get exactly the Government, plus the established order they rightfully deserve, and if they are largely satisfied with that state of affairs then that is their business. Or is it now that Europe and a peaceful and commercial Globalisation threatens Britain with something better?

I trust that this controversial updated publication may be of interest to those who have for one reason or other allowed the Scots Guards Regimental History of the Invasion of the Crimea in1854, to pass them by, but may now stop and read the updated version for a while!?

Purchase of Commissions

A Price for Loyalty or Horse Trading?

From Wikipedia

The sale of commissions was a common practice in most European armies where wealthy and noble officers purchased their rank. Only the Imperial Russian Army and the Prussian Army never used such a system. While initially shunned in the French Revolutionary Army, it was eventually revived in the Grande Armée of Napoleon I (mainly in the French allied and satellite states). The British Army, which used this practice through most of its history, was last to abolish it.

In the Austrian army, the sale of commissions was abolished in 1803. Nevertheless, it remained legal if two officers agreed to «exchange» their ranks. This system existed up to the middle of the 19th century. The practice begun in 1683 during the reign of Charles II and continued until 1871, being abolished on 1 November as part of the Cardwell Reforms.

Commissions could only be purchased in cavalry and infantry regiments (and therefore up to the rank of Colonel only). Commissions in the Royal Engineers and the Royal Artillery were awarded to those who graduated from a course at the Royal Military Academy at Woolwich, and subsequent promotion was by seniority only. Such officers (and those of the Army of the British East India Company), were often looked down upon as being «not quite gentlemen» by officers who had purchased their commissions.

There were several key reasons behind the sale of commissions:

It preserved the social exclusivity of the officer class. Not only were the poor necessarily excluded from the commissioned ranks, but regimental colonels were permitted, and often did, refuse to allow the purchase of a commission in their regiment by anyone who had the necessary money but was not from a social background to their liking. This was especially the case in the Guards regiments, which were dominated by aristocrats. Elsewhere however, it was not unknown for Colonels to lend deserving senior non-commissioned officers or warrant officers the funds necessary to purchase commissions.[1]

It served as a form of collateral against abuse of authority or grave negligence or incompetence. Disgraced officers could be cashiered by the crown (that is, stripped of their commission without reimbursement).

It ensured that the officer class was largely populated by persons having a vested interest in maintaining the status quo, thereby reducing the possibility of Army units taking part in a revolution or coup.

It ensured that officers had private means and were unlikely to engage in looting or pillaging, or to cheat the soldiers under their command by engaging in profiteering using army supplies.

It provided honourably retired officers with an immediate source of capital.

It was not unknown for officers who incurred or inherited debts, to sell their commission to raise funds. In theory, a commission could be sold only for its official value, and was to be offered first to the next most senior officer in the same regiment. In practice, desirable commissions in fashionable regiments were often sold to the highest bidder after an unseemly auction. A self-interested senior officer might well regard his commission as his pension fund, and would encourage the inflation of its value.

Even the official values of commissions varied by regiment, usually in line with the differing levels of social prestige of different regiments. In 1837 for example the costs of ranks in regular infantry regiments were: Ensign £450, Lieutenant £700, Captain £1800, Major £3200, Lt Colonel £4540. In the same year the costs of ranks in the Life Guards were: Cornet £1260, Lieutenant £1785, Captain £3500, Major £5350, Lt Colonel £7250. These prices were not incremental, so to purchase a promotion an officer only had to pay the difference in price between his existing rank and the new one.

The worst potential effects of the system were mitigated during intensive conflicts such as the Napoleonic Wars by heavy casualties among senior ranks (which ensured that the vacant commissions were exchanged for their face value only), and the possibility of promotion to brevet army ranks for deserving officers. An officer might be a subaltern or Captain in his regiment, but might hold a higher local rank if attached to other units or allied armies, or might be given a higher Army rank by the Commander-in-Chief, or the Monarch, in recognition of meritorious service or a notable feat of bravery. Officers bearing dispatches giving news of a victory (such as Waterloo), often received such promotion, and might be specially selected by a General in the field for this purpose.

The malpractices associated with the purchase of commissions reached their height in the long peace between the Napoleonic Wars and the Crimean War, when

Purchase of Commissions

Lord Cardigan paid £40,000 for his commission. It was in the Crimea that it became most obvious that the system of purchase often led to incompetent leadership, such as that which resulted in the Charge of the Light Brigade. An inquiry (the Commission on Purchase) was established in 1855, and commented unfavourably on the institution. The practice of purchase of commissions was finally abolished as part of the Cardwell reforms which made many changes to the structure and procedures of the Army.

For much of the period over which commissions were purchased, it was no more unfair as a system than the processes of royal or political patronage which applied in most other European (and American) armies. The rigid system of promotion by seniority, as applied in the army of the East India Company, had its own drawbacks which became evident when intense conflicts such as the First Anglo-Sikh War or Indian Rebellion of 1857 broke out after long periods of peace, and many senior officers proved too elderly or infirm to command effectively in the field.

Crimea War, Beginnings and the Endings

A Sad Story In The Telling

The British Invaded the Crimea in September 1854 in league with their French and Turkish Allies. The original war the British were to fight on the River Danube in the 'Principalities' was at an end with the Russian Armies in the course of making their way back to Russia.

There was also a four point peace plan on the Diplomatic agendas, with Czar Nicolai recognising that the opportunity to cure Turkey 'The sick man of Europe' was no longer an option open to him. Therefore losing his prospect of taking over Constantinople, and the further aim of making certain that both the Black Sea and the Mediterranean could then become 'Russian Lakes'. This result being the sole intent for making religious, political and military expediency around the religious issues during the early stages of the argument, and then his 'fervour' for protecting the Greek Orthodox population in the demographic arena of the ongoing diplomacy. Which policy then lead to war with the Allies when he sent his troops to do his diplomatic work for him.

However, the British were now able to confirm an opportunistic opening for themselves. Having then decided that the Russian Black Sea Fleet Port at Sevastopol posed a threat to both Turkey and their own British Interests. Then leading them to plan an invasion of the Crimea to destroy the Black Sea Port at Sevastopol. But it had to happen quickly!

The Military invasion of the Crimea by the Allies then took place with speed and political expediency being rather more important than the military requirements needs satisfied to mount such an invasion. However the British could always depend on their French Allies to offer much needed support if and when required!

Thus the Allied Invasion of the Crimea was mounted, unprepared, uncertain, and with its Armies very, very sick with the Cholera. Though better in the Crimea than bringing the diseased Army home in time for Xmas 1854, with thousands dead, and not a dead Russian to be counted in exchange. So sooner rather than later were relative to the despatch Lord Raglan was to receive on his orders for the Invasion of the Crimea.

The war was to officially end in April 1856, with the Treaty of Paris, and so the British contingent headed away from the Crimea, straight into the Indian Mutiny. With the Guards Brigade headed back to their Public Duty routine via Aldershot, where service could be resumed as normal to the Monarchy rather than the British peoples homeland security.

The British were not to return to the Crimea as friends and visitors until the early 1990s, and the City not opened officially to visitors until 1997. Thus it has only been for the last ten years or so that the Crimea War, (as it become known by the British), could be re-visited and examined.

Neither did the war between the Russians and the Allied contingents comprised of the Turks, French and British, and later the Sardinians, arrive suddenly, for all the events which led to the war had been collecting themselves together culminating in the final pieces of the jigsaw leading to the particular phase of the overall conflict since 1853. But there were other tenuous happenings and events which also lent themselves to the Allied adventure in the Crimea, and the Great Exhibition of May 1851, was one such event. For this special event was to stir the hearts and mindsets of many fervent members of the British establishment which added to their subjective beliefs that the British people through their far flung Empire, had been given the right to police the World.

The Great Exhibition was very probably prompted by the success of the French Industrial Exposition of 1844, when at that time it was suggested to the British Government that it would be most advantageous for British industry to have a similar exhibition in London. However the British Government showed no interest. That being said, they would have kept an ever open eye on the French Exhibition, and then by 1851 when Great Britain was arguably the leader of the industrial revolution, and feeling very secure in that ideal, would have fallen victim to the noble British political art of thinking again, having probably got it wrong to begin with. And so it came to pass that the Exhibition then under the direction of the Society of Arts and the management skills of Prince Albert, consort of Queen Victoria was to go ahead. The Great Exhibition of 1851 in London was thus conceived to symbolize this industrial, military and economic superiority of Great Britain. However adjustments would have to be regulated, for Just representing the feats of Britain itself would have excluded many of the technological achievements pioneered by the British in its many Dominions, Colonies and Protectorates around the Empire, so it was decided to make the exhibition truly international with invitations being extended to almost all of the colonized world that may have something of service to offer. The British also felt that it was important to show their achievements right alongside those of "less civilized" countries. This patronising attitude manifesting the prevailing thought control and mindset in England at the time, and was ripe for the somewhat arrogant parading of accomplishments. This opening curtain of British World Dynamics left many of the strongly emerging 'Middle Classes' feeling secure, economically and politically, and Queen Victoria was eager to reinforce the feeling of contentment within her reign.

It was also during the mid-1850s that the word "Victorian" began to be employed to express a new self-consciousness, both in relation to the nation and to the period through which it was passing.

London, the capital city which was also home to a British Military Garrison at that time, with the Brigade of Guards very much in visual evidence around the Royal residences, and their ceremonial parading.

There was also the daily routine of the 'Bank of England Picquet' which was not to come to an end before 1973. Therefore the Military Establishment would have been involved in the work, and also the sideline management of the Exhibition, and thus fully conscious, and no doubt very much a part of their countries feelings of pride, superiority, and arrogant mind sets.

To bolster their attitude of disdain for all things Russian during this period, the Russian collections of exhibits were still at sea (or not sent at all according to some commentators) when the Exhibition was officially opened on May 1st 1851. The information that Russia would not be present at the Exhibition due to their own misfortune would have sent disdainful smiles through some sections of the British Establishment, and Russia's lapse therefore seen as somehow to reinforce the emergence of another English mindset in taking for granted that Russia and its peoples were somehow inferior to the English way of life and aspirations of the time.

However, I would argue from a present day and hind sighted perception that most of the agricultural workers and farmers toiling away in Rural England, whilst forming a large and powerful minority of the overall mainland and Northern Irish population at that time. (and still all being collectively termed as English) whilst knowing of the Great Exhibition, would accept that it should be primarily shown as very much part of leading to the upgrading of their own specialised, and in general terms, subject of agriculture and commerce. Therefore seeing the facility of the Great Exhibition in that light of their ever developing need to speculate further abroad, and in doing so have very little knowledge, nor interest of military and political matters outside of their professional interests.

The idea however that the forthcoming war, in national, and in general terms, was in any way popular, I believe is false. The notion that the conflict with Russia and its problems with Turkey really interested the British public at that time probably came about Largely due to some sections of the news sheets publishers. These news sheets were printed to sell, and war 'sold' copy.

However there will always be those people of the minority who were thinking in terms of relevant establishment mindset rather than commercial reality, needs, and the true unheard of feelings from the vast majority of the British population at that moment in time. But as always those of the minority with the loudest voices are heard the most, especially if they originate from the elitists of British society.

And yet Richard Cobden MP, and other members of the 'House' were not to applaud this war, and spoke out loudly against it, but just as the invasions of Iraq and Afghanistan in present times the people in power were not listening for compromise nor options. So once again we are to observe, and make note of a British government that serves its people in parallel, rather than within the crowd. So war with Russia it was to be, and the Scots Fusilier Guards were taken from their London and Windsor sentry boxes to be sent on their way to fight it.

Sir F Maurice Regimental History begins

Chapter III

THE CRIMEAN WAR TO THE BATTLE OF THE ALMA

The ostensible cause of the disputes, which culminated in war with Russia, was the ongoing quarrels between the Greek and Roman Churches in Jerusalem. The Czar Nicholas took up the position of protector of the Greek Church, and with the help of the Russian clergy of that church stirred up religious enthusiasm in his dominions. This developed into a campaign on behalf of the Greek Christians, who inhabited what are now Romania, Bulgaria, and Yugoslavia, and were then provinces of turkey. The Christians living on Turkish territory undoubtedly were often maltreated, and it was not difficult for the Czar to present a case for intervention, which had the advantage of being in accord with Russian aspirations. The freeing of the European provinces of Turkey might well bring Russia to Constantinople, give her control of the Dardanelle's, and provide her with the long-coveted entrance to the Mediterranean. The opportunity for realizing this ambitious program seemed to have arrived, for the young Emperor of Austria was under personal obligations to the Czar, who thought it unlikely that he would interfere, while France was still in the throes of the political disturbances which had resulted in the coup d'etat of 1851 and the restoration of the empire under Louis napoleon. In 1851 too the Great Exhibition held in London had been heralded as introducing a new era of peace and goodwill, and the British government under lord Aberdeen made no secret of its pacific tendencies. Looking around Europe, the Czar could find no one who would be likely to thwart his designs upon Turkey.

Accordingly, in the spring of 1853 Nicholas put forward a claim to the protectorate of all the Christian subjects of the Sultan, who numbered not less than fourteen millions. The sultan very naturally refused the demand, which would, if agreed to, have, in effect, authorized political interference by Russia in a large part of the Turkish Dominions. The Czar's reply to this refusal was to send troops across the River Pruth into the Danubian provinces of Turkey. Great Britain, France and Austria intervened and tried to prevent war, but in vain. The sultan then sent an ultimatum to the Czar requiring the withdrawal of the Russian troops, and when this was disregarded he declared war on Russia on October 23rd 1853.

There is considerable difference of opinion as to the motives and intentions of Louis Napoleon during this crisis, and Kinglake, who hated him, imputes to him the most Machiavellian designs. But I do not think that there is now much doubt but that he sincerely believed that if France and Great Britain took a firm line the Czar would hold his hand. At any rate he induced the British Government to join him in a Naval demonstration, and the Allied fleets entered the Dardanelle's the day before the Turkish declaration of war. This step, as Queen Victoria saw, but her Ministers did not, practically committed us to war,. While the French and British ships were off Constantinople a Russian fleet attacked and destroyed a Turkish Squadron off Sinope in the Black Sea on November 30th. This act aroused such a storm of indignation in Great Britain, as Lord Aberdeen, with all his desire for peace, was unable to withstand. The French Emperor had addressed to the Czar a final proposal for a peaceful settlement, pointing out that if were rejected great Britain and France must declare war. He received the reply that *'Russia will prove herself in 1854 what she was in 1812,'* this allusion to the fate of his great ancestor's Grand Army made it impossible for Louis Napoleon and the French to turn back.

Early in 1854 the British Government began to move troops to Malta, though apparently without any very definite idea of what they were to do, for they left England without transport, supplies, or medical equipment. As a part of this force a Guards Brigade composed of the 3rd Grenadiers, 1st Coldstream and 1st Scots Fusilier Guards, was sent to Malta under Brig-General Bentinck. The 1st Battalion of the Regiment paraded at Wellington Barracks early on February 28th and marched to Buckingham Palace, where it was inspected by her Majesty and the Prince Consort, in the presence of the Duke of Cambridge as Colonel of the Regiment. The battalions then entrained for Portsmouth, where it embarked the same day on the *SS.Simoon.*

The embarkation state of the 1st Battalion shows a strength of 26 officers, 45 sergeants, 40 corporals, 19 drummers, 829 privates, 25 women and 4 horses. The Officers who embarked were Colonel G.Dixon in Command, Colonels, Moncrieff and Sir C. Hamilton; Lieut-Colonels W.J. Ridley, the Hon. C.G. Scott, F. Seymour, J. H. Dalrymple; Captains H. Hepburn, F. Haygarth, the Hon. W. Scarlett, G. H. Shuckburgh, H.F. Drummond, who was Adjutant, J. D. Ashley, W.C. Bowler, D.F. Buckley, the Hon. A. E. Fraser; Lieutenants R. Gipps. F. Baring, S.L. Damer, S. J. Blane, WW. knollys, G. Gordon, R. Lindsay, Viscount Ennismore, the Hon. H. Annesley; Quartermaster G. Allen; Battalion Surgeon J.A. Bostock. Assistant Surgeons F. Robinson and A.G. Elkington.

We have seen that while the Regiment was on the Scottish establishment some at least of the Company Commanders provided themselves with pipers, and from what Sergeant Fraser tells us it appears also to have been the practice, at least until the early part of the nineteenth century, to employ pipers with recruiting parties which were sent to the Highlands, but there is no record of pipers being with the Regiment in England until 1853, when the 1st Battalion appointed one of its Sergeants, Ewan Henderson, Pipe-Major. Henderson was the son of a Sergeant of the 92nd, who had fought in the Peninsula and at Waterloo, and was a native of Armat, near Fort William. He embarked with the 1st Battalion and played his pipes both at the Alma and at the Battle of Inkerman. This was a purely private enterprise of the 1st Battalion, and Sergeant Henderson's status as Pipe-Major was not officially recognized, but as we shall see, the enterprise was not long in producing results of a more permanent character

Update

The Journey of the Scots Fusilier Guards to the East

It's all Systems Go!

We pick up the Regimental History above in time for the talk of 'pipers' ,which is evidently more important than the voyage to the assembly points far away in strange waters. Pipers obviously being a Regimental priority at that time, and a point that the modern reader should think about in relation to regimental insights and soldiering needs and requirements.

It must also be taken into consideration that pipers the same as 'bandsmen' become part of the medical staff during the conflict.

I have however included the sea going preparations within the pages of this update, for I believe that the transit of the British Forces from mainland Britain to their new overseas stations is important as part of the Regimental History. It then gives a further insight and a more overall vision of the coordination and the efforts involved at the beginnings of this war yet to come.

The reader will also note that this fleet being assembled also included the transportation of men and materials to the Baltic where British Forces were to also to spend the duration of the needless war in apprehension, futility and little positive aim.

That action is but another sad story in the telling of British military history.

The preparation for the transit and the move to Malta itself is hardly given a mention in the Scots Guards History. However if this first major step on the journey to the East is not included, then the move from Britain to Malta in the Regimental History becomes a non-event. When in fact it was part and parcel of the British Forces at work, and should be understood as an intrinsic piece of the detail of the construction of the British Invasion forces during those importantly historic events. Therefore the transit of the 'Army of the East' should have been given a significant entry into the F Maurice history;

Once again we thank the Internet for the information which follows

Preparations for war Feb 1854

Southport Visiter

Jan 21st 1854

Preparations for War

'England and France are preparing two powerful fleets to take naval possession of the Baltic sea to defeat the Russian fleet should it show itself out of the harbour at Cronstradt and to place St Petersburg in a state of close blocade.

The screw steamship JAMES WATT and CAESAR, each 90 guns have been commissioned, the first on Friday the second on Saturday. The ILLUSTRIOUS, 72 guns also commissioned in order to serve as a training ship for newly-raised seamen of the navy.

Two steam frigates, the BULLDOG and the DRAGON were commissioned on Monday.

The CUMBERLAND, 70 guns, flagship of Vice Admiral, Sir G. F. SEYMOUR. K.C.B. Commander-in-Chief in the West Indies, will come to England immediately, and the ship intended to relieve her, the BESCAWEN, 70 guns, flag ship of Rear Admiral FANSHAWE, C.B, now fitting at Chatham, is to be detained in England.

It is estimated 2,500 blue-jackets are required to man the ships now fitting out at home ports.

It is intended by the Government to enrol 20.000 Irish Militia, to these 10,000 Scotch Militia will be added.

H.M.S APOLLO an old 42 gun frigate has been fitted as a store ship under the command of Mr JOHNSON, Master R.N. Filled with provisions it was towed out at Portsmouth harbour on Saturday for Spithead, whence she has sailed for Euxine.

22 recruiting parties have left Woolwich garrison on Friday and Saturday last, and 17 on Monday to enlist young men for the Royal Artillery.

February 17th 1854

The Cunard's Co, steam ships CAMBRIA and NIAGRA have been chartered to take out the guards, carrying 1,000 guards each.

The Peninsular and Oriental Companies are likely to supply the Government with one or two of their ships, the RIPON probably being one of their number.

The great screw ship HIMALAYA expected back in the next few days from Alexandria, her services will be put into requisition. There are also available the General Screw Companies JASON and GOLDEN FLEECE.

Preliminary orders for enrolment of the Greenwich Pensioners have been issued by the Admiralty. All pensioners are to attend on Tuesday next for inspection to ascertain their fitness for service. Failure to comply will result in losing their pensions.

Update

The Pensioners were to be called upon to volunteer for service during the war as medical orderlies. In fact they were to require more medical treatment than they ever gave once having joined operations. This was to be another pathetic episode of Britain at war, whilst adding insult to injury by exploiting these old soldiers, marines and sailors. That little bit was all about saving money on medical services!

Continue, Sailing Order of Battle

Coast guards are to be made available for manning the navy. Rear Admiral CHADS. C.B just promoted from Captain of the EXCELLENT, Gunnery ship, is appointed to command of the division of the fleet intended for the Baltic. Lieut J. H. CHADS has been nominated Flag-Lieut to his father.

It is said the NILE, 90 guns, screw, will be one of the Baltic flag ships. Sir C. NAPIER is mentioned as a probable commander and His Royal Highness the Duke of Cambridge will be in command of the Brigade of Guards.

The SPITFIRE Surveying, steamer, Commander SPRATT, has been ordered up to the Black sea, no doubt for surveying operations.

The Journey of the Scots Fusilier Guards to the East

The DUKE of WELLINGTON, 131 guns, St JEAN D'ACRE, 101 guns, ROYAL GEORGE, 120 guns, AGAMEMNON, 91 guns, PRINCESS ROYAL, 91 guns, CAESAR, 91 guns, JAMES WATT, 91 guns, NILE, 91 guns, CRESSY, 81 guns, SANSPARAL, 71 guns, HOGUE, 60 guns, AJAX, 60 guns, BLENHEIM, 60 guns, EDINBURGH, 60 guns, 14 such screw ships, properly manned, are a match for 28, sail, of the canvas fleet of Russia.

Another addition to this fleet is the MAJESTIC, 81 guns, to be commissioned at Sheerness, commanded by Capt James HOPE. C.B, the Capt of the FIREBRAND, who led the way up the Parana and cut the chain across the noble river at Oligando Point, giving freedom to the commerce of the Country.

The following regiments will be on their way to the Mediterranean before the end of next week. 3rd Bat, Grenadier Guards, 2nd Bat, Coldstream Guards, 1st Bat, Scots Fusilier Guards,

4th, 28th, 33rd, 50th, 77th and 93rd Highlanders, with the 2nd Bat of the Rifle brigade.

The 9th and the 62nd regiments are on their passage from Cork, the 39th, 89th, 17th and 14th have formed companies and await transport accommodation.

The regiments already at the Mediterranean stations are the 1st [1st Batt], 3d Buffs, 13th Light infantry, 30th, 31st, 41st, 44th, 47th, 48th, 49th, 55th, 57th, 68th, 71st [1stBatt] and 92nd.

There is a shortage of ship's clerks an pursers in the R.N, all those in that class on ships in harbour will be sent to sea, and invalided officers will undertake the duties on home stations. All excusing themselves from service through ill health will have to be examined at Greenwich, Haslar etc, by the Naval physicians.

Orders arriving at Portsmouth on Saturday, vessels to form the fleet to the North sea and Baltic to assemble at the Downs by the 6th of March and they will also rendezvous in the Yarmouth roads. The expedition will be one of the most powerful ever sent northward;

DUKE OF WELLINGTON, screw, 131 guns, NEPTUNE, 120 guns, ST GEORGE, 120 guns, ROYAL GEORGE, screw, 120 guns, ST JEAN D'ACRE, screw 101 guns, PRINCESS ROYAL, screw, 91 guns, CAESAR, screw, 91 guns, NILE, screw, 91 guns, JAMES WATT, screw, 91 guns, PRINCE REGENT, 91 guns, MAJESTIC, 90 guns, MONARCH, 84 guns, CRESSY, screw, 80 guns, BOSCOWEN, 70 guns, BLENHEIM, screw, 60 guns, HOGUE, screw, 60 guns, EDINBURGH, screw, 58 guns, AJAX, screw, 41 guns, PIQUE, 40 guns, AMPHIAN, screw, 34 guns, DAUNTLESS, screw, 33 guns, TRIBUNE, screw, 18 guns, SIMOON, troop screw ship, 18 guns, MAGICIENNE, 16 guns, VALOROUS, paddle, 16 guns, DESPERATE, screw, 8 guns, VULTURE, screw, 6 guns, VULCAN, troop screw ship, 6 guns, DRAGON, paddle, 6 guns, BULLDOG, paddle, 6 guns, BASILISK, paddle, 6 guns.

Recruiting for the navy is being carried out at Liverpool with great energy, but moderate success, the high wages obtainable in the Mercantile marine being an obstacle towards the enlistment of good sailors in H.M Service. Capt BEVIS sent off to London, 34 able bodied seamen from Liverpool on Monday night and 30 yesterday.

On Saturday the Cunard steamer NIAGRA will sail for Malta with a regiment at present stationed at Leeds, 900 strong.

Recruiting parties are active in Manchester, but with moderate success, numerous candidates have offered themselves but the majority, have been refused, being below the standard height. The 7th Regt of Fusiliers stationed at Regent Rd, barracks, Salford, expect to be sent to the east in the course of next month. (Timothy Gowing's Regiment)

In the Metropolis on Wednesday, shortly after 12 o' clock the 1st Bat, Coldstream Guards, marched out from St Georges Barracks, Trafalgar Square, en route for Chichester, preparatory to their embarkation for the Mediterranean. Col BENTINCK commanded the battalion, which as it passed along the Strand, was enthusiastically cheered by a multitude, so great was the excitement that the thoroughfare was for some time entirely suspended. At Waterloo Bridge the toll-keepers were overwhelmed by the torrent of people accompanying the troops, who were not stopped in their farewell by any number of turnstiles, and the men appeared in high spirits and marched cheerfully along to the familiar air of, "The girl I left behind me."

At 2pm the 3rd Batt of the Grenadier Guards removed from the Tower to St Georges barracks and they, too, in their passage along the streets, were accompanied by crowds of people.

On Wednesday 350, picked men from the 2nd Batt, Scots Fusilier Guards, now stationed at Windsor, arrived at the Wellington barracks, which proceeds at once to the Mediterranean.

The expedition are, Lieut Col DIXON, Lieut Col MONCRIEFF, and Quarter Master ALLEN.

Besides Mister DUNBAR'S ship the CANTERBURY, the government have chartered for the transport of stores to

Malta, the ORIENT, 1050 tons, the SIR JOHN POLLOCK, 640 tons, the GEORGIAN, 780 tons.

The embarkation will be effected on Saturday at noon, as soon as the troops are on board, the steamers will proceed on their voyage. Only a few of the Officer's horses will be taken, and women and children will accompany each detachment. About 2,500 troops it is said will sail from Southampton and these will be distributed between the RIPON, MANILLA and ORINOCO, the latter being an emigrant ship, will take the largest number. The ships have been victualled for 15 days, but with good weather should reach their destination in 11 days, the ordinary duration of the voyage.

The Highland Brigade of the 42nd, 79th and 93rd Highlanders, are under orders for the east. The order for the 63rd Regt to embark for The Cape of Good Hope has been countermanned.

The Regiments for foreign, service will not relieve the corps in the Mediterranean, but will proceed to the neighbourhood of Constantinople.

On Saturday morning a war steamer arrived at Belfast Lough for the purpose of taking on board the coast guard men of the several stations of Antrim and Down. She left on Sunday evening with 60 men, smart fellows, well accustomed to the sea, and to the use of arms, better still delighted at the change in their service. The steamer proceeded to Cork with a body of spare coast guards of the Southern districts waiting for embarkation, she will then proceed to Portsmouth.

Update

We may note the complexities of the move, and It is also of interest to note that many of the ships mentioned above were to stay in post at the new station, whilst some of them were to be lost, especially during the great storm of November 14th 1854 in the vicinity of the small port at Balaclava. Many of the ships are also mentioned on the ships plaques at the British Monument at Cathcart Hill. During modern times two RN ships visiting Sevastopol have sent working parties up to the Monument for tidying up duties on behalf of the British Embassy, which is acting on behalf of the British nation?

Reg Hist

The Journey to the East is now Continued

The day before the Battalion sailed, Great Britain and France had sent an ultimatum to Russia demanding the evacuation of the Principalities by April 30th. The Guards Brigade spent six weeks in Malta, and there Captain the Hon. JS Jocelyn joined from home. But when by the third week of April it became clear that Russia had no intention of complying with the demands of the Allies, the British Government decided upon a military concentration in Turkey and the Guards sailed from Malta on April 21st, and after a short stay in Gallipoli, where they had their first sight of their French Allies, who were in occupation of the town, reached Scutari on the 29th. The next day, no reply coming from Russia to their ultimatum, Great Britain and France declared war.

Lord Raglan arrived at Scutari to become Commander-in Chief of the British Expeditionary Force, and there its organization in Division and Brigades was developed. A number of Officers of the Regiment received appointment on the staff:

Lieutenant-Colonel C.F. Seymour was Assistant Adjutant-General of the 4th Division, Captain Kingscote became ADC To Lord Raglan, and Lieut-Colonel C. Tyrwhitt, ADC. To the Duke of Cambridge, who commanded the 1st Division. Captain F. Stephenson had sailed from England as Brigade-Major of the Guards Brigade, and Captain E. Neville become ADC. To Sir R. England, who commanded the 3rd Division. Lt/Colonel-Colonel Berkeley and Captain the Hon. W.C W Coke joined the 1st Battalion while it was at Scutari,. Though some attempt was made there to form the Regiments and Battalions into an Army, the force was still almost entirely deficient in transport and in reserves of stores and supplies. while Lord Raglan was there some attempt was made to form the regiments and battalions into an army, the force was still almost entirely deficient in transport and in reserves of stores and supplies. while Lord Raglan was organizing his force at Scutari, Russia began active operations in the principalities, and after some early successes her force crossed the Danube and on May 19th began the siege of Silistria, as a preliminary to an advance through the Balkans on Constantinople. Everything then pointed to a campaign on the Danube or in the Balkans, and the Allied Governments decided to move their forces to Varna to support the Turks. The Guards Brigade left the Bosphorus on June 13th and landed at Varna the next day. There it found the French contingent under the command of Marshal St Arnaud

Meantime the Turks in Silistria, ably directed by two British Officers, Major Nasmyth and Captain Butler, had put up a stout defence and on June 3rd, Austria, which had assembled 50,000 men on the frontier, summoned the Czar to evacuate the Principalities. After some hesitation the Czar, finding that Austria was in earnest and was concerting plans with the British and French commanders, threw up the sponge, abandoned the siege of Silistria, and by August 2nd had withdrawn his troops across the Pruth.

By this time England had been seized with a raging war fever. The gallant defence of Silistria had aroused enthusiasm and Nasmyth and Butler had become popular heroes. The British government was thus reluctantly forced into more active measures and decided not to make peace until the Russian fleet in the Black Sea and the defended harbours on which it was based had been destroyed. So at the end of August the order went forth sending the Allied forces to the Crimea with the object of destroying the defences of Sebastopol.

Update

The main reason for the Allied invasion of the Crimea now becomes clear. The Port of Sevastopol traditional home of the Russian Black Sea fleet had the potential to make mischief at some time in the future, and therefore was to be destroyed by an Allied invasion of the Crimea. However there still remained the option of blockading the Port from the Black Sea entry. At this time of August 1854 Odessa and Kherson, as well as Sevastopol were under Allied blockade (as were the Russian Ports on the Baltic far to the North), ensuring that the Allies had complete control of the Black Sea, and the Mediterranean. This provided the guarantee that the Russian Black Sea Fleet bottled up in the Sevastopol harbour presented no significant nor immediate threat. This would be known by the Allies at that time.

There is also the aftermath of the victory at the Alma when the Russians had scuttled part of their fleet in order to narrow the gateway in and out of the harbour. However in so doing they had also reduced the number of ships in their fleet, and furthermore restricted their own comings and goings, making it an easy and almost entirely risk free task for the Allies to continue the blockade and so maintain their vigilance of the Black Sea and the Mediterranean, and at very little cost to the nation in terms of finance and lives?

However with the Alma battle now being hard fought and won, and therefore access to the destruction of Sevastopol to be the next short move, the advance around Sevastopol by the Allies continued, and then came the point of no return during the early part of the investment which led to the continuation of the siege for the next year.

We have now arrived at the point of a totally unnecessary Invasion which was nothing less than Victorian Gunboat Diplomacy, and furthermore relied heavily on the suspect motives of the French support, for without that support the Invasion could not go ahead.

There was also the Cholera epidemic which continued unabated slowly but surely depleting the Allied Forces, and so because of, or in spite of the epidemic the half planned Invasion of the Crimea was to go ahead. I again make the point that these present updates are not from hindsight, for these facts were readily available at that time to any British Government that was really interested in peaceful negotiation. There was a peace plan on the diplomatic tables at that point, but it was too demanding of the Russian's, almost as if a continuation of the different Allied self interests was to continue as a self fulfilled legacy and prophesy. In other terms the invasion was going ahead anyway!

Reg Hist

Before that decision was reached those forces had faired badly in Bulgaria. The British troops, after a short stay in Varna, were encamped at Aladin, near the lake of Devna, a very picturesque but singularly unhealthy spot. Surgeon Major bostock thus describes the place and its effects.

'A great portion of the valley consists of low marshy land, is liable to inundations of the river and produces a rank vegetation when exposed to the powerful action of the sun during the summer month. Exhalations arise from the land, which become manifest as outbreaks of fever, and cholera amongst the troop in the vicinity. Exposed to this influence the battalion which up to this period had been excellent now began to deteriorate. Several cases of fever, all of an intermittent character, occurred and bowel complaints become prevalent. On July 1st the Battalion marched to Aladyn about 10 miles inland on the Devna road and encamped with the brigade on ground recently occupied by the Light Division, a little elevated above the head of the lower lake and surrounded by wooded and highly picturesque country but abounding in the sources of disease. Fever and bowel complaints become more prevalent and more severe. On July 19th the first draft of 159 men joined the Battalion. They were mostly young soldiers and soon felt the injurious effect of the climate and the sudden changes of circumstance. The first death that took place in the Battalion, since it left England, occurred in the case of one of the young recruits from cholera after a few a hours illness on July 27th.

During august, fifty-four men of the Battalion succumbed and Surgeon-Major Bostock records that there were few who were not affected by illness of one sort or another. 4 on august 16th the Brigade was ordered to Varna to give it the benefit of sea air. Captain Haygarth, who kept a diary, says under Wednesday, August 16th;. *'Up early, tents struck at 4.30 as we commenced our march at 5.30 for Varna. Our packs carried for us on horses and arabis on account of the weakness of the men. Very short marches only about six miles a day.'* Three days were taken to cover the distance of seventeen miles from the camp at Aladyn to the new camp near Varna, which is striking evidence of the effect of a badly chosen camping ground on the efficiency of the battalion, and its losses from disease were below the average. We have seen that the battalion left England twenty-nine officers and nine hundred and thirty-two other ranks. Three Officers had joined en-route and it received in Bulgaria a draft of three officers, lieutenant-colonel Onslow, Captain Viscount Chewton and Lieutenant Thistlethwayte and one hundred and fifty-nine other ranks. It embarked at Varna for the Crimea with thirty-four Officers and seven hundred and one other ranks present and fit for duty, and a number of Officers who were doing duty were affected by illness, Lieut-Colonel Onslow and the Hon.C.A. Scott were invalided home and lieutenant Thistlethwayte crawled out of hospital to embark, so that time spent in Bulgaria was more deadly than was any battle of the Crimean war'

Update
Ravages of the Cholera and of Politics

A poisoned mix of Cholera, Military Politics and Gunboat Diplomacy

The question being, was the Allied Invasion of the Crimea with the sole objective of destroying the Port and the Russian Black Sea fleet in Sevastopol implemented because of, or in spite, of the British and French armies Cholera epidemic, and was then the needless Invasion all about an implementation of pure and undiluted British gunboat diplomacy, thus leading to the invasion of the Crimea being carried out by an unprepared and diseased British army?

The Russians had lifted the siege of Silistria around the last week in June 1854, and so the war the British had come to fight was over. Yet by the end of June the British Government had decided to continue the war against Russia by Invading the Crimea in order to destroy the Russian Black Sea Fleet Port at Sevastopol. This was their sole intent for the Invasion. So why the Invasion of the Crimea on the main Russian Motherland, and this sole purpose in destroying the Black Sea Fleet Port at Sevastopol really all about in terms of the safety and security of the British public back in Britain?

Kinglake had suggested at that time;

'If France had been mistress of herself, or if England had been free from passion and craving for adventure, the war would have been virtually at an end on the day when the Russian army completed its retreat from the country of the Danube and re-entered the Czar's dominions. How came it to happen that, rejecting the peace which seemed to be thus prepared by the mere course of events, the Western Powers determined to undertake the invasion of a Russian province'?

The Times newspaper was later to carry out much hind sighted reviews based on Kinglake's 'Invasion of the Crimea', which in my opinion tells of the 'Gunboat Diplomacy' which was inbuilt into the invasion of the Crimea. This Gunboat Diplomacy which was to straighten out wayward opposition to the British Governments wishes and policies overseas had been carried out principally by the British Navy, combining with British troops to ensure the wishes of the British Government, and were common policy by the middle of the 19th century, so much so that the principle had become embalmed in an unwritten British constitution where the need to make up the rules as the British Monarchy and Government went along the imperialist road had been deemed necessary. Therefore the Gunboat policy now being underwritten was for the British to finally safeguard the security of British shipping through the Mediterranean and Black Seas;

The Invasion of the Crimea Sept 1854

Times Review of Kinglake, the British 'Reason Why', for the Invasion of the Crimea

'The Ministry had resolved that the Crimea should be invaded because they were anxious to check the arrogant pretensions of Russia. They obeyed not only the popular impulse, which was rampant for war, as Mr Kinglake loudly

declares, — they availed themselves of an opportunity to strike a blow at an enemy who excited their apprehensions in the East, who threatened to disturb the balance of Europe, and menaced us in our Indian Empire.

It was because in the vast arsenal of Sebastopol Russia held uplifted a mailed hand for ever ready to strike the sick Turk, and to grasp his inheritance, that the Ministry and the people designated it as the point of attack. The despatch merely put in an elaborate form the orders which the Cabinet thought fit to give Lord Raglan to carry out their views. It contained no new principle, embodied no novel direction, made no alteration in plan. St Arnaud was at the same time ordered by the Emperor not to advance towards the Danube, and was directed to support the English in an invasion of the Crimea.'

Orders for the Invasion had been given to the Cabinet by the Duke of Newcastle at Pembroke Lodge, Richmond on June 28th, so the British Government were losing no time in ordering the invasion. The orders were then sent to Lord Raglan and reached him at Varna, about which time Cholera had entered the British camp via the French in July 1854. It had first occurred among the French on their troopships passing from Marseille to the Dardanelle's, stayed with them while they were quartered at Gallipoli, and followed them to Bulgaria where it spread to the British. In less than a month the British lost over 500 men whilst a French Staff Officer estimated that 10,000 of their Army lay dead or struck down by sickness. Dysentery and diarrhoea was to stay with both Armies for the rest of the War: Cholera was to abate and then return in April 1855. It was under these diseased and stressful conditions that the army would now have to undergo the Invasion of the Crimea which had been predetermined by the British Government, and Lord Raglan

Ravages of the Cholera and of Politics

had received the despatches for this Military operation at his HQ in Varna.

Can we begin to imagine the dilemma and pressure that Lord Raglan was now under!.

Now begins the catalogue of Crisis management leading to further incompetence which was to virtually destroy the British Army of the East during this campaign. Lord Raglan on receiving the despatches and after some reflection on their contents, had then sent for Sir George Brown for a meeting between the two old comrades and brothers in arms. This was not a secret meeting, but a quiet space and time in which to deliberate on the situations and problems now inherent in agreeing to undertake this invasion of the Crimea. Lord Raglan was also under the extra pressure of being privy to the dormant commission now residing in Sir George Cathcart's left hand breast pocket. After some discussion between themselves George Brown remarked that if Lord Raglan would not accept the command of the invasion, then the Government would find a replacement. Thus Lord Raglan was then reminded that the replacement was already in command of the 4th Division, and would in all probability not hesitate to accept the challenges of the invasion. Thus Lord Raglan now had an extra and subjective problem, for if he was to resign there is no doubt that Sir George Cathcart would immediately contrive to taking over command of the army and then Sir George Brown would soon know the facts of the secret dormant commission, and Lord Raglan would lose further face amongst his dearest comrades and the army. Could this situation have tipped the balance between an invasion and a quiet withdrawal of the Allies, whilst just leaving a token force to support the Turks and with the Allied fleets handy to provide back up should the need arise?

Another factor and part of the puzzle was that Brigadier General Airey had reported on the ravages of cholera to the army command in Britain, and the doubts as to the wisdom of invading the Crimea. These doubts he resurrects later when he is blamed for the winter troubles. He was later exonerated from any blame by an official enquiry. The rest is now history, in that the Invasion of the Crimea and the Gunboat Diplomacy required to destroy the Russian Black Sea Fleet at Sevastopol was implemented in spite of the cholera.

So what about Cholera?

Cholera, a severe infectious disease endemic to India and some other tropical countries and occasionally spreading to temperate climates. The symptoms of cholera are diarrhoea and the loss of water and salts in the stool. In severe cholera, the patient develops violent diarrhoea with characteristic "rice-water stools", vomiting, thirst, muscle cramps, and, sometimes, circulatory collapse. Death can occur as quickly as a few hours after the onset of symptoms. The mortality rate is more than 50 per cent in untreated cases, but falls to less than 1 per cent with modern effective treatment. With severe symptoms of cholera the suffering patient would have called out for death to come as a relief from the agony, and knowing that there was to be no cure. Just imagine the foreboding of this evil disease and how it would have played on the minds of all ranks of the Allied armies, as they went about the dreadful task of burying their friends and comrades, and wondering who would be next.

The causative agent of cholera is the bacterium Vibrio cholerae, which was discovered in 1883 by the German doctor and bacteriologist Robert Koch. Virtually the only means by which a person can be infected is from food or water contaminated by bacteria from the stools of cholera patients. Prevention of the disease is therefore a matter of sanitation. Cholera epidemics swept through Europe and the United States in the 19th century but did not recur in those areas after improvement of the water supply. The connection between the disease and infected water sources was discovered by a London anesthetist, Dr John Snow, during an epidemic that occurred in London in the 1850s, when he established that the source of infection came from contaminated water in a water pump in Broad Street.

Thanks to; Journal of the Society for Army Historical Research 75 (1997) 240-245

Cholera and Dysentery in the Crimean War:
A Layman's View
By Major Colin Robins.

During the Crimean War death rates in the 'Army of the East' from disease were nearly four times those from Enemy action. 16,297 out of total deaths, 1854-56, of 20,813.

Over half the deaths from disease were recorded as from dysentery or cholera.

It is tempting for the modern reader to assume that someone, the High Command, the Commissariat or the Medical Services must have have been to blame for this. But in considering the matter one must do so in the light of contemporary medical knowledge, not with the advantage of twentieth century hindsight,

For the causes of cholera and dysentery were not yet known; treatments were inappropriate and ineffective.

How was cholera then viewed, and were the deaths from from disease unavoidable?

This essay is an attempt to consider the question from the layman's point of view and to set it in its historical context.

Even John Shepherd, whose masterly work is essential reading for any student of the Crimean War, not just of medical services, writes as a qualified and experienced doctor, and takes much for granted which needs explanation to the layman, who may well have mental picture of the cholera victims having a black and bloated face-not a symptom of cholera at all!

Cholera was then thought by some to be due to a change in the ponderable or imponderable elements of the air, others regarded it as as the result of 'a vegetable miasma arising from the soil' or even due to volcanic or other changes in the crust of the earth.

A few realised that it was contagious but others thought that it came from 'animalcules' in the air.

Cholera reached the British Army at the camp at Varna in July 1854.

It had first occurred among the French on their troopships passing from Marseille to to the Dardanelle's, stayed with them while they were quartered at Gallipoli, and followed them to Bulgaria where it spread to the British.

In less than a month the British lost over 500 men whilst a French Staff Officer estimated that 10,000 of their Army lay dead or struck down by sickness.

Dysentery was to stay with both Armies for the rest of the War: Cholera was to abate and then return in April 1855.

Did the Army Doctors realise at any stage of the campaign how the diseases were really spread? There is no evidence that they did. They must be excused for old fashioned views in 1854 when these were widely held in England; thus, some of the moves of camp made while the Army was in Bulgaria were attempts to escape the 'Malarial exhalations and miasmata' rising from the two lakes near Varna.

But as late as August 1855, when the second epidemic of Cholera was at its height, they thought it was due to a combination of heat, 'tainted air' from tainted water, and general filth.

Was that then an accepted point of view?

Study of the English Medical press shows that controversy still raged. It is sufficient to quote from the Medical Times and Gazette, which was the chosen medium of Dr Snow himself. Lengthy extracts were printed from a 'Report on Cholera in the Baltic fleet in 1854' by Sir William Burnett, Director General of the Medical Department of the Navy.

'Copious use of zinc chloride in the bilges', etc., was apparently beneficial, but perversely, the report stated that 'Cholera prevailed extensively in those ships in which distilled water was used', whereas the ship Magicienne remained cholera free though taking on water from the River Neva which had been criticised as as polluted with sewage from from Cronstadt.

Snow wrote at once, seeking to interpret these statements favorably to his theory, but not all readers would have been convinced.

An Assistant Surgeon wrote from the camp before Sevastopol on 12th March 1855, expressly denying that water was the cause of dysentery 'Since there is one common source from whence the Officers and men procure their supply, and the former have been comparatively exempt from dysenteric disease'.

He was sure that it had been caused by *'The exposure of the autumn, the rations of meat and green coffee, the severity of the weather and the absence of all comfort, warmth and dry clothes on returning from duty'*.

This theme reinforced a powerful leader of 10th March which noted inter alia that 'The harbour of Balaclava must by now be a vast cess-pit' and warned Lord Raglan that if he continued to allow sanitary matters to be neglected then he would command an Army 'Of invalids, worn down by diarrhoea and dysentery, covered with the fatal spots of plague, or raving with the delirium of fever and quartered in the hospitals of Scutari and Smyrna'.

By then at least the cleaning up of the Harbour had been started under Colonel Harding, and expert civilian help from James Newlands, the Liverpool City Engineer, was on the way.

Finally, in April 1855, Snow submitted a paper to the magazine on the subject of contamination of water supplies which could hardly be faulted today. In particular he noted that whereas at Varna the French had suffered more from cholera than the English, the situation had been reversed at Sevastopol, and he attributed this to the fact that they had soon after their arrival there, laid down a piped water supply from the hills above their camp.

What of the English water supply?

Water had to be taken where it could be found and there was no way of purifying it. The wretched attempts of the soldiers to heat their food and roast their coffee are well known, and boiling all their water would have been totally impracticable. Combating the dehydration of the diseases with impure water would have been useless, and in any case it seems likely that in the Army the spread of disease was as much from contaminated food as from water. Standards of personal hygiene obviously varied and this is perhaps one the reasons why the incidence of the disease was less among the Officers. But it was almost impossible for the men to keep clean anyway.

Were the Medical Services to blame in any other way?

The possible confusion between cholera and dysentery will almost certainly have made no difference as the same (Ineffective) treatment was provided for both diseases. The toleration of filth everywhere (Even in the Hospitals, until Florence Nightingale arrived) is a fair charge, but one which the High Command and every Regimental Officer must also answer.

Their defence would no doubt be that the soldiers were living in conditions which were nowhere as bad as those in the slums in every major city in Britain. This is not an excuse that any modern Officer trained to look after his men before himself would accept for a moment: and the Naval Brigade did conspicuously better.

True they had some advantages, but Commodore Lushington's arrangements for the comfort and well-being of the sailors ashore were in sharp contrast to the apparent indifference of Army Commanders, and the casualty figures show the same divergence.

Thus it is the non-cholera diseases (Including dysentery) where contemporary commentators found the High Command and the Commissariat guilty, for the way some Regiments were worked to death.

Their soldiers went for long periods of exacting duty without proper food or shelter, which must have reduced the strength and resistance to disease of many to the point where they died from an illness which if not exhausted they would not have caught, or would quickly have shrugged off. The point had been made in the Medical Times and Gazette,

'Our soldiers have had bad shoes, miserable quarters, a scant supply of fuel, and provisions of a very indifferent quality. They have been exposed to a very low temperature, overworked and underfed. Under those circumstances, the mortality has been exactly what might have been anticipated (Colin Robins Italics for emphasis)

The indictment contained in the the Report of the Commissioners, Sir John McNeill and Colonel Tulloch, appointed by Parliament is well known, as is the answer to it from the so-called Chelsea Board of General Officers, who exonerated all the Officers concerned and put all the problems down to 'A shortage of pressed hay from England'. Much less well known is Colonel Tulloch's printed response to the criticisms in the latter of him and his fellow Commissioner. In it he quotes of the actual evidence which was necessarily omitted from the first report as the War was then still going on. And the bare facts were dispassionately stated the 'Technical' Medical report prepared for Parliament.

In some conclusion, however unlucky the scourge of cholera, thousands of men were allowed to perish through overwork, and for want of wholesome food and proper protection from the weather.

Little wonder then that the greatest danger came not from the enemy but from its own lack of structure and organisation. An army of 28,000 men under Lord Raglan landed at Varna on 29 May 1854 when the practical difficulties of maintaining that number without adequate preparation and co-ordination soon became evident. Within a matter of weeks large numbers of the men fell ill with diarrhoea and sickness brought on by polluted water supplies and unsanitary conditions;

within two months over five thousand men had been admitted to hospital. In June cholera made its first appearance and by mid-July an epidemic was raging. At the military hospital that had been established in Varna the death rate reached 86%. The effect on morale was devastating, for without a shot being fired the army lost at least 900 men with many more being laid low by sickness and lassitude.

Internet

Reg Hist.

It was with very real joy that the battalion received on august 28th the news that it was to quit Bulgaria to embark for the Crimea. Actually the move was delayed for more than a week and the fleet weighed anchor for its new field of adventure on September 7th. while the 1st battalion was at Varna the Gazette of June 20th arrived from home with the news that lord Rokeby, Colonel G. Dixon and Colonel G. Eden had been promoted Major-General and that Colonel G. Moncrieff had become Lieutenant-Colonel of the Regiment. Colonels Dixon and Moncrieff went home on promotion on July 10 and the 1st battalion sailed under the command of major and Lieut-Colonel Sir C. Hamilton, Bt. In the same gazette Lieutenant Stephenson was promoted Captain and Lieutenant-Colonel. He thereupon resigned his position as Brigade Lajor and took over command of the Left Flank Company.

The expeditionary force moving to the Crimea under Lord Raglan had been organized in five Infantry Divisions and a Cavalry Brigade. The 1st Division, commanded by the Duke of Cambridge, was composed of the Guards Brigade under Bentinck, who had been promoted Major-General, and the 42nd, 79th, and 93rd under Sir Colin Campbell, with two field batteries. Sir De-Lacy Evans commanded the 2nd Division with Pennyfather's and Adams's Brigades, each of three line Battalions. The divisional artillery consisted of two field batteries. The composition of the 3rd division was the same. It was commanded by Sir Richard England, with Campbell and Eyre as his Brigadiers. The 4th Division under Sir G. Cathcart was incomplete and had only four line Battalions and one battery. The Light Division commanded by Sir G. Brown had two Brigades under Codrington and Buller, with the 2nd Rifle Brigade, one Horse Artillery Battery and one field Battery as Divisional troops.

The Cavalry under Lord Lucan, with Lord Cardigan as his Brigadier, had five Cavalry Regiments and one Battery of horse Artillery. The 4th division, being incomplete, was at first left behind, but lord raglan brought it up in time for the landing for which his available force was 1,000 sabres, 26,000 infantry and 60 guns.

The French Army, under Marshal St. Arnaud, consisted of 30,000 infantry organized in four Divisions, under Prince Napoleon, Canrobert, Forey, and Bosquet, with a Turkish Division 7,000 strong attached. The French had sixty-eight guns, but no Cavalry. Lord Raglan had some difficulty in persuading St. Arnaud to accompany him to the Crimea, for the destruction of the Russian naval power in the Black Sea was not a French interest; but he managed to convince him that the Allies could not make peace honourably without striking a blow at Russia, and that Sebastopol was the best target.

Update

I believe the last paragraph above makes it very clear that without gaining French Support the invasion of the Crimea could never had gone ahead just formed by the British and Turks acting with each other, and that state would have been the end any invasion plans, and the termination of the Eastern question, at least for the time being.

Furthermore It was not difficult for Lord Raglan to gain French support from the Emperor in Paris, nor from the French Commander St Arnaud, the real difficulty lie in trying to persuade many of the senior elements in the French forces to understand the reason for this invasion and its benefits to France on a long term footing.

There is also another matter which is not referred to within the Scots Fusilier Guards journal, and this was to be one of the main events leading up to the decision to embark on the invasion.

1) The Duke of Newcastle had despatched orders for the invasion of the Crimea. For the details of the initial cabinet discussion of the orders to be sent on to Lord Raglan, and one of the major reasons for the invasion of the Crimea going ahead is contained in a little realised British Government Cabinet meeting in the relevant chapter of the updated journal.

2) There was also the private, though not secret, meeting between Lord Raglan and Sir George Brown at Varna, in which they discussed the Newcastle despatches, and their reservations against the invasion at such a late period of the year, the continual outbreaks of cholera, lack of information and knowledge, and a French officer resistance against the invasion. An opposition which had in fact been quelled from Paris. Then the circumstances which would have arose if Lord Raglan had refused the command of the army and the commission, with the probability that someone else would take it on, and then of the dormant commission in Cathcart's breast pocket, which Raglan was well aware of, though Brown was not. Which unorthodoxy begs the question;

Ravages of the Cholera and of Politics

Was the dormant commission, sparked by Queen Victoria herself in order to keep command of the Army from the Duke of Cambridge, to actually tip the point of balance between an invasion of the Crimea, or a winter deployment in the area away from the Crimea?

Consider the options available If there had been no dormant commission. Lord Raglan could have then well argued against the Invasion, and the French command could have then told Paris that Raglan was the defaulter of the Invasion, and Raglan would have informed Newcastle that the French had withdrawn their support, which was true enough given all the ingredients of the situation. Or some other dual arrangement have been made to suit all camps. Thus in the end result there would have been no invasion of the Crimea, and no War?

Therefore if the Monarchy in the shape and form of the Duke of Cambridge had not been part of the expedition as Commander of the 1st Division, then there would have been no need for the Dormant commission, no need for the underhanded conspiracy that went along with the package, and so no Invasion of the Crimea, and no war?

And then for a moment or two consider the aftermath of a Crimea war which has long preyed upon history, and still serves to provide reasons why war should never be an option open to the monarchy, politicians and diplomats, without the public at large being given a neutral and detached forum open and transparent to all sides of the question. Or was it the British peoples' enthusiasm for the continuing war against Russia that formed the main causal for the invasion of the Crimea?

I believe it most unlikely, for if the government had no wish for continuing the war with Russia there would have been no invasion at that time. Or shall we continue to refer, and be of the opinion that the Invasion of the Crimea was nothing more, nor less, than 'Gunboat Diplomacy' once again called into action by the British administration, which had included Queen Victoria, though Consort Prince Albert was firmly against the affair?

Reg Hist

So on September 9th the Allied flotilla assembled off the coast of the Crimea. Of that country their ignorance was complete, for the French, not expecting a move in that direction, had collected no information, and in those days had no military intelligence department. Such news, scanty enough, as was available about the enemy's forces, the nature of the country, and the defences of Sebastopol, came from the Foreign Office and naturally enough was not such as a Commander-in-Chief would require.

The Hon. J.S. Jocelyn wrote home this account of the voyage from Varna to the Crimea:-

'I shall leave these few lines with Mr Halpin, who remains on board at present, to forward to you by the first steamer to Constantinople. We left Ballshieh Bay last Thursday, steered north east till we were off Cape Jarkhan, a cape on the north-west coast of the Crimea which we reached on Saturday evening. We cast anchor there in 25 fathoms, out of sight of land, and stayed at anchor there all Sunday, till Lord Raglan, who went on in a small steamer to reconnoitre the coast, came back to us on Monday morning. On Monday we steamed again down the coast of the Crimea, and it was a wonderful sight to see all those magnificent ships, about 400 of them altogether, but, if bad weather had come, very dangerous. As it was we had a short squall on Monday night that took the two ships that we towing so suddenly that we were obliged to cast them adrift, and in so doing it brought us right round, and at that moment an immense steamer

towing two large ships was coming right across our bows. I thought it was all up with us. But the second ship just caught us on our figure-head, carrying it and the whole of our bowsprit away, and the motion sent us away from the ship that was towing after her. As it was we lurched very heavily and altogether it was a most providential escape- the second we have had since we left Malta on board this ship. On Tuesday night we all cast anchor in Koslof or Eupatoria Bay, and are now steering direct for Sevastopol about 20 miles off. I shall add a few lines when we stop opposite the exact place where we land. As we carry nothing on shore but what we carry on our backs, our cloaks, and three days biscuit and pork, I may not be able to write so soon again as I could wish for, for I shall have nothing to write on until I get my baggage up, which may not be for some time.

Update
His Royal Highness Prince George, Duke of Cambridge
B 26 March 1819 –D 17 March 1904

'Know your enemy'!

The individual perception of the understanding of knowing your enemy, is perhaps more complex than the notion of gaining that knowledge and experience may at first suggest. For your enemy may well be close to you, but not seen nor recognized as such, and in fact may be easier seen and recognised as a friend at the superficial level, simply put, all those who appear to be on your side may not in fact be so, but are part of a social illusion created more by individual and group dynamics added to expectations rather than true reality. For 'friendship' may only be acknowledged in the minds and terms of functioning goodwill between those who volunteer for the social contract of kindliness between the leaders, members and followers, and in terms of honest mutual respect, one for another

Let me give an example. In the modern British Army, soldiers, and in fact all serving members of the armed Services are encouraged to know their enemies. This 'skill' becomes principle in their learning curve as an intrinsic element of the maturing as fully skilled and ever developing human piece of a military team. A team which begins with individual's, and then moves through a process, and system of becoming part of larger grouping of individuals. Eventually therefore the serving person becomes a component piece of the complete jigsaw of an Army, or even a joint service group perhaps as a member of NATO or some other international command element.

So knowing your enemy as a tool of knowledge and information becomes second nature, and if in doubt, say nothing. And so do we presume that the nearer you are to your enemy the more you get to understand them, or do you, and therein lies the rub?

Unfortunately for myself, and many thousands of those others who have been serving British soldiers, the early training and mindset of originating this personal skill of knowing your enemy normally begins close at hand, and I had an indication of this unraveling of friend from foe during my time at the Guards Depot, Caterham, back in 1957. During those days of National Service, when those you would have thought had your best interests at heart, being the officers and NCOs responsible for your performance during basic training actually executed the duties of an 'Enemy', with an even better unconscious intent than that of being a friend. In other terms they set out to make themselves unpleasant, rather than as enablers, facilitators or just supporters of the recruit's undergoing their basic training. Thus the contest between those training the recruit that should have been your friends, became your enemies of not only of the individual recruit, but also the collective group of recruits all undergoing the same 'friendly fire' of the instructors. This process of the 'enemy' being close at hand continued during my time in the Battalions where *'watching your back'* became 2nd nature, and now as I update this journal, and turning on occasions to research the present Scots Guards Chronicle, titled *'Among Friends',* I am again reminded that that title framed in the realness of life and my personal experience was to be some way from the absolute truth.

This inconsistency then of knowing your friends and your enemies, both on your side of the fence and the other side, then attaches itself to your physic, and lo and beheld you have it taped, and may then plan your moves and social grouping accordingly. However the problem may be unbeknown to the individual soldier in the shape and form of their senior officers, who they very rarely get to know, which brings me nicely to the point.

HRH George Duke of Cambridge was to be the Commander of the 1st Division for a while, that is until he deserted his command, and presumably all of his friends, in November 1854, and sailed back to Britain where he was to be ushered into Queen Victoria's presence where she was heard to exclaim *"Shame, Shame"*! However it was not too long before the affable and friendly George was to take over as the new Commander in Chief of the British Army with the death of Lord Hardinge the previous incumbent of that post. Certainly the C in C duties were all about administration rather than command, and George was probably placed in that managerial position to safely ensure that he would never command troops (or friends) in the field again, and so it proved. What a way to manage an Army!

And we know that the Royal procedure and links to the armed forces continues even to this very day when it cannot be good nor sensible policy for the forces to become linked to the monarchy in any shape or form. And I may speak especially for the Brigade of Guards, as the relationship continually gets in the way of developmental training. Plus the British Royal family and politicians are bad enough without complicating the set up even further by also adding them up as part of the leadership equation, and do not forget the media in this contamination and growth of collective obstructions. Whose army is it, anyway?

So let us now have a look at the profile of our supposed friendly George, and learn more about him during his time as Commander of the 1st Division during the Crimea Campaign

George was a member of the British Royal Family and Army Officer who served as Commander-in-Chief of the British Army from 1856 to 1895.

A male-line grandson of King George III, the Duke of Cambridge was a first cousin of Queen Victoria and the maternal uncle of Princess (Victoria) Mary of Teck, the consort of King George V.

There now follows his CV;

Field Marshal His Royal Highness Prince George William Fredrick Charles, KG, KT, KP, GCB, GCMG, GCVO, KJStJ, ADC, Duke of Cambridge, Earl of Tipperary, and Baron Culloden was born at Cambridge House in Hanover, Germany, the only son of Prince Adolphus, Duke of Cambridge and his wife, the former Princess Augusta of Hesse-Cassel. He was styled Prince George of Cambridge until he succeeded to his father's dukedom on 8 July 1850. King George IV created him Knight Grand Cross of the Royal Guelphic Order in 1825. King William IV appointed him a Knight of the Garter on 15 August 1835. Queen Victoria conferred the following honors upon him: Knight Grand Cross of the Order of St. Michael and St. George (1845); Knight Grand Cross of the Order of the Bath (1855); Order of St. Patrick (1861); and the Order of the Thistle (1881); and Knight Grand Cross of the Royal Victorian Order (1896). He became a personal aide-de-camp to the Queen in 1882 and to King Edward VII in 1901.

Prince George of Cambridge was educated in Hanover by the Rev. J. R. Wood, a canon of Worcester. Like his father, he embarked upon an army career. In November

1837, after he had served for a short time in the Hanoverian army, he received the rank of colonel in the British Army. He was attached to the staff at Gibraltar from October 1838 to April 1839. After serving in Ireland with the 12th Royal Lancers (the Prince of Wales's), he was appointed colonel of the 17th Light Dragoons (now Lancers), in April 1842. From 1842 to 1845, he served as a colonel on the staff in the Ionian islands.

The Duke of Cambridge became inspector of the cavalry in 1852. He held that post until 1854, when, upon the outbreak of the Crimean War, he received command of the 1st Division (Guards and Highland Brigades) of the British army in the East. In June 1854, he was promoted to the rank of lieutenant general.

He was present at the battles of the Alma, Balaklava and Inkerman, and at the siege of Sevastopol.

On 5 July 1856, the Duke was appointed *general commanding-in-chief* of the British Army; a post that was retitled commander-in-chief of the forces by Letters Patent in 1887. In that capacity he served as the chief military advisor to the Secretary of State for War, with responsibility for the administration of the army and the command of forces in the field. However, the commander-in-chief was not subordinate to the secretary of state. He was promoted of the rank of field marshal on 9 November 1862.

The Duke of Cambridge was the longest serving head of the British Army, serving as commander-in-chief for 39 years. Although he was deeply concerned about the welfare of soldiers, he earned a reputation for being resistant to doctrinal change and for making promotions based upon an officer's social standing, rather than his merit. Under his command, the British Army became a moribund and stagnant institution, lagging far behind its continental counterparts.

In the late 19th century, whereas 50 per cent of all military literature was written in Germany and 25 per cent in France, just one per cent came from Britain. It is said that he rebuked one of his more intelligent subordinates with the words: *"Brains? I don't believe in brains! You haven't any, I know, Sir!"* He was equally forthright on his reluctance to adopt change: *"There is a time for everything, and the time for change is when you can no longer help it."*

In the wake of the Prussian victory in the 1870-71 Franco-Prussian War, the Liberal Party government of Prime Minister William Gladstone and Secretary of State for War Edward Cardwell called for major army reforms.

The resulting War Office Act, which Parliament passed in 1881, formally subordinated the office of commander-in-chief of the army to the secretary of state. The Duke of Cambridge strongly resented this move, a sentiment shared by a majority of officers, many of whom would not have gained their posts on merit alone.

Under the Order-in-Council of February 1888, all responsibility for military affairs was vested in the office of commander-in-chief. An 1890 royal commission led by Lord Hartington (later the 8th Duke of Devonshire) criticized the administration of the War Office and recommended the devolution of authority from the commander-in-chief to subordinate military officers. The Duke of Cambridge was forced to resign his post on 1 November 1895, and was succeeded by Lord Wolseley, whose duties were considerably modified.

The Duke of Cambridge served as colonel-in-chief of the 17th Lancers, Royal Artillery and Royal Engineers; the Middlesex Regiment and King's Royal Rifle Corps;

colonel of the Grenadier Guards; honorary colonel of the 10th Duke of Cambridge's Own Lancers, 20th Duke of Cambridge's Own Punjabis, Royal Malta Artillery, 4 Batt. Suffolk Regiment, Middlesex Imperial Yeomanry, and 1st City of London Volunteer Brigade. He became the ranger of Hyde Park and St. James's Park in 1852, and of Richmond Park in 1857; a governor of the Royal Military Academy in 1862, and its president in 1870.

The Duke of Cambridge died in 1904 at Gloucester House, Piccadilly, London. He was buried next to Mrs. FitzGeorge in Kensal Green Cemetery, London. With his death, the 1801 creation of the dukedom of Cambridge became extinct.

The Duke is today commemorated by an equestrian statue standing on Whitehall in central London; it is, somewhat ironically, positioned outside the front door of the War Office that he so strongly resisted. It is also sad to relate that nowhere in Britain is there a statue to Lord Raglan who died at his post outside Sevastopol in June 1855?

Now perhaps another version of HRH George from further research, not so kind, but fits in with events.

Death or Glory. The Legacy of the Crimea War

Robert B. Edgerton Westview Press 1999

With the exception of the American Civil War in which thousands of men suffered a psychosomatic stress reaction called *nostalgia,* as well as many other kinds of psychiatric disorders, stress reactions were seldom reported during wars of the nineteenth century." The Crimean War was no exception. Personal accounts by men who survived this war rarely even hint at any stress reactions by them or by other, comparable to the "shell shock of World War I, the "combat fatigue" of World War 11 or the "post-traumatic stress syndrome" of the Vietnam War.' However, one evident exception was His Royal Highness, the Duke of Cambridge.

Needless to say, accustomed to the utmost in luxury, he thought nothing of arriving in Turkey trailed by seventeen carts filled with personal baggage. In letters to his wife, he complained despairingly about the cold, the mud, the hunger, the endless fatigue, and the ghastly horrors of war, saying that the war had "completely worn out my nerves and spirit." However the Duke of Cambridge cared intensely about the welfare of the Brigade of Guards, which he commanded. At Inkerman, he led the Guards with reckless bravery during the day-long battle, having his horse killed under him as he rode through the Russian troops surrounding him. He escaped with only a minor flesh wound, but his exhaustion after the battle was profound. He began to obsess about the Guards losses, which amounted to some 40 percent of the brigade, bursting into tears in public when he visualized the dead bodies he had seen. When he became unable to sleep and physically ill with diarrhoea, doctors ordered him aboard the ship *Retribution* to recuperate. The hurricane struck only a few days later, the battered ship very nearly sinking. As the storm ravaged the ship, the duke lost control, clutching the hand of a steward and wailing over and over, "Oh! We shall be lost!"[1] He then developed a fever and could not bear to think about the war, which he referred to as a "dreadful thing," He insisted that he could not bear to remain in the Crimea and asked the Queen's permission to leave for England, citing ill health. She told him that she had already heard the rumours said to be flying about the clubs of London that the Duke had lost his will, adding that his departure from the Crimea was unthinkable. Disregarding her wishes, he returned to England and, despite disdainful gossip, was eventually forgiven sufficiently to serve as Commander in Chief of the army for thirty-nine years.

In all probability, the Duke *of* Cambridge was not the only man to react as he did. Perhaps some of the officers who found ways to leave the Crimea were suffering distress comparable to his. But if so, they left no memoirs, and doctors in the various armies made no mention of symptoms of what would now be called post traumatic stress among their patients. It is tempting to speculate that soldiers in the armies of the Crimean War had led such horrific lives that they simply could not express what they may well have felt. But we know that many soldiers were aghast at what they saw at least early in the war, and that some officers did exhibit cowardice. It is also possible that because there was no concept like *shell shock* that would legitimise stress-induced symptoms, men could not show their symptoms without fear of scorn or punishment. It is apparent that as the twentieth century progressed, and stress-related incapacity for duty became increasingly legitimate in Western armies, more and more men were diagnosed with this disorder. Still, there is good reason to believe that the symptoms of post traumatic stress syndrome were known in antiquity.

When one now considers the difference with hindsight in quality of service and endeavour over a period of time between the Duke of Cambridge and his subordinate during the Crimea Campaign, Sir Colin Campbell, it is not too difficult to work out who was the true leader of the two.

Yet family prestige was to hold all the cards for those that made it to the top as a matter of 'right' through the privileges attached, whilst there were those that worked hoping that they may be noticed for well deserved promotion, a prime example being the relationship between the Duke and Sir Colin Campbell, leading onto the regiments of Guards and Highlanders being partners within the ranks of the 1st

Division, which brings me back to the question of 'knowing your enemy'?

I believe that this example is as good as it will get as we look at the two men from the perspective of the Crimea War, where it may have been that Sir Colin Campbell was to 'look after' the Duke of Cambridge, and so Highlander and Guardsmen fought together in the same Division?

And they were certainly no friends to each other!

And so get know your enemy, for they could be commanding, or governing you, wherever you may be!?

There is a further indicator to be acknowledged, questioned and then answered when paying detailed attention to the command structure of the 1st Division to be commanded by his HRH the Duke of Cambridge.

This Division, comprised of three Guards Battalions under the command of Brigadier Bentink of the Coldstream Guards, plus Three Highland Regiments, under the command of the well known and highly experienced Sir Colin Campbell, who was perhaps the best commander that Lord Raglan had. (I will be discussing Sir Colin Campbell further on in an update) But in my opinion his job was not only to command the Highland Brigade, but also to take care of the Duke of Cambridge, his immediate senior and Commanding Officer.

There is much evidence, especially via Kinglake to demonstrate this guiding relationship between Cambridge and Campbell.

This situation within the command elements would then contain some logic of the unholy mix of Guards and Highlanders making up the 1st Division. for here we have two seemingly well separated soldiering cultures supporting each other, when in actual fact suspicion would have weighed heavily on the Highlander poachers turned gamekeepers, especially so amongst the officers, and again there is evidence to support this claim that the Guardsmen who were the Queens favourites (especially so the Scots Fusilier Guards) would have instinctively shunned the Highland Clansmen. The Jacobite rebellion was only 3 or 4 generations past after all!

During my lifetime so far, and as far as I am concerned, the British Monarchy have treated the country of my birth and all of its peoples with a certain patronizing arrogance and self righteous proclaim, and now as I gaze out of my Dining Room window in Sevastopol and look upon the British Memorial Monument crumbling and neglected at Cathcart Hill in the distance, it would seem to me that I should grant no loyalty towards the monarchy, or what they are supposed to stand for in the governance of the people of Britain, and in recent times, the Commonwealth of Nations, plus they are certainly no friends of mine!

Update
A Very Special Cabinet Meeting.

"Anybody for a smoke"

The author George MacDonald Fraser, (1925-2008) was to enjoy acclaim and popularity along with 'Flashman', the hero of fortune he had created. Flashman the cowardly soldier who always made good, in the Victorian times of British Imperialist Empire building. An Empire building structure which was very closely and factually linked to the practical application of *'Gunboat Diplomacy'*. But perhaps, and now somewhat unfortunately, his hero also fits too neatly into the perceptions that present day cynical historians carry with them when thinking of character profiling during this particular phase of somewhat infamous British Political and Military History. The Lord's Lucan and Cardigan providing an example, and leading to these present times of still unfinished business, Cock-Ups and Conspiracies treading those important historical paths leading to demographic, religious and political turmoil, which even in these present times continues to spark into violence around this present troubled World, and may be traced back to the 'Empire', and all it stood for. All caused by British administration, long past, past, present and no doubt into the future.

I was drawn to this particular cabinet meeting when going through the index of one of Fraser's books *'Flashman at the Charge'*, and I came upon the reference to this particular Cabinet Meeting held at Pembroke Lodge, Richmond, on the evening of June 28th 1854. A Cabinet Meeting in which the Duke of Newcastle, the British Secretary of State at that

A Very Special Cabinet Meeting.

time, was to discuss his orders to be sent to Lord Raglan for the prompt Invasion of the Crimea. This discussion with the Cabinet assembled for the very purpose of debating the dispatch, and every person at that auspicious gathering would have been well aware of the facts that were to be seriously and well thought about and debated.

However it should be noted that at that time the war that the British Forces had voyaged to fight was now concluding with the Russians' hesitantly headed home from the hapless siege of Silistria with their tails between their legs. Whilst being led from St. Petersburg by a Czar who had now lost the opportunity to 'cure (Turkey) the sick man of Europe' by taking it over. The cabinet assembled would then have been made aware of this opportunity to cancel out the war and then turn to peaceful approaches to compromise the situation between the Russian Empire and the British interests in that demographic and territorial area of the World. Unfortunately however for the Czar at this time with his opportunity lost, was an opportunity to be gained by the British, and they quickly took advantage of the Czars disadvantage by very quickly exploiting the situation leading on to the Allies Invasion of the Crimea, rather than looking for peace terms. Therefore under these conditions the Duke of Newcastle had expected to be given a questioning and probing time by the assembled cabinet members. After all the orders were explicit in their positive appraisal of the opportunity that the British Forces now had to Invade the Crimea. Quickly besiege the Port of Sevastopol, which was the base of the Russian Black Sea Fleet, and destroy it, thus ensuring the routes to the East were left open to Britain through the Mediterranean and the Black Sea.

The cabinet were expected to deliberate on this issue, for though it would seem that according to the history of the times the people were enthusiastic for the invasion and destruction of Sevastopol, some politicians and senior Military Officers could foresee the dangers of an action that was not prepared fully. There was also the lateness of the seasonal cycle with winter soon to come. Also the health of the Army which was in a state of Cholera epidemic, plus the almost academic point that the Russians were still in occupation of the area of the Pruth River, and could return to fight on, though all the indicators and diplomatic signals were against this happening. So, there was much to discuss that June evening if troubled times ahead were to be avoided.

The next phase of my research to unravel what happened during that important cabinet meeting was to directly approach the writings of Kinglake himself for the full story of the mysterious events at that very special cabinet meeting

The Invasion of the Crimea. Kinglake

The Duke of Newcastle took the Despatch to Richmond, for there was to be a meeting of the members of the Cabinet at Pembroke Lodge, and he intended to make this the occasion for submitting the proposed instructions to the judgment of his colleagues. It was evening—a summer evening—and all the members of the Cabinet were present when the Duke took out the draft of his proposed despatch and began to read it. Then there occurred an incident, very trifling in itself, but yet so momentous in its consequences, that, if it had happened in old times, it would have been attributed to the direct intervention of the immortal gods. In these days, perhaps, the physiologist will speak of the condition into which the human brain is naturally brought when it rests after anxious labours, and the analytical chemist may regret that he had not an opportunity of testing the food of which the Ministers had partaken, with a view to detect the presence of some narcotic poison; but no well-informed person will look upon the accident as characteristic of the men whom it befell; for the very faults, no less than the high qualities of the statesmen composing Lord Aberdeen's Cabinet, were of such a kind as to secure them against the imputation of being careless and torpid. However, it is very certain that, before the reading of the paper had long continued, all the members of the Cabinet, except a small minority, were overcome with sleep. For a moment the noise of a tumbling chair disturbed the repose of the Government; but presently the Duke of Newcastle resumed the reading of his draft, and then again the fated sleep descended upon the eyelids of Ministers. Later in the evening, and in another room, the Duke of Newcastle made another and a last effort to win attention to the contents of the draft, but again a blissful rest (not this time actual sleep) interposed between Ministers and cares of State; and all, even those who from the first had remained awake, were in a quiet, assenting frame of mind. Upon the whole, the Despatch, though it bristled with sentences tending to provoke objection, received from the Cabinet the kind of approval which is often awarded to an unobjectionable sermon. Not a letter of it was altered ; and it will be seen by-and-by that that cogency in the wording of the Despatch, which could hardly have failed to provoke objection from an awakened Cabinet, was the very cause which governed events.

And so it came to pass that in the fullness of time and British political expediency, the Allied Invasion of the Crimea was to take place.

But what was the reason that had caused the cabinet to lose interest in a discussion around the events and circumstances of a conflict that though now ending at Silistria, could begin again at Sevastopol. Surely this particular Cabinet Meeting could be thought of as both fundamental and crucial. And yet rather than steep themselves in this issue of a National Crisis, the Cabinet had induced sleep and torpor amongst themselves until they had been overcome, and so by default the Duke of Newcastle now had the bit between his teeth for his objective, the Invasion of the Crimea and the destruction of the Russian Black Sea Port at Sevastopol.

In my opinion the reason for this singular lapse by the assembled British Cabinet is not too difficult to assume, for if the Cabinet was present then so was Lord Palmerston, (according to Flashman he was?) who at that time was Home Secretary. Which brings me directly onto the question of the trading of Opium, which was yet another major issue included as an important element of the National debate, and also of the wider Victorian population of those times. The use of opium for both medical care and for use as a recreational drug was rife throughout the land, and Palmerston had already involved himself in the first opium war of 1839-1843, and was to again between 1856-1860, when Prime Minister. Therefore the cabinet as part of their ongoing agenda would collectively have been made well aware of the smoking of opium, and the taking of the drug would probably have been prevalent even amongst members of the government. So there was no harm, nor nothing untoward, in a relaxing smoke of opium whilst waiting for the Duke of Newcastle to arrive, and indeed could be considered as normal.

However, perhaps the Duke had been too late and the opium smoked too long?

And so by the Invasion of the Crimea in September 1854, Britain went to prolong a war that was now over, with an army that was militarily unprepared, and very sick with the cholera, Though perhaps rather than finish at the war they had gone to fight, there was also conspiracy in the political air, for bringing an army home to Britain, or indeed taking it elsewhere when riddled with cholera would not be a good idea neither, nor with any dead Russians to show for the effort, But the loss amongst the British Army had been very significant. No, better that the invasion goes ahead, and then there is always the French to either rely on for the victory, or blame for the failure of the invasion.

In December 1854, Richard Cobden MP was to make a speech in Parliament. A statement of composed parliamentary rhetoric which tore to pieces any sense the Government may have had for their expedient Invasion of the Crimea. Meanwhile and at the time of the Cobden speech in December 1854, the British Army was lying stagnating outside Sevastopol, and on the Plain of Balaclava. They had lost all their momentum, and began to feel the real difficulties of coping with yet more disease, added to the severity of winter, and after the great storm of November 14th at Balaclava, had lost their supply of winter clothing. Something then had to happen, and in the true path of British parliamentary method the Prime Minister was eventually changed, Aberdeen for Palmerston. Thus the war was to continue, and still true to form in these present times, for in any crisis management parliament they still tend to change the oil rather than the engine, and so the lame duck procedure for British political management continues from before those times to these present times by the very simple formula of changing Prime Ministers.

Update continues

A 'Dormant Commission'

Appropriately, and by Conspiracy, passed on to General Sir George Cathcart

Since when did the British Army ever approve the policy of a *"Dormant Commission',* which is then to be kept secret from the army and its structure of command. To do so would surely undermine the complete and understandable function of any *'Chain of Command',* A *'Standard Operational Procedure'* known, expected and appreciated throughout the British Army from its earliest beginnings, for this sacred chain of known command fully ensures that any casualty at all levels of commanding communication could be quickly filled by someone who understands exactly what the Strategic and tactical positions are at that time, and then their part to play in any renewed hierarchal structure. This was, and is, especially so at the top management level where 2/ICs were kept in close proximity to their Commanders, so that the Command structure could be continued quickly and cohesively in the event of the Commander, at any level, being called away or becoming a casualty.

So why the deviation from that age old and very trusted British army policy?

Begging the question of exactly why, and what was the main purpose of General Sir George Cathcart, Commander of the 4th Division being secretly given the *'Dormant Commission',* which he had also been instructed to carry at all times from that time on. He had been called on to the post of Commander of the 4th Division. A somewhat reactionary command, for it was to be kept as the hind leg in reserve during the early part of the Crimea campaign, and especially so at the Alma where his Division was not only at the rear of the Army, but was also short of a further battalion which had not yet joined up with the main force and was required to make up its numbers. Furthermore the 4th Division were still only issued with the smooth bore musket, when practically every other battalion in the force had been issued with the Minie Rifle, and which was about to find a new place in Infantry Strategy and tactics, with Cathcart not being in close proximity to the new teachings and practice as it was to be put into effective usage by the British Army, and for the first time in anger!

It would seem that Cathcart was given the rough stick under the command of Lord Raglan, and there is much evidence to point to this conclusion. There is also enough evidence to make the point that Cathcart was indeed unhappy with this appointment, or certainly the secret manner in which he had been made to accept it. The feelings of insecurity and then neglect would have also played on George Cathcart's mind and perhaps through his coming trials and tribulations, and as a result of this piece of State manipulative nonsense would in essence lead to his untimely death at Inkerman. Though by the time of that carnage at Inkerman he had been relieved of the dormant commission.

General Sir George Cathcart would have been angry and frustrated inwardly at his treatment by Lord Raglan. Perhaps leading onto his disobeying Lord Raglan's specific orders to fill the gap between the Sandbag Battery and the Barrier, and then went on to motivate the small remainder of his division which he still had with him, having distributed his main force around the British defences. This action of

Cathcart's which prompted the 'False Victory' at the Kitspur during the rash advance motivated by himself, was to lead directly to his death. Unfortunately it also led to other death's. Know your enemy indeed. Perhaps Cathcart had carried out this act of defiance with the prime intention of winning the battle and thus demonstrating his abilities as the next army commander?

We will never know, will we?

(The Dormant Commission could have also led to the very Invasion of the Crimea, which is discussed during this updated history)

So let us try to find the reasoning behind this unorthodox move from the accepted function of the senior chain of command by asking the question 'where did this order originate from'?

Certainly not from the Army, so where?

My research gives an indication that the order for the Dormant Commission was dispensed from the Monarchy, and then endorsed through some political and military mechanisms.

But why from the Monarchy?

Surely they could leave command structures to the Politicians and the Army command. So what was to be so different in this situation?

In my opinion the answer lies in the person and personality of the Commander of the 1st Division, HRH the Duke of Cambridge, who at Queen Victoria's command must not under any circumstances be allowed to take over as Commander in Chief of the army in the event of Lord Raglan being incapacitated. Or for any other reason of not being available to command the Army, and this situation was to be kept secret between HM Queen Victoria, Lord Raglan, Sir George Cathcart, and the Duke of Cambridge himself.

If this course of events is in any way correct it would mean that the Duke's mental state was even at this early stage of the army's move to the East known to be suspect, and to his nearest and dearest, and also taking into consideration that he was the Queen's cousin, that lady would be well aware of any inadequacies in the Duke's mental make up. In fact sometime prior the Duke had been a suitor for marriage to the young Queen Victoria, though she had vetoed the idea after some superficial courting. However I must make the further point that this assumption made by myself that the Duke was to make a poor Divisional Commander, now comes well loaded with hindsight, which would not have been appreciated at that time.

My personal conclusion is simple, yes, he may well have been a 'Jolly good fellow' but he was no divisional commander, and as an army commander?

To all other intents and purposes the next natural leader of the British Army in the East, was Sir George Brown Commander of the Light Division who more than any other in the expeditionary force enjoyed Lord Raglan's confidence and trust. Yet Lord Raglan was never to inform George Brown of the dormant commission given to Sir George Cathcart, which was to place a strain upon Lord Raglan in his close relationship with George Brown, and thence further pressure on his command of the British Army of the East. What effect then on both Raglan and Cathcart, and try to ascertain exactly what effect the strain of keeping Sir George Cathcart's secrecy of the dormant commission was having on Lord Raglan's overall leadership capabilities, and Cathcart's command of the 4th Division responsibilities. I begin by suggesting that once in the campaign field the significance and priority of the dormant commission would be moved slowly to the back of Raglan's mind as the list of priorities ranged themselves into a never ending and changing basis from one day to the next. I think it should also be kept in mind that this campaign was being fought by crisis management rather than pro-active positive thinking and action. Thus the Dormant Commission fairly quickly become of a low priority grade as more immediate matters were to set upon Lord Raglan's mind. Lord Raglan would continue to assume his normal, almost casual manner of his own form of diplomatic mismanagement of the Army, and thus lose mind sight of the Sir George Cathcart personal predicament. Though in the camp of the 4th Division the issue of the dormant commission would be keeping Cathcart alert for any indications that he was to be given a command more suited to his star rating as 2/IC, or at least called to Lord Raglan's side for advice and confidences. But this was not the case, and so General Sir George Cathcart was no more than the other divisional commanders awaiting their master's orders and their promotion opportunities.

The Dormant Commission being given in secret to Sir George Cathcart, and so keeping it away from the Duke of Cambridge, had to happen in the opening stages of the campaign as the army of the East was forming and preparing. The conspiracy would also be better kept secret, or known only to those who could implement this handing over of the Dormant Commission whilst ensuring that no-one else would be aware of the subterfuge being committed. Thus the Duke of Cambridge would save face, but also know that he had to prove himself before he could assume his own ambitious motives, should he have any. It could well be argued that at that time, and considerations, that Sir George Cathcart was the obvious choice to be the 2nd in command but the army still had to prove itself, so it was not felt appropriate to designate a 2/IC at that stage, but just to ensure that the Duke of Cambridge could not be a candidate for the position at that precise time.

So In very simple terms the dormant commission was given to Cathcart to keep it away from Cambridge

I have yet to read any other realistic or authoritive reason for the dormant commission being given to Sir George Cathcart. Thus the Monarchy in collusion with the political and military establishment kept the Royal induced conspiracy from the British Parliament and the people.

The argument I have put forward could also be seen as the reason for the invasion of the Crimea which would have led indirectly and in subterfuge to the Crimea War.

(See the meeting at Varna between Raglan and Brown).

Update continued

The Dog 'Bob'

A regimental doggie story indeed.

Whilst we journey towards the Crimea Campaign we might well spare a thought for the dog 'Bob', who was to remain in the Regiments care until he to was killed, not whilst on active duty outside Sevastopol, but sadly whilst on Public Service duty outside Buckingham Palace?

The Dog Bob also gives an insight into the Public Duty role of the Guards Brigade at that time for some interesting detail of its format and role play, as Queen Victoria's latent and ceremonial security shield at the Royal residences.

I have also included this chapter to make the point that soldiers are human, and always have been. Sometimes however they may be taken out of the order and expectations of the human social contract, whilst serving in the contemporary soldiering society in which they find themselves. This phenomenon may occur under the harsh and brutal conditions they have to live with, and become part of; therefore making the point that it is only by their socialisation process once serving that changes the individual from one person to another, and in essence the soldier may become a 'Jekyl and Hyde' character!

This first article is taken from an item published in the 1960 edition of the Scots Guards Magazine.The second article which follows on is to be the true story of the 'Dog Bob', written by Colonel Francis Haygarth, himself a 'Lion' of the Scots (Fusilier) Guards, an article contributed by L/Cpl Keith Gorman of the Archives, RHQ Scots Guards We shall meet up again with Colonel Haygarth at the Alma

The Dog Bob by J A Elliot

'Bob' was the name and title of a hero whose exploits have never found their way into official despatches or been blazoned forth to an admiring world by the loud tongued trumpets of Fame. He was a faithful dog, who was as modest and unassuming as he was brave and bold, and it now becomes the duty of his historian, and those who love courage and fidelity in dumb animals, to lay a chaplet on his memorial. Poor Bob's birth was a mystery to his military friends, but he was found one night in the winter of 1852/3 under the following melancholy circumstances, and to the hour of his death he never ceased to be grateful for his timely rescue.

The sentry posted in the gardens of St James's Palace on the night of our story was a Scots (Fusilier) Guardsman and he went on duty at two o'clock in the morning. All was quiet for a time, but Jock had not been very long at his station before a most unusual disturbance took place outside the Palace walls on the side farthest from the gates. The sentry had no means of ascertaining the cause of the uproar, but it seemed like a short sharp struggle between two persons, while blows, like those produced on the body of a man or animal by a heavy stick, were frequent. Above all was heard the constant barking, and occasional howling of a dog, which gradually became fainter and fainter, until it grew into a prolonged and dismal moan. Then the sentry heard the deep thud of a heavy body falling within the Palace grounds, and a sad wail, like the cry of a deserted child, fell strangely upon his ear.

The sound of receding footsteps and the murmur of voices were heard for a moment in the distance, and then again all was still, except for the low wail mentioned above. The sentry's heart was moved to pity and forgetting his 'orders', he left his post to serve the cause of humanity. Proceeding to the spot from whence the agonised sound seemed to come, he found

The Dog 'Bob'

there a poor dog, lying bleeding in the snow, and evidently severely injured. 'Puir deil!' exclaimed the generous-hearted Scotsman, 'It shall never he said that Jock Anderson refused his succour to a puir dumb-creature in distress. Come, then, get on thy legs, mon, an' we'll find a house for ye.'

The poor dog seemed to appreciate the Guardsman's kindness, for he licked the great rough hands that gently lifted him upon his legs, and made a strenuous effort to walk towards the sentry box. At this moment the gates opened and a light twinkled dimly through the darkness. It was three o'clock 'Rounds', and the sentry was a long way from his post. 'By Heavens!' he exclaimed, in a low voice. 'You are in for it now, Jock, and no mistake; but never mind, mon,' he continued, addressing the dog, 'I'll not desert ye.'

The Sergeant of the party stamped his foot hard upon the frozen snow as he approached the sentry-box, in order to attract the attention of the sentry, who was supposed to challenge with a stamp of the foot also, instead of the usual. 'Who goes there?', a system adopted in palaces to avoid disturbing the inmates.

No reply being returned, and the usual salute and cry of 'All's Well', being missing, the 'Rounds' went right up to the box. There is no sentry here!' said the officer, as the Drummer held up the lantern and allowed the dim light of the candle to expose the vacant receptacle.

'Here am I, Sergeant', exclaimed the generous soldier, as he appeared, leading the poor wounded animal along at a very slow pace. 'This puir doggie has been thrown over the wall by some brutes, and his cries were so pitiful that I couldna' leave him there to dee in the could snow.

"Am I to understand', said the officer in a stern voice, 'that you left your post, contrary to orders, to attend to that dog?"

Aye, sir, I did', replied the sentry, in a broad Scots accent, as he brought his musket to the shoulder, 'and I hope ye will excuse me for rescuing a puir, half-murthered doggie frae death. Indeed I thocht it was acheil at first.'

The officer's heart was touched with sympathy, and he turned to consult the Sergeant on the matter, while the latter, proud of the reference, and clothed for the nonce with that 'little brief authority' drew himself up to his full height and said, 'This man, having left his post contrary to strict orders, sir, and against the provisions of the Articles of War, should be relieved from his post and marched back a prisoner to the-guard-room.

"Very well, then,' replied the officer a young Lieutenant of not very long standing, "Let him be relieved".

Jock Anderson was then relieved from his duty, and his musket and bayonet being taken from him, he was marched back as a prisoner. After all, a soldier is but a man, and Jock, who had seen many years' service in his Regiment, found his eyes filled with tears as he was thus, for the first time, disgraced in the presence of his comrades. While he was thinking of this, however, he felt something warm touch his hand, and looking down, he beheld the poor dog whom he had rescued, gazing steadily at him with such a sympathetic look, that he felt his heart bound within him, and he could not help exclaiming, 'Puir beastie! Thy gratitude is my best reward. "Silence!' thundered the Sergeant 'To the right face! Quick march!' And the 'Rounds' marched back to the guardroom, visiting the other sentries on their way, all of whom wondered who it was that was thus made a prisoner, and for what reason.

Meanwhile the poor dog, still bleeding from the effects of its ill treatment, limped painfully along some distance behind the 'Rounds', and never lost sight of them once they reached the guardroom. On their arrival, the disarmed sentry was further denuded of his belts, and dismissed to the genial comfort of the guard-bed for the remainder of the night. He went and sat down by the fire, however, and had scarcely done so, when the poor dog limped in, and going straight to his benefactor, began to show such unmistakable signs of delight that the Sergeant again exerted his authority and said, 'Turn that dog out!' But the officer, amused at the incident which had occurred during his Round, and not liking the idea of making the man a prisoner, had remained at the door of the guardroom to watch the proceedings of the dog, and on hearing the Sergeant's order, he stepped forward and expressed a desire that the dog should remain and be well cared for. 'God bless ye sir! - thank ye, sir!' exclaimed Jock Anderson as he patted the dog, and made a bed for him before the blazing fire with his greatcoat - which he took off his own back for the purpose.

'Yes, sir, very well, sir,' said the Sergeant in an obsequious tone. 'I will see the Colonel about it in the morning, Anderson', said the officer, 'and will do what I can for you,' and turning on his heel he left the guardroom, and retired to his own feather-bedded and carpeted chamber.

As soon as he had disappeared, and the Sergeant had gone to that part of the room set apart for the Non Commissioned Officers, Anderson's comrades crowded round him to hear the story of his adventure. And while he was narrating it the generous fellow himself got a sponge and some warm water from the cantiniere's (canteen woman's) stall, and gently bathed the poor dog's wounds, while others picked out some choice pieces of meat from the tin plates with which the tables were strewed, and toasting them at the fire, made a savoury supper for the poor animal. It was a touching sight to see poor Bob, for by this name he was at once christened, endeavouring by all means in his power to show his gratitude for all this kindness. When the morning

The Dog 'Bob'

came, the Lieutenant true to his promise, sought the Colonel and gave him an account of the incident which had occurred, taking care to make the soldier's offence appear as light as possible. The Colonel, luckily, was not a martinet, otherwise it would have fared hard with Jock Anderson (who would certainly have been tried by court martial, and sentenced to a long term of imprisonment), and he resolved to overlook the offence, on condition that the culprit promised never to leave his post again, except according to orders.

The young officer was not long in imparting the good news to the prisoner, who gave the promise required, and was allowed to resume his duties without any further interruption. The dog, which was of no particular breed, was not a bad looking animal, but whatever he was deficient in appearance was amply atoned for by his subsequent conduct. A very brief period of kind treatment served thoroughly to restore him to a life of activity; and for ever afterwards, though he remained faithful to his preserver, he was considered as Regimental property and was dubbed, both by officers and men, with the title which stands at the head of this history.

Bob's fidelity was destined soon to be put to a much sterner proof than it had yet experienced. He had already been through a soldier's, or rather a dog's life, at Chobham Camp, and had shown his aptitude for a military career, but scarcely was his first campaign over than a real one had to be undertaken, and he accompanied the 1st Battalion Scots Fusilier Guards, to which he belonged, to the Crimea.

On the disembarkation of the allied armies in the Crimea, Bob's campaigning life began in earnest, for he had to pass the first night in the open air, along with the men of his battalion, amid a continual downpour of rain. But the following days were luckily fine, and the march to the Alma was almost of the nature of a pleasure-trip. It lasted but one day, and on 20th September 1854 was fought the battle of that name, at which

The Dog 'Bob'

Bob saved the life of his preserver, and so repaid the debt of gratitude he owed him, besides contributing to the preservation of other valuable lives. It happened in this wise. In the most critical period of the fight on the heights, the 1st Battalion Scots Fusilier Guards was suddenly thrown into disorder by the retreat of a regiment in its front which was caused by some mistaken order, and falling back for a short distance it became exposed to a most terrible fire from the Russian batteries. In the confusion which ensued Cpl Anderson and others, with the dog, had got separated from the Battalion, and before they were aware of it, a party of Russian soldiers, belonging to the great Vladimir Column, attacked them and endeavoured to make them prisoners. The Guardsmen fought valiantly for their lives and liberty, and Anderson was engaged with three Russians at one time. He succeeded in bayoneting one, and had clubbed his musket to deal with the other, when the dog, who had been watching the scene very intently, seeing the third man levelling his gun at his preserver, sprang fiercely upon him, and seizing him by the arm compelled him to drop the musket instantaneously. At the same moment Anderson disposed of his other assailant and took the third fellow prisoner, and by this time the Battalion, which had recovered from its momentary mistake, came dashing bravely forward to victory. A few minutes afterwards its Regimental Colour was planted upon the hard-won heights, and Bob stood at the foot of that proud standard, not the least amongst the many heroes that glorious day had made.

The Dog 'Bob'

At Inkerman, Bob was wounded in the right forefoot. He turned out on that dark November morn and followed his friends to the field. Grenadiers, Coldstreamers and Fusiliers fought there like the heroes of old, until their ranks dwindled to a 'thin red streak' of single file, and in the thickest of the battle Bob, in his own modest fashion, performed prodigies of valour. Many a Russian soldier felt the keen edge of his teeth on that memorable occasion, and perchance, came to the conclusion that the little British Army who stemmed that living tide of 70,000 stalwart Muscovites, must have had demons fighting on its side. Bob's generous protector was that day numbered among those whose lives were sacrificed, and the poor dog's grief was heartrending to see. Though wounded himself, he took no heed of the fact, but sat by the side of his friend's body until the burial party removed it. He followed, and when poor Anderson was laid in the grave, he leapt into the pit and could only with difficulty be removed. But Anderson's comrade, a Sergeant of the same Company, took the faithful dog in his arms and carried him, in spite of his pitiful cries, to his tent, where he had his leg washed and bandaged, and where he was also kept a prisoner until he had regained the use of his leg.

His favourite resort, until the Army quitted the Crimea, was the mound where poor Anderson was buried on Cathcart's Hill, named after Sir George Cathcart, Commander of the 4th Division, who was killed at Inkerman. (He was a kinsman of the former Lieutenant Colonel Commanding.) It was from that spot he was unwillingly led when the Guards embarked at Balaklava, and turned their bronzed and bearded faces homewards. At Aldershot, to which station they were ordered on their arrival in England, Bob had the honour of being introduced to Her Majesty The Queen, who was pleased to take great notice of him, and to stroke him gently with her parasol and at the subsequent review held in Hyde Park, he marched proudly behind the Colours of his Battalion to the

The Dog 'Bob'

tune of 'See, see, the Conquering Hero Comes'! To his collar was attached the two war medals, and an imitation of the Victoria Cross with which his friends had solemnly invested him, and which was made from spent Russian rifle bullets.

After serving faithfully with the Battalion for so long, he was allowed to march at the head of the Queen's Guard whenever it was found by the Scots Fusilier Guards. But Bob did not long survive his return from the Crimea. marching at the head of the Guard on 4th February 1860, he was run over and killed by a butcher's cart outside Buckingham Palace. His death was a sad blow to the Regiment, and his body was subsequently stuffed and mounted in order that Scots Guardsmen could see him and be proud of him for all time. Bob now sits, looking as intelligent and proud as ever, in the Scottish United Services Museum, Edinburgh Castle. On 4th February 1960, on the centenary of his death, the Lieutenant-Colonel Commanding the Regiment presented a plaque to the Museum from the Regiment to be placed on his showcase.

An amusing sequel to this story turned up after the presentation of the plaque was publicised in the newspapers. A Miss Coward of Edinburgh found a letter written by her grandfather, who had seen service in the Regiment in the Crimea. He had written home about the dog 'Bob,' and wrote that he was called 'Bob' during the week, and 'Robert' on Sundays and would not answer to his weekday name on the Sabbath!

The Dog 'Bob'

Scots Guards Magazine Editors Note;

The poem below has been transcribed from a recently recovered original script, circa 1860s.

On the death of the Scots Fusilier Guards dog Bob

Go lift him gently from the wheels and soothe his dying pain, For love and pain can yet he feels Though love and care be vain.

'Tis sad that after all these years Our comrade and our Friend, The Brave dog of the Fusiliers should meet with such an end.

Up Alma's hill among the vine we laughed to see him trot, Then frisk along the silent lines to chase the rolling shot.

And when the work waged hard by day and hard and cold by night, When that November morning lay upon us like a blight.

And eyes were strained and ears were bent against the muthering north, Till the grey mist took shape and sent Grey scores of Russians forth.

Beneath that slaughter wild and grim nor man nor dog would run, He stood by us and we by him till the great fight was done.

And right throughout the snow and frost he faced both shot and shell, Though unrelieved he kept his post and did his duty well.

By death on death the time was strained by want, disease, despair, Like Autumn leaves our Army waned but still the dog was there.

He cheered us through these hours of gloom we fed him in our dearth, Through him the Trench's living tomb rang loud with reckless mirth.

And when peace returned once more after the city's fall, That veteran home in pride we bore and loved him one and all.

With ranks refilled our hearts were sick and to old memories clung, The grim ravines we left glared thick with death stones of the young.

Hands which had patted him lay chill, voices which called were dumb, And footsteps that he watched for still never again could come.

Never again, this world of woe still hurries on so fast, They come not back, 'tis he must go to join them in the past.

There with brave names and deeds entwined which time may not forget, Young Fusiliers unborn shall find the Legend of our pet.

And when some grey haired soldier tells how through that night of fear, The City tolled its sullen Bells warning that death was near.

How with the Fog that shrouded foe rolled round us nigh and nigher, Like mouldring smoke which gathers slow to burst in floods of fire.

Hence wandering through the past at will before our children's eyes, To frame each living picture still just as he sees it rise.

How bearing down to many a soul after a long delay, The great siege of Sebastopol began at break of day.

The Dog 'Bob'

How with full knowledge of the fate that dogged their desperate track, The Balaclava horsemen straight rode into Hell and back.

How o 'er the bleakhills bloodstained crest as Boys at football run, The Guards and Highlanders abreast raced for the Alma Gun.

How sudden our each fevered bed delight like sunrise broke, When soft hands propped the dying head and tender voices spoke.

And then awakening from despair at length the soldier knew, That to her children suffering there the Mother's heart beat true.

Marked by the Medal, his of right and by his kind keen face, Amid these histories grave and light Poor Bob shall keep his place.

And never may our honoured Queen for love and service pay, Less brave, less patient, or more mean than his we mourn today

"BOB," THE SCOTS FUSILIER GUARDS' DOG. By COL. FRANCIS HAYGARTH, S.F.G., 1841-1860

The article below which appeared in the 1933 Household Brigade Magazine, concerning the 'Dog Bob' was kindly sent to me by
K Gorman, BA (Hons)
Lance Corporal
Archivist
HQ Scots Guards
Wellington Barracks
London
SW1E 6HQ

The Dog 'Bob'

"BOB" was a native of the Royal Borough of Windsor, and passed his puppyhood in the service of a butcher of that town. Like many others who have won distinction in the British Army, he started in a humble station of life. He gave early token of a liking for a soldier's life, and in the spring of 1853, the 1st Bn. Scots Fusilier Guards being at Windsor, "Bob" was frequently found in the barracks and taken back by his master, but returned as soon as opportunity offered. His master, finding that" Bob" had made up his mind to follow the drum, at length gave up all thought of reclaiming him, and when the Battalion marched to Chobham Camp in June, "Bob" marched with it, recognized as belonging thereto. Here he gave promise of that excellence for which he was afterwards distinguished as an old campaigner. Always first on parade, and when the duties of the day were over, no old soldier was a better hand at "foraging" and looking out for himself.

At the Wellington Barracks during the winter of 1853-4, some officers allowed "Bob" regular rations; and when the Battalion embarked on H.M.S. *Simoom,* at Portsmouth. On February 28th, 1854, "Bob" was among the first on board. Here his career was nearly brought to a close. For the First-Lieutenant, seeing "Bob," inquired, " Who's dog is that ?" and no one in particular claiming him, the order was given to "Throw him overboard," but before this could be carried out, it was explained that" Bob" belonged to everyone, and he was allowed to remain.

He soon became as great pet on board as he had been on shore. "Bob" served at Malta, Sartari, and in Bulgaria. When the Army embarked at Varna, for the Crimea, " Bob" got on board the wrong ship, and, his whereabouts being ascertained after the arrival at Baljik Bay, an escort of officers went after him and brought him back in their boat, a prisoner.," Bob" was at the landing in the Crimea and at the Battle of the Alma was returned among the "'missing.". He rejoined the Battalion at Balaklava, after the flank march; was present at the Battle of Balaklava; and at Inkerman he distinguished himself by chasing spent balls and shells, for which he was given a medal. He served in the trenches up to the fall of Sevastopol.

"Bob" returned to England with the Battalion, and marched into London at its head in July, 1856, having shared the fortunes of the Corps during a most eventful period. After that "Bob" did duty in London, Windsor and Portsmouth. He had a large circle of acquaintances and admirers. At Guard Mounting at St. James's or at reviews and field days in Hyde Park,' his portly form and decorated breast attracted considerably attention. While stationed at the Tower he patronized the steam-boats in performing the journey between that fortress and the West End, and as he was known to the steam-boat people, no objection was made.

Poor" Bob" met with an untimely death at the beginning of February, 1860, while marching out with his Battalion. He was run over by a cart and killed on the spot, to the regret of the whole Regiment. He was looked on as a comrade by all, and in the minds of many was associated with the most exciting events of the Russian War. Many were the expressions of sorrow as "poor old ' Bob' "was conveyed past the Battalion by a Drummer who carried him to the Buckingham Palace guard-room.

"Bob" was a great favourite from the time he joined, but he showed partiality to no one in particular. He would not go out of barracks with a single individual, except on duty. In commemoration of his faithful service, the- officers of the Regiment had him stuffed and presented to the Royal United Service Institution Museum, where he may be seen among the mementos of the Crimean War. Bob:' with his Inkerman medal, is now in the Scottish National War Museum at Edinburgh Castle

Update

I feel it sad that the RHQ at the time the history was compiled in 1934 forgot the dog Bob, but fortunately Col Haygarth's reminder, plus the other article above places 'Bob' back to his rightful place as a member of the SFG.

Its a humane story and demonstrates the goodwill in the hearts and minds of the soldiers.

Update continues

Sir Colin Campbell, of the Highland Brigade

The best are sometimes treated the worst, especially if serving with the Guards Brigade

The Internet is now a wonderful place to search for those little known publications leading to erstwhile added information which brings a fresh complexion to be added to previous publications. Therefore I like to mention authors who in the past have made this particular Scots Guards update possible with some human colouring and detail, and I now introduce you to Colonel **Sir Anthony Coningham Sterling** KCB (1805–1871) who was a British Army officer and historian, the author of *The Highland Brigade in the Crimea.*

Sterling, was the eldest son of Captain Edward Sterling, by Hester, daughter of John Coningham of Derry, was born at Dundalk in 1805. John Sterling was a younger brother. After keeping some terms at Trinity College, Cambridge, he was on 18 February 1826 gazetted Ensign in the 24th Foot. From 21 March 1834 to 5 December 1843 he was a Captain in the 73rd Foot, and was then placed on half-pay. He was on active service during the Crimean campaign of 1854–5, first as brigade major and afterwards as assistant adjutant-general to the Highland division, including the battles of the Alma, Balaklava, and Inkerman, and the siege of Sebastopol. He received the medal with four clasps, the order of the Legion of Honour, the Turkish medal, and the fourth class of the Medjidie.

On 17 October 1857 he sold his commission, retiring with the rank of Colonel; but during 1858–9 he was again employed as military secretary to Sir Colin Campbell, 1st Baron Clyde, in the suppression of the Indian Rebellion of 1857, and received a medal with clasp.

In 1861 Lord Clyde accused Sterling of willfully neglecting to insert the name of Colonel Pakenham in a list of persons recommended for reward by the bestowal of the KCB at the close of the mutiny.

This led to many letters, which are given in *Correspondence concerning Charges made by Lord Clyde against Sir Anthony Sterling*, March 1861 (privately printed 1863). He was gazetted CB on 5 July 1855, and KCB on 21 July 1860.[1]

He died at 3 South Place, Knightsbridge, London, on 1 March 1871, having married in 1829 Charlotte, daughter of Major-general Joseph Baird; she died on 10 April 1863.

Sterling was also the author of:

Russia under Nicholas I, a translation, 1841

Letters from the Army in the Crimea, written by a Staff Officer, 1857

The Story of the Highland Brigade in the Crimea, founded on Letters written during 1854, 1855, and 1856 by Lieut.-Col. A. Sterling, a Staff Officer who was there, 1895.

I was gifted the book during the Autumn of 2008 by a Dundonian business gentlemen who was visiting Sevastopol with the intention of paying a visit to Cathcart Hill. The book in question was first published in 1895, and tells it as it was then known with very few variables from that time to this, thus providing the reader with some unknown truths and facts that have been kept at arms length by the less emotional modern authors who have followed on to present times with their copyright publications with the sole intention of making money from the bones of those who fought and died in the Crimea during that conflict, whilst maintaining the status quo in order to endear themselves to the established order.

The specific reason I had asked for that book to be delivered was because I was sure it would make mention of the relationship between the Guards and the Highlanders, and I was not to be disappointed in this assumption, for the relationship between the Guards and Highlanders was not to be a friendly affair, with the book confirming what I already suspected of the initial make up and command of the 1st Division led by the Duke of Cambridge. A Divisional Commander very probably advised by Sir Colin Campbell, the real divisional leader commanding the Highland Brigade, who in their turn were the real soldiers of the 1st Division, and the action at the Alma was to demonstrate that as fact. Again adding to my thinking that the Division had been pasted together with the intention that Sir Colin could look after the Duke.

The first showing of this leadership sideshow was at the Alma battle which left the Scots Fusilier Guards claiming to be awarded 4 Victoria Crosses for getting it all wrong, and the Highlanders none at all for getting it right. Whilst at the heights of the Kourgane Hill the Highlanders rightfully claimed the final victory for the Allies at the Alma Battle, leaving the road and the miles to Sevastopol relatively left open for the advance onto the destruction of the port.

In any Infantry Division the combination and mix of the Regiments to be joined together is fundamentally important, for whilst rivalry leading to the competitive spiritual element is important between regiments and supporting groups and arms, so is the communication and respect between the officers and men of all the Regimental combinations within the Division, this convention especially applies to the officers. Therefore in compiling this update research of the relationship between the Guards Brigade and the Highlanders, I had the instinctive thoughts that neither that twain should have met especially at that time and in this place outside Sevastopol, though already there had been problems in the relationship. The mix between the regiments comprising the two halves of the 1st Division could not have been more culturally divisive with the Highlander Clansmen Scots joining company with the English monarchists of the Guards Brigade, for It must be taken into account that the '45 rebellion for Prince Charles James Stuart had only concluded some 3 or 4 generations past, and with the Highland clearances still being continued even as the Crimea War was being contested. This inhumane act of the clearances being part of the probable economic reason why the Highland Brigade was in existence, for the kilted soldiers had to earn money for their families in the Highlands from somewhere. Though ideally never to the extent of fighting alongside the 'Aulde Enemy' inner core of the English monarchist Guards. A deformity which would have surely bruised their Highland pride!.

So what was the political and military reasoning for this make up of the 6 Battalions of the 1st Division, and was the main reason to enable the experienced Sir Colin Campbell of the Highland Brigade to look after the inexperienced Divisional Commander, HRH the Duke of Cambridge. I will begin by taking the reader through the campaign in general terms.

Sir Colin Campbell was without doubt the only senior general officer to consistently perform to the expectations of his seniors and to the men he commanded throughout the Crimea War. He is also the soldier that had been passed by on promotion lists, sidelined by the established military and political order of the era because of his working class roots. Trying to unravel his passage through the Crimean campaign is difficult for he seems to belong to everybody, and yet no-body in terms of consistency, neither has any author to my knowledge totally dedicated himself to the detail of Sir Colin's career during the year long siege of Sevastopol. I have therefore drawn on information of a general nature to be found in many books and from other sources, but the one book that speaks with an authoritive pen was first published in 1895, so corresponds with the events as the author of the book who served with Sir Colin was to understand them. This book also fills in some of the gaps that have been left by the chronicle of the Scots Fusilier Guards.

The Highlander chronicle book's contents also includes the authors thoughts on what seems to be the warped and jaundiced relationship between the Guards Brigade and the Highlanders of the 1st Division, and I may mention yet again that I suspect that the 1st Division was put together in that way solely for Sir Colin to look after the young and inexperienced Duke of Cambridge, the Divisional Commander of the 1st Division, who was a good-natured man, industrious, well-liked and affable. That he could lead men under fire was yet to be seen.

On 11th February 1854 Sir Colin Campbell was offered the command of one of the two brigades which were to be sent to the Crimea. he accepted the command, but by the time he reached Turkey the 'Division' was an army, and he was appointed as the commander of the Highland Brigade of the 1st Division under the command of the Duke of Cambridge.

The Division consisting of the Guards Brigade, 3rd Bn Grenadier Guards, 1st Bn Coldstream Guards and the 1st Bn Scots Fusilier Guards, commanded by Brigadier Bentinck of the Coldstream Guards, and the 42nd, 79th, and 93rd Highlanders commanded by Brigadier Sir Colin Campbell. On 20 June 1854, while Sir Colin was at Varna, he was promoted to the rank of Major-General. He landed in the Crimea and fought at the battle of the Alma, during the battle and at the crucial phase he led his brigade against the lesser redoubt which had still to be taken by the Highland Brigade and overthrew the last columns of the Russians. Immediately Post Alma Battle he asked permission from Lord Raglan for permission to wear the highland bonnet instead of the cocked hat of a general officer. Lord Raglan agreed to this unconventional request, but in doing so confirmed Sir Colin Campbell as a 'Highlander'.

This uncompromising gesture by Colin Campbell would have led to an even more acrimonious relationship, between the Guards and the Highland men, for the Guardsmen were very aware that Sir Colin was the best the Division had and he was now further removed, and remember Sir Colin was a lowland Scots, so the Scots Fusilier Guards would have felt betrayed by this move of Sir Colin with his now confirmed loyalty to the Highlanders.

After the Alma Sir Colin Campbell was appointed as commander at Balaclava; his services were recognised by his promotion to the colonelcy of the 67th regiment on 24 October 1854. As commander at Balaclava he was responsible for the repulse of the Russian Cavaly column by the 93rd Highlanders, now famously termed as the 'Thin Red Line', but his Highland Brigade were not involved in the action at Inkerman on November 5th 1854. In December 1854 he assumed the command of the First Division, consisting of the Guards and Highland Brigade's when the

Duke of Cambridge returned to England having deserted from his 1st Division Command.

Lord Rokeby however was soon to arrive from Britain taking command of the Guards Brigade in January 1855, for the Monarchists back in London could not have a Lowland Scots disguised as a Highlander, in command of a Guards Brigade?

Sir Colin Campbell continued to command at Balaclava, which also included the Cavalry, under the command of Lord Lucan with his Cavalry Division, or what was left of them after the Battle of Balaclava. Surprisingly Sir Colin was able to enjoy a good and working relationship with Lord Lucan, who was always applicable to accepting advice reference the defence and detailed administration of the Balaclava area of command from Sir Colin. Sir Colin was to receive continual thanks for his services from Lord Raglan. On 18th June 1855 he led the 1st Division up to the front, and commanded the reserve at the storming of the Redan on 8 September. He was made a G.C.B. on 5 July 1855

However back in Britain, Campbell's military position was being undermined by Lord Panmure (Head of the British War Department and a member of Lord Palmerston's Cabinet) had proposed that he should become governor of Malta, and then further suggested the option that he should serve under Codrington the next army commander after the resignation of Sir James Simpson. Codrington of the Coldstream Guards, had never heard, nor seen, a shot fired in anger until the battle of the Alma. In disgust, Campbell left the Crimea on 3 November 1855. He was persuaded to rethink his position and on 4 June 1856 he was promoted to the rank of Lieutenant-General, returning to the Crimea to take command of a corps under Codrington. Campbell only commanded the Highland Division for a further month and then returned to England.

Update continues

The Highland Brigade in the Crimea

'Poachers turned Gamekeepers'

Founded on letters written during the years 1854, 1855, and 1856

By Lieut-Colonel Anthony Sterling a staff officer with Sir Colin Campbell.

Below is taken from his Preface with my added comments

'The manner in which the system prevailing in the regiments of Guards has acted upon, the interests and efficiency of the rest of the British Army'

Unfortunately the bad feeling that existed between the Guards and the Highlanders was mostly sparked by the favoured and privileged order of things as laid out by the Army Command, with blessings from the Monarchy which gave much preferential favour to the three regiments of the Guards Brigade.

I shall now go through the book being researched and give examples of the reasons why there was this ill feeling to the Guards by both officers and other ranks of the Highland Brigade, and indeed throughout the line regiments. Another fact to remember is that the Brigade of Guards at that time consisted of the Grenadiers, Coldstream and Scots Fusilier Guards.

Contd.

The double rank held by officers of the Brigade of Guards was found to be detrimental to the Service. Had each Brigade taken its tour of duty, as a unit, the difficulties would not have arisen; but, detached parties having been ordered from different Regiments, the extra rank of the Guards' Officers frequently put them in command of older and more experienced officers: friction and dissatisfaction constantly arose.

When Sir Colin Campbell was sent up to the siege with his Division—in the middle of June 1855—he found this system of detachments existing, and of course he had no power to alter it; but he did make a demonstration, for at the same period the Division of the French army commanded by General Canrobert came to the siege, and took the trenches immediately the right of our attack. In the French army the trench duty was taken by Divisions; and General Canrobert, who had been Commander-in-Chief, took himself his turn of the trenches every third day. One of his two Brigades took the advanced trench, and the other was in reserve—alternately. This was the Division which afterwards stormed the Malakoff. When Sir Colin Campbell found this, he also took his turn in the trenches, instead of detailing a brigadier. He did so three times; but the example was deemed contagious, and an order came out directing the Generals of Division to remain in their camps in reserve with the cooks. I do not know the precise date of this order; for the printed general orders which 1 had were all destroyed when my hut was burned down. But I perceive that in one of my Letters it is mentioned that, in August, there were then in the army a Commander in-Chief, a Chief of the Staff, three Generals of Division, and three Generals of Brigade, all Guardsmen—total eight (Simpson, Barnard, Bentinck. Rokeby, Craufurd. Ridley. Codrington and Windham. Lord Rokeby was appointed to command the 1st

Division 13th August. 1855. Colonel Ridley (a Guardsman] to 2nd Brigade, 1st Division, [Line Brigade] 13th August, 1855. Colonel Drummond [a Guardsman] to Brigade of Guards, 11th August, 1855. The latter was superseded in this command by General Craufurd, also a Guardsman 29th October. 1855). and only twelve of the Line.

Now 1 think it surprising that some of these gentlemen, who had all been brought up together in the same corps, did not suggest to the Commander-in-Chief the propriety of imitating the French, who sent into the trenches a Division complete, with its General, its Brigadiers, and every Staff Officer, as well as the Lieutenant-Colonels. Majors. Captains, and subalterns of each regimenl. The importance of having a large number of officers present with the men in the trenches was immense; for the soldiers were almost all young, some of them not three months from their homes, and the example of officers was very necessary for them.

When in a division one of the brigades is a Brigade of Guards, detachment duty is only taken by the other brigade. This was unfolded to us in Bulgaria, where the Highland Brigade furnished a detachment of two Companies to headquarters; and when Sir Colin Campbell applied to have it relieved, he heard the remarkable fact, that the Guards did not take that sort of duty.

Having explained as well as 1 can, how the example of the Guards is likely to act upon and to spread through the army to the detriment of discipline, I will just mention the point of the tremendous privilege, that every ensign in the Guards is Lieutenant, ipso facto, in the army, every Lieutenant a Captain, and every Captain a Lieutenant Colonel.

Next in the unholy alliance between the Guards Brigade and the Highlanders came the business of the packs and their carriage from one camp site to another. (Another sad phase of this next shortcoming of the Guards physical fitness was to resurrect itself during the Falkland Campaign of 1982 when again their inability to march over distance and take their kit with them was to prove the operation inoperative, and so the Two Guards Battalions of the Scots and Welsh Guards took to the sea, and we all remember what happened to Sir Tristan and Sir Galahad in the area of Bluff Cove!?)

This paragraph below speaks of the move of camp sites;

There are too many forms, too much time lost in obtaining any object, however important. The Guards are very much more unhealthy than we are, and do not march as well. When we marched from Varna to Aladeen, only twenty of the Highlanders who started with the Column did not march in with it; of the Guards one hundred and fifty at least were behind. Now I hear on this new march the Guards are to have their packs carried for them— a most fatal blunder, and the beginning of blunders. We shall refuse for our men, as they are perfectly fit to carry their packs, and do not wish to be separated from their property.

The next contribution to this work comes from John Skinner a British citizen now resident in Tasmania who has written a biography of Sir Colin Cambpell

Dear Norry,

quoting from the Nat. Biog Dictionary - 11th Feb 1854 sent to Crimea as Brigade Commander. Commanded Highland Brigade, 42nd: 79th: 93rd. under the command of D. of C. June 20th 1854 promoted to major-general, when at Varna. Prior to Sebastopol promoted to Commandant at Balaclava and made Colonel of the 67th Regiment on 24th Oct 1854. Did not take part in Inkerman.

Dec. 1854 assumed command of First Div. consisting of Guards and highlanders when D. of C. went to England.

Sir Colin left Nov 1855 after the row with Codrington. He was made Col. of the 67th Reg on 24th Oct. 1854. He went back to the Crimea in June 1856.

Further to this however, Lord Lucan needs to be factored in. He was not popular, unlike the Duke. of Cambridge. and they were rivals for the loyalty of the men. Lucan used brute force, Cambridge provided the beer!

John continues;

Kinglake at the Alma

He [Sir Colin] rode into battle at the head of the army, with the Duke of Cambridge at his side to the left of the column. He remained with the Duke until the guards had crossed the river, giving encouragement to the Duke, who wanted to halt to address his troops, because of the confusion caused by the disorderly retreat of the Light Division. Sir Colin's earnest desire was to make no such delay but to press forward on the enemy with the natural impulse and the advice was followed with triumphant result.

From this it seems that the Duke of Cambridge was in command in name only

And at Balaclava;

Out riding early in the morning of 25th October Sir Colin and Lord Lucan were the first to notice the advance of the Russian cavalry lines. Later that day they advised the D. of C. to wait awhile before assembling his men and taking the offensive.

After Lucan ordered the Charge of the Light Brigade debacle, he was 'sent for'. In March 1855 he had to defend himself in Parliament [House of Lords] to avoid a Court

Martial being called for by the general public. He blamed others, namely his ADC Captain Nolan and his brother-in-law, Cardigan. Did he in fact, due to previous knowledge of the inadequacy of the Duke of Cambridge privately blame the Duke as well?

I think that family connections will continue to protect the Duke of Cambridge. He was not functioning as an effective leader by the time he left, Sir Colin was really the power behind the scenes (of the 1st division).

I think that a lead in might be through Lord Lucan. What happened to him after the spoke in the House of Lords? etc.

Hope this helps. Regards John.

The Highland Brigade in the Crimea continues

Lieutenant - Colonel Anthony Sterling

Letter XXVII

Bivouack, Balaclava, 28 September 1854

I wrote you a hurried note after the battle of the Alma, which I could not even look over. We have since seen nothing of the Russians, except the tail of a column which marched out of Balaclava to meet their reinforcements from Anapa, We have now marched completely round Sebastopol, and have gained possession of the harbour of Balaclava, where the Agamemnon is now moored. This becomes our new base. They are landing the siege train; and we shall no doubt advance immediately to break ground and begin. It is probable they will make an obstinate resistance; but all sieges come to an end in a time which can be calculated. War is a horrid thing; not merely the field battle is a horrid thing; not merely the field of battle is hideous, but the ruin *of the poor helpless inhabitants. We came down here unexpectedly; the men were not drunk, and were quite obedient to their officers. The orders were distinct as to not injuring property; yet the village (Kadikoi) close to the camp of this division where the Duke has his quarters, was completely gutted in half-an-hour the inhabitants had run away. The men seemed to do it out of fun; they broke boxes and drawers that were open, and threw the fragments into the street. The battle of the Alma must during its progress, have been a grand sight to spectators who had time to admire. The cool advance the English under fire surprised out French allies. It is acknowledged by them that we had much the worse part of the position to take. Our Brigade was very lucky in not losing many officers or men. Some other regiments suffered frightfully, the 23rd lost thirteen officers, of whom nine were killed. this regiment and the 19th and 23rd, bore the brunt of the enemies first fire from the centre battery. After passing the river they were not allowed to form, but attacked in confusion, and were driven back, then our Division, which was behind them, after some hesitation, was advanced. I believe Cs advice, and his war-experience, found very useful. In the Brigade of Guards, the Fusilier regiment, which was the centre one, was broken, and driven back with great loss. They got mixed with the beaten regiments of the Light Division, which retreated through them, and put them into confusion. The moments our bonnets topped the hill, on the left of the Guards, the Russians gave way. But it was pretty critical, if we had waited ten minutes, or even five minutes more, the Russians would have been on the crest of the hill first, and God knows what would have been the loss of the Highland Brigade, even if we had succeeded in pushing them back. When we got halfway up the hill, I saw it was alright. We killed an enormous number Russians; the whole ground to our front, for hundreds of yards was strewed with dead*

LETTER CVIII.

Camp, before Sebastopol, 14th August, 1855.

The new arrangement of the Division is, I believe, made. We shall have the Highland Division, and it will consist of—1st Brigade, 42nd, 79th, 92nd, 93rd Kilts; 2nd Brigade, 1st and 2nd Battalion Royals, 71st and 72nd Trews. The Royal is the 1st Regiment, or Royal Scotch; but they are not Highland. The 71st is to be sent back from Kertsch, when replaced by the 82nd, hourly expected; the 92nd is not arrived. I have not heard of the other Divisions yet, nor who will have the luck of being with the Guards. I have just hauled down the 1st Division flag, and sent it to Lord Rokeby, who will now command the 1st Division. I shall be Assistant Adjutant-General to the Highland Division; and we shall, I suppose, hoist St. Andrew's Cross.

In simple conclusion It's a sad story, but stems from the same causes of a long drawn out conflicting process that has for many hundreds of years bred suspicion and warfare between the self interests, culture, religion, of the fractions involved, and to still ignore the fact will only ensure it lives on in the Hearts and Minds of many people in Britain, and then passed on to the next generation.

Update cont.

The Minie Rifle

Thank goodness for the Hythe Musketry School.

The issuing of the Minie rifle to the 1st Bn. Scots Fusilier Guards is not given a single mention in the F Maurice history.

It is something of an embarrassment In my opinion, and based on my experience when serving with the Scots Guards, that new equipment never seems to warrant, or perhaps deserve a mention in the Scots Guards Histories of the past, This failing is obviously the fault of senior officers at the Scots Guards RHQ who render information and advice to which ever unfortunate is writing the contemporary history. It is certainly not from security reasons that these tools of the trade are neglected as part of the Regiment's history, but probably more to do with the general officers understanding and little knowledge of such detail. Also to blame for this shortfall of information would be the serving officers within the Battalions, who were either not involved in the writing of the history, or could not be bothered at that time, nor in the future when the history was finally published. Yet another case of short sightness, or perhaps a total lack of the appreciation of priorities, or even worse, that there is no cause to intervene for the Regimental History was a matter of small concern for the greater majority of serving, or past members of the Scots Guards, Who whilst being outwardly proud of their history knew very little of it, and certainly not the wider picture, and know even less detail. And so yet a further reason that the Lady Butler painting of saving the colour at the Alma was to stay as truth until present times?

The School of Musketry

Back in Britain the Musketry School at Hythe had first opened in 1853 and was giving priority instruction on the uses of the new Minie rifle, which foresighted and pro-active practice was to more than prove itself in the forthcoming war.

This strategic and tactical view was taken by the administration at Army HQ under its new Commander in Chief Lord Hardinge (1785-1856) who had taken over from Lord Wellington after his death in 1852. This take over proved to be very beneficial for the British Army as Wellington had not been a believer in the new rifle, whereas Lord Hardinge was. So once again by a change of fortune more than any good judgment from command elements the British Army were to have the Minie Rifle, and then to learn the new expertise that went along with the new technology all closely over seen by the new 'hands on' Commander in Chief, Lord Hardinge.

I believe that it was during their stay in Malta, or Varna that the Minie Rifle was first issued to the Scots Fusilier Guards, and selected Bn Officers and NCOs were given the necessary instructions on the new rifles use and practice, which they then passed onto their company groups who then passed it onto individual soldiers with appropriate use and training.

With the war breaking out in 1853 between the Russians and the Turks, Britain sensed that it was only a matter of time before they would be drawn into the conflict. At this time the British Army was in the midst of a significant weapons transformation from smoothbore muskets to rifled muskets. While a number of regiments had already been supplied with the pattern 1851 Minie Rifled musket, the majority of the army still carried the 1842 pattern smooth bore musket. By the end of 1853, the Enfield Rifled musket as approved by the War Department for the army was also put into production. In 1854 the political situation deteriorated, and on March 27th Britain, along with France, declared war on Russia.

In 1847, Captain Claude Etienne Minié of the Chasseurs d'Orléans had invented the blunt lead bullet; in 1849 he invented the rifle that was named after him. It had a percussion lock and weighed 10 lbs 9 ozs, fired a hollow based bullet of .702 inch calibre. The rifle fired a conical bullet with a cavity in its base plugged with a piece of iron. By the explosion of the charge the iron plug was driven further in, expanding the sides to fit closely the grooves of the barrel. Reasonable accuracy could be achieved at distances up to 600 yards and the 500 grain bullet could penetrate 4 inches of soft pine at 1,000 yards. These weapons had sights installed for correct holding, aiming and firing by the individual soldier.

An interesting result of the general introduction of the (Minie) rifle was the establishment in various countries of specialised schools of instruction to teach its proper use. In the days of the smoothbore musket, individual accuracy under battle conditions had hardly been possible, and the instruction of volley firing had largely been a matter for the drill-sergeant for controlled volley fire at short range. The charge would then follow with the use of the bayonet on closing with the enemy ranks.

The Rifle Regiments had evolved their own systems, but by 1852 it was clear to the British Commander in Chief, Lord Hardinge, that something more permanent was required, and in 1853 a school of Musketry was set up at Hythe on the Kent coast. Suitable barracks existed there, and miles of shingle beaches provided ample space for ranges without taking over agricultural land. The primary object of the new school was to study military rifle shooting in all its aspects and to pass on the necessary knowledge to carefully selected regimental instructors, who would then pass in into their Bn. ranks for implementation and training.

There was a second object; Lord Hardinge, who had taken over from Wellington on his death in 1852 as Commander in Chief wished to be sure that the weapons provided were the best possible, and he ordered this assurance to come from an establishment under his direct management control.

The school of Musketry's first Commandant was Lieutenant-Colonel Charles Crawford Hay (Later Major General) of the 19th Regiment, the Green Howards, who bought with him two more members of the Regiment, Lieutenant Currie, who acted as Adjutant, and Colour Sergeant John McKay. Three Sergeant Instructors joined almost immediately and from this modest nucleus the School of Musketry sprang. Hay was not initially a great expert on rifle shooting but he soon became an enthusiast who established sound methods which hardly changed for fifty years. A great deal of the initial doctrine was based on the French *Ecole De Tir* at Vincennes. A pioneer in the establishment of such schools. Although it was naturally modified in the light of practical experience.

Hay and his Staff were dedicated Officers, WOs and NCOs and were to receive the greatest support from successive Commanders in Chief. Never less their initial efforts to spread the doctrine of the rifle met with much obstruction. It was less than a dozen years since the British Infantry had finally discarded its flintlocks and there were a good many Officers who deployed the change, believing that the proper way for British Soldiers to fight was to deliver a series of swift volleys at point blank range as a preparation for a decisive charge with the bayonet. It was an attitude which was to linger into the twentieth century and influence military tactics.

The system evolved by Hay and his instructors at the Hythe musketry camp was on sensible scientific lines which would still be valid in modern times. It involved a good deal of theory, perhaps more than would be acceptable now, but the accurate long-range rifle was then such revolutionary concept that a good deal had to be explained that would nowadays be taken for granted. There was also a good deal of 'Dry training' to teach the soldier to adopt the best positions from which to shoot, together with aiming from a rest and instruction in trigger release. It was still anticipated that most shooting would be done standing up, so this was taken as the basic position. Although Hay was a great believer in the kneeling position which could be quickly adopted without loss of time and certainly gave a steadier shot, since the left elbow was rested on the left knee. After some preliminary snapping of caps and the firing of blank charges to accustom the soldier to the noise and recoil, he was allowed to progress to practice with the specially designed Minie ball. The targets were of cast iron 1.8 metres high .6.09m wide, and were marked of by deep grooves into 152mm squares. these targets in numbers up to six could be locked together to form a target at the maximum range; this representation would allow the targets to be seen as the enemy moving in column. The range was around 800 Metres, a range at which few modern soldiers would think of opening fire, yet even during the Boer War 1899-1902, the British were being targeted and outshot at these ranges by the 'Boer Kommandoes' with their German produced Mauser rifles

For the first time the application of this type of accurate and individual rifle fire demanded add-on skills from the soldiers, such as a great deal of time on the judging of distance. Black powder was not a particularly powerful propellant and at longer ranges the bullet traveled in a high ark. It then descended so steeply that a miscalculation of even a few yards in range would cause the bullet to fall at the foot of the target or pitch behind it. This was somewhat less serious than it sounds, because troops in battle moved in columns or successive lines, presenting a target of some depth, and especially so when targeting the cavalry where a number of men on horses constituted an even larger target area. Nevertheless, any major miscalculation of range could waste a high proportion of shots. These days we term this barrage of small arms fire and where it lands as the 'Beaten Zone', and it was to play its own memorable part in the saga of the 'Thin Red Line', at Balaclava, where Sir Colin Campbell had placed his men of the 93rd and the attached personnel deliberately in the file formation to enable maximum effective fire to be brought down on any form of attacker..

Suffering from a chronic shortage of rifled muskets, regiments not going to the Crimea were stripped of their Minie Rifles which were given to the troops going. By the time the British force left in September they were armed with a mixture of the three different muskets. In an attempt to standardize the handling of various arms in the Army a revised Platoon (loading and firing) exercise was issued in the previous June. By the time the Regiments embarked they would have been well versed in the new loading and firing drill. Much is made of the problems of supply for the British army during the Crimean War and having three different types of muskets in use worsened the situation, especially with ammunition. The Pattern 1842 Musket used a round lead ball for its .753 calibre barrel while the pattern 1851 Minie Rifle needed a .702 calibre conical bullet. The addition of the pattern 1853 Enfield musket brought the need for smaller lead balls for its .577 calibre barrel. Getting the right ammunition to the right soldier must have been quite confusing.

There were to be four main manifestations marking the advantages of the Minie Rifle during the siege of Sevastopol, as well as the overall psychological victory of the rifle becoming being much feared by the Russian defenders. The main successes however were Initially at the Alma River's Great Redoubt by the Light Division, followed up by the 1st Division, (better late than never!) And then the Highland Brigade assaulting and taking the Lesser Redoubt on the Kourgane Hill which was to confirm the Alma battle being won convincingly by the Allies. But the victory owed much to the well used Minie Rifle at that time.

There was then the work carried out by Capt. Goodlake assisted closely by Sgt. Ashton both of the Coldstream Guards, and his section of Sharpshooters selected from the Guards Brigade. This little known revelation deserves a much detailed report for an update which is essential if the Scots Guards History of the Crimea War is to become credible. Without that evidence the History lacks important structure. However perhaps the most crucial use of the Minie Rifle was in its defensive role at Inkerman, which was to initially hold, and then wear down the continuous determined Russian assaults whilst the French were able to bring their forces to bear and finally drive the Russians from the Inkerman Heights.

The so called Minie ball, was not a ball at all, but rather a cylindro-ogival bullet with three angular grooves filled with lubricating tallow and a cavity at the base, shaped as an upright cone, the powder charge exploding against the cone in the bullet base would expand the grooves to make a tight fit against the rifling in the barrel. The rifling imparted a spin to the bullet, thus vastly improving accuracy.

The Minie Rifle

These were the tactics used at the battle of the Alma River by some of the line Regiments and the Guards Brigade, but already the new teaching begun at the new school of musketry at Hythe just a year earlier, around the longer ranges and much increased accuracy of the Minie rifle was having its effect in changing these old 'musket' formations into individual rifle fire, where skirmishing, and in line advances became almost the same configuration.

The British Commander and his Divisional Officers were veterans of Waterloo, and the accuracy of the new Minie bullet had not yet made its impression on these Generals. Some of the more senior were also short sighted and so unable to conceptualize the advantages of the new rifle's use at the much longer ranges. But fortunately the soldiers of the Light Division, and the Rifle Brigade were versed in the new use and advantages that the Minie rifle was capable of, and used it to good effect, not only at the Alma but throughout the Crimea Campaign. However this loose formation adopted by the Light Infantry, the Rifle Brigade and many of the line regiments was not for the Guards Brigade who went to extraordinary lengths to ensure their 'lines' were as per the parade square before advancing upon the enemy in line. The rifle was now a weapon to be used to gain the advantage on the advance when the fire fight had to be won, but closing on an enemy in order to capture that defended position was still to be also fought by the aggressive use of the bayonet. However The Minie rifle was to change the face of battle strategy and tactics in the meanness of the field. No longer would an infantry battalion have to form square to take on cavalry, but only to verify that they had range and space in which to form line with the purpose of bringing maximum effective rifle fire against cavalry at the longer distance advantageous to the rifleman. Also to understand the science of the 'beaten zone', the area which could be covered by any number of rifles firing singly, in unison, or volley fire against an enemy advancing in groups

The infantry could also now skirmish forward in 'section' or even pairs, coming together 'in line' when concentrated fire at the longer ranges was called for. The important factor here was that 'advances' could be kept moving forward as the 'fire fight' was being won against an enemy forced to 'keep their heads down'. 'Fire and movement' had now come to stay during the Crimea War, and it all began at the Alma direct from the School of Musketry at Hythe, with fresh thinking from the Horse Guards and the new Commander in Chief, Lord Hardinge!

Another significant factor was that for the first time gun batteries could be 'taken out' at a longer range than those guns could fire, demonstrated by the Russian main guns at the Alma's Great Redoubt being removed quickly. The trick was to get close enough to disarm the gun carriages by sniping the horses. The gun crews themselves could then become targets, or taken prisoner. Thus making it almost impossible for them to escape with the guns. The guns were now very much inside the battlefield, and no longer on the outside firing in!

Update

The French participation in the invasion of the Crimea

"Ahh, those Frenchies"!

It now days seems somewhat ludicrous that the reincarnated, renewed, and reinvigorated French Army of that time of 1854, supported by the politics and supreme military leadership back in Paris, would actually allow themselves to be caught up in the invasion of the Crimea with the intent of destroying Sevastopol, without having their own motives for so doing?

It may also be realised that the French, far from being followers of the British, were in practice not only intent on fulfilling their role but becoming the real command element during the invasion and investment of Sevastopol. The literary situation being that the idea of the French leading the invasion was never to be part of any British writer's who were recording the efforts of the British Army contingent, so once again perhaps the situation of who was commanding who during the campaign should be viewed with an open mind. For it could be well argued from a modern point of view that history has been rewritten in order to bolster the British part to play whilst undermining the French effort. It may even be suggested that it was the French whose hidden agenda finally persuaded the British forces not to blockade the Russian Port of Sevastopol, but invade, for the French were undoubtedly still nursing the terrible memories of defeat by the Russians of 1812, and were now intent on hitting back at the Russian mainland, and this invasion of the Crimea was their opportunity for the revenge they earnestly sought.

We may also note as we follow the adventures of the Allied Armies during the Crimea War just how many occasions, and when it critically mattered, that the French stepped forward to save the British, and in doing saved themselves, especially at Inkerman.

Without any doubt the invasion could never have taken place by the British and a relatively small Turkish contingent without the main line aid and support of the French. With special attention being paid to the last battle of the campaign at the Tchernia Retchka, and the final storming and capture of the Malakov Tower, The front door of Sevastopol Fortress, by the French.

Now to bring the French part to play up to date. During the preparations for the 150th commemoration of the Crimea War in 2004, new reconciliation monuments were built by the Ukraine government in Kiev. The French government however wanted to put forward their own proposition, and so paid the extra cost necessary for a French monument designed by them. The new monument was built on the site of the original French cemetery which had been desecrated during the 2nd World War. The finished landscaping and monument is a fitting tribute to their soldiers of the campaign, The French also put into operation the security and maintenance required to ensure the monuments future.

The British Embassy attempted to do the same as the French with their monument at Cathcart Hill, but were turned down by the Ukraine Government when the British expected the Ukraine government to complete and upgrade their original monument up at Cathcart Hill. Instead the Ukraine government built the new British monument in the low ground below Cathcart Hill where the Light Infantry were based, but not too far from the Guards camp as well. Major J Dart in his British Embassy report on Cathcart Hill of June 2007, laid out several options. One of the options was to bring the movables down from the British monument and lay them out as part of the 2004 Ukraine reconciliation monument. I have heard nothing of this option since?

Reg Hist

The Landing at Calamity Bay and the advance to the Alma

Update

A landing not too far removed from the British invasion of the Falklands of 1982, except by the number of years past, but the flavour tastes the same.

(It would seem to me that if a group of people of their own free will decide to live on a piece of real estate which is contested in terms of ownership, such as the Falklands, then they must take responsibility for any movement onto that land by the contestants, and suffer the consequences. In the Falklands situation however it was the people of mainland Britain who had to suffer the consequences by yet another showing of British 'Gunboat Diplomacy'?)

Reg Hist.

A landing-place was chosen on a strip of open beach about twenty miles south of Eupatoria and thirty miles north of Sevastopol. There on September 14th the first troops were put ashore without any opposition from the Russians, but in the afternoon a heavy ground swell set in and the landing was not completed until the 18th. The only transport landed was pack animals, and indeed there was little enough to land. The experiences at Varna had shown that the men were not fit to carry their packs and these were left on board, each man taking a few necessaries wrapped in a blanket. Even the officers had to carry everything they required. No tents were landed except for General Officers and a few for the sick. About three hundred and fifty local vehicles were captured or secured immediately after the landing, and with this meagre equipment the army set out to take Sebastopol. Heavy rain set in on the night after the first day of the landing, and the troops had to sleep without shelter on sodden ground while the Army was assembling, which did not improve the health of the Army, already not too good.

The Allied Commanders had agreed that as we alone had Cavalry, the French should advance next to the coast and we on the outer flank. The country being open rolling down land the forward movement was made on a broad front. The French on the right had their Army in a lozenge formation, the 1st Division leading, then in second line came the 2nd and 3rd Division and the bulk of the Artillery, with the Turks and 4th Division in line in rear. The British advance was led by the 11th and 13th Hussars under Lord Cardigan, followed by the 2nd and Light Division as the first line of the Infantry in that order from right to left, the 3rd and 1st Divisions formed the second line of the Infantry with the 4th Division, less a Brigade, in rear. The three remaining Cavalry Regiments under Lord Lucan covered the left flank and rear. The march began on the 19th under a blazing sun and as there was no transport for water the men were soon falling out in numbers and did not obtain relief until, after a march of some fourteen miles, the Bulganak stream was reached. On the heights south of the stream the Russians were first sighted. An advance guard had been sent out from Sebastopol, but it withdrew after exchanging a few shots with our leading troops, and the force passed the night quietly in bivouac on the Bulganak. The Allied Commanders had decided to form no base on landing, probably because they had no transport to bring up supplies from a base if it

The Landing at Calamity Bay and the advance to the Alma

were established. Instead the army was to be fed from the ships, which were to move parallel with it. They could not therefore afford to lose touch with the coast and this decided the form of the battle which was about to take place. On the morning of September 20th the Allied force began to move forward over the plateau between the Bulganak and the Alma, in the same formation as on the previous day. The contact obtained with the enemy on the Bulganak and the news of Russian movements obtained from observers in the ships, made everyone realise that the enemy was likely to be encountered in force and it was no surprise when, soon after noon, the Russians were seen to be in position on the far bank of the Alma

The Alma, a winding and sluggish stream, fordable anywhere except just at the mouth, flows generally east and west across the line of advance which the Allies had taken. On their side the ground slopes gently down to the river, but on the Russian side it rises sharply and gives the enemy a commanding position. In the centre of that part of the valley to which the Allies were advancing lies the village of Bourliouk, which formed the point of contact between the right of our 2nd Division and the left of Prince Napoleon's Division. From Bourliouk to the sea was then the French front of attack. On this front the ground rises steeply, directly from the valley, and is only accessible to troops in formation in places. From Bourliouk westwards the main ridge recedes and on the British front is in places about a mile from the river. Just west of the village the main road from Eupatoria to Sebastopol crosses the river by a bridge and proceeds on its way through a gap between Telegraph Hill on the east and Kourgane hill on the west.

The Russian force which had come out from Sebastopol to dispute the passage of the Alma comprised about 3,400 sabres, 33,000 infantry and 120 guns, under the command of Menschikoff. Against this Lord Raglan, after deducting the detachments left at the landing-place, was bringing 1,000 sabres, 23,000 infantry and 60 guns, and St. Arnaud about 35,000 French and Turks. Menschikoff did not wish to expose his left to the fire of the Allied ships and apparently thought that the cliffs east of Bourliouk were too steep to admit of an attack in force from that quarter. He therefore posted none of his troops west of telegraph hill and had the bulk of his force on the ridge east of the main road, with his reserve behind that road and behind his left centre. He made no attempt to entrench a position for his infantry, contenting himself with throwing up two earthworks for the protection of his guns. Of these the most important was on the north-eastern slope of the Kourgane hill and contained the heavy guns, which commanded the bridge over the Alma and the gap through which passed the road to Sebastopol. This became known as the Great Redoubt, a rather flattering title for a very simple work. The other earthwork was rather more than half a mile east of the great redoubt and contained a field battery sited to cover the Russian right

Upon sighting the enemy the Allied forces remained halted for some time on the ground north of the Alma, while Lord Raglan and St. Arnaud reconnoitred the position and made their plan of attack. It was found that it would be possible for the French to cross the river and climb the cliff opposite to them in three places. It was then agreed that the French should move off first and climb up to the plateau under the covering fire of the guns of the fleet and that when they were well on their way the British should attack the Russian position in front. The Allied Commanders apparently thought that the Russian front extended much nearer to the sea than was the case, for there were no Russians within reach of the ships' guns and the French Army as a whole was lightly engaged. We may dispose of its part in the battle at once. St. Arnaud ordered his men to leave their packs on the ground to lighten them for the climb

The Landing at Calamity Bay and the advance to the Alma

up the cliff. About 1pm. One of Bosquet's brigades, followed by the Turkish Division, advanced and crossed the Alma by a ford near its mouth. These troops after a toilsome climb got up on the plateau to find no Russians anywhere near them, and they never fired a shot. Canrobert's division climbed up by a track midway between Bourliouk and Almatamak and, came out on the plateau about three-quarters of a mile west of telegraph hill to find no enemy opposite them. But when Menschikoff saw the movement and understood its menace to his left flank he moved his reserve against Canrobert, who, finding the track by which he had ascended too steep for guns, had sent his artillery to follow Bosquet's 2nd brigade. As Bosquet was already using this track for his artillery Canrobert's was much delayed and did not get up till the battle was nearly over. Being without guns, Canrobert fell back to the edge of the cliff, where his men suffered some loss from the Russian artillery, but were not, except for skirmishers, otherwise engaged, as Menshikoff's reserve considered that it had done its duty in stopping the turning movement, and did not attack. Prince Napoleon's Division had some fighting with the Russian left at and above Bourliouk. In brief, all that the French achieved was to place themselves in a position to out flank the Russians, which, as we shall see, St. Arnaud refused to do.

The British advanced with the 2nd Division on the right and the Light Division on the left of the first line. In the second line the 3rd Division followed the 2nd and the 1st Division the light division. The 4th Division followed in rear and the Cavalry was on the left flank, drawn somewhat back. The portion of the valley of the Alma to which our troops were advancing was that between the villages of Bourliouk and Tarkhanlar, a distance of about two miles. Almost the whole of these two miles on the north bank of the river was occupied by gardens and vineyards enclosed with low stone walls. As the skirmishers of the 2nd and

Light Divisions advanced they were met in the village of Bourliouk and in the vineyards by Russian skirmishers, who were driven back, but not before the village of Bourliouk had been set on fire. The 2nd and Light Divisions were deployed with some difficulty owing to the fire and the enclosures in the valley, and lay for some time under the pounding of the Russian guns. Lord Raglan, then hearing from St. Arnaud that the French skirmishers were on the plateau, ordered the 2nd and Light Divisions to attack and, that done, galloped off with a few of his staff round the burning village, across the Alma to a knoll north of Telegraph Hill, where he was in considerable personal danger and could exercise no control whatever over the battle. The 1st Battalion of the Regiment was to suffer heavily because of this wild action of the Commander-in-Chief.

Update

With hindsight to make a present day judgment in the light of more information and research, I have reached the conclusion that Lord Raglan had no other option during that phase of the battle than to seek a location where he could observe as much of the ongoing battle that was now raging around him. And after all, who are we to judge the Commander in Chief on his efforts at that particular time, or is this to be but another cover up for the inadequacies of the Duke of Cambridge which were to come later?

The British part to play at this stage of the battle could be handled by his staff, and as we now know Lord Raglan's man Friday Brig. General Airey was taking a firm hand around the British Divisions, leaving Lord Raglan to control and command the flow of the British part of the battle with his staff from his high point of observation where he could also see what the French and Turks were up to. However what did happen with this situation in relevance to the 1st Division, was that the Duke of Cambridge somewhat unnerved by his part to play as Divisional Commander whilst under severe and close battle conditions, was seeking guidance from all who came into his sphere, and we know for a fact that he had consorted with both General Buller on the extreme left of the Light Division, and of course his confidante of the Highland Brigade, Sir Colin Campbell.

Some time before the battle had been joined at the Great Redoubt, Sir George Brown commanding the Light Division, had requested the Duke of Cambridge not to send his 1st Division onto the Great Redoubt until he had asked for support. However this instruction which had seemed a clear cut and straightforward directive before the Light Division had become heavily committed on the Great Redoubt, was no longer the simple matter it had been prior to the battle's main phase. Then came the time during which the Great Redoubt was being assaulted by the Light Division and elements of the 2nd Division, which left the Duke floundering around the battlefield seeking assistance and advice.

The phase of the battle which then came into play on the Great Redoubt with the ill fated action of part of the Scots Fusilier Guards rash advance onto the slopes of the main Russian position, was to turn itself from the initial cock-up into a conspiracy at the de-briefs, which were no doubt held in discreet debate between those of the leadership who had been most directly involved. The result being the award of no less than four Victoria Crosses and a convenient Regimental 'Retreat' custom dispensed to the Scots Fusilier Guards, two ill designed favours which have stood the test of time even unto these present times?

Later was to come the Lady Butler painting to add further effect to the cover up.

And perhaps that is the truth of the matter, so why spoil a good historical story of valour and defending the Regimental colours with the modern truth. Which in practical terms was nothing but a brutal fight for survival by men cut of from the remainder of their battalion, and the division, after allowing themselves to become dangerously exposed to the Russian Infantry, who were awaiting their opportunity to swoop down on this isolated group of the Scots Fusilier Guards?

In other terms the Scots Fusilier Guards were in fact a 'habble' rather than 'heroes' at that particular phase of the Alma Battle

Reg Hist

The 2nd Division was delayed by the burning village, and Brown's Light Division was the first to attack. Buller held back his Brigade to cover the left, but Codrington went on with his two Battalions, the 95th and the 55th, of Pennefather's Brigade of the 2nd Division advancing on his right. These men swarmed up the slope towards the Great Redoubt. To their amazement the Russians made no attempt to defend this work. Horses with lassoo harness were brought up hastily and dragged the guns, save two which were captured, out of danger, had Codrington been supported promptly the battle might well have been won sooner and with much less loss. But there was no one keeping a watchful and directing eye on the battle such as Wellington had kept at Waterloo.

Update

This battle was not Waterloo, and Cambridge should have been the commander to immediately sense that it was time for the 1st Division to advance and give much needed support to augment Codrington's efforts

The Landing at Calamity Bay and the advance to the Alma

Reg Hist

The 1st and 3rd Divisions, without orders, lay in the valley under the long-range fire of the Russians guns. When the enemy saw that the British were in the Great Redoubt they turned their guns upon them and soon forced them to take cover on its northern side, where they were attacked on either flank by Russian columns. Just then a British bugler blew the 'cease fire' and then 'retreat', and upon the calls being repeated the left and centre of Codrington's Brigade fell back slowly until, as they came out upon the slope they were harried by a heavy fire from the Russian batteries, and thereupon they tumbled back in a confused mass right upon the advancing line of the Scots Fusilier Guards. This brings us to the part of the 1st Battalion in the battle.

Update

In my opinion this sounding of the 'Retreat', was to clear the Great Redoubt of all the British troops still fighting up at that hard won position. That would leave the way clear for the 1st Division to form up and assault the Great Redoubt in line taking with them the remnants of the Light Division who had retired back down the slope as a direct result of the rallying 'retreat' being sounded. There would then be no masking of the Minie Rifle fire by any other British Infantry which would have all retired down the hill, leaving the way completely clear for the 1st division advance up to the Great Redoubt. Perhaps more by luck than good judgment this was the main effect anyway, and the rest is now manipulatively informed Scots Guards Regimental History equaling a preservation of the old adage, 'Alls well that ends well'. Plus a 'Regimental Custom' at the daily sounding of the 'Retreat' that was to be included in the complete Scots Fusilier Guards cover up. And then followed up with the Lady Butler painting as part of the ceremonial during the change of the

Scots Fusilier Guards to that of the 'Scots Guards' in 1877, a ceremony held at the RHQ Scots Guards lorded over by the Commander in Chief, the Duke of Cambridge, as he sought to finally exorcise the last of the ghosts from his unfortunate time as the 1st Division Commander during the Crimea campaign. With the Lady Butler painting close by to confirm his part to have played to his satisfaction, and to the newly ordained Scots Guards pride of regiment.

Alma Battle Map

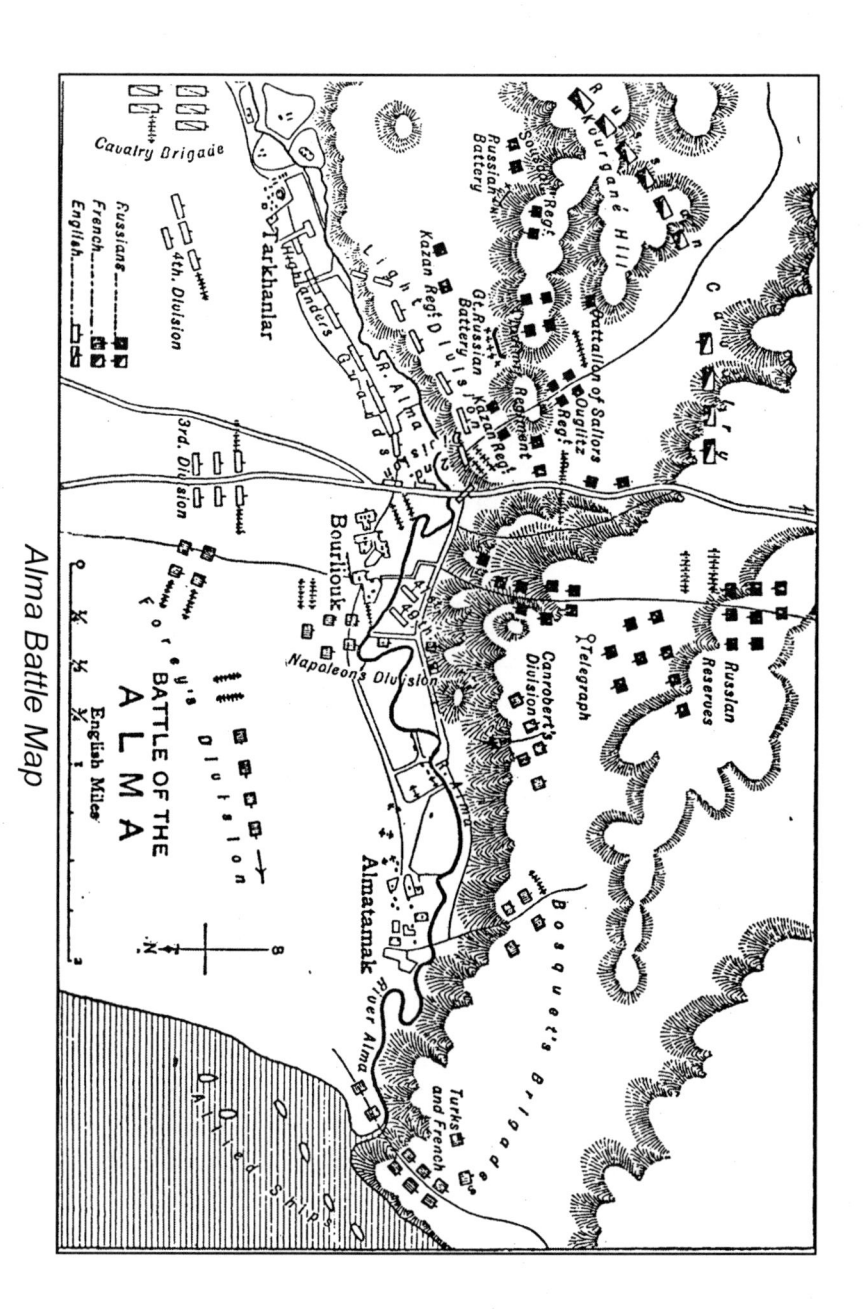

Update continues
The Battle for the Alma Continues
20th September 1854

We may see from the map reproduced above from the F Maurice History that the Russian Infantry Regiments at the Alma were not in a defensive position, nor screen, but rather formed in columns ready and waiting to advance down onto the Allies having halted them with cannon shot in the killing ground that Menshikov the Russian Commander in Chief, had mapped and measured out previously on the North side of the river. In simple military terms the Russian Army on the high ground South of the Alma River, was at the 'ready', and at the point of standing prepared to begin advancing down onto the plain forcing the Allied invaders to retreat as they advanced, or what was to be left of the Allies after the Russian guns had finished with them.

You will also notice in the top left hand corner of the map the Russian Cavalry screen at about four times stronger than the British Cavalry at that time, waiting to ride into the British from their right flank and take the British in their left flank, with the ultimate aim of pushing the Allies back to the Black Sea., and all that was to stop them at that part of the battlefield were the Highlanders, but they would be enough, for the Russian cavalry by this time had seen at first hand the carnage that the Minie Rifle in the hands of skilled soldiers and firm leadership could do, as the British continually advanced onto the Great Redoubt, and nothing the Russians could do was going to stop them, and so decided that discretion was the better part of valour, and living to fight another day was more appropriate at that very early stage of the invasion. This is also another pointer to the fact that this was not a Russian defensive plan. For you will also note that the bridge road across the Port Road had been left open for the Russians to cross with guns and infantry and attack the Allies once their guns had completed their task of stopping the Allies in the killing ground below the Great Redoubt, and north of the Alma river.

THE MAP ABOVE'S TOP EDGE IS POINTING SOUTH TOWARDS SEVASTOPOL.

(The map below has been taken from the Regimental History of the Scots Guards, by Sir F Maurice published 1934)

THE CRUCIAL ACTION WHICH TOOK PLACE ON THE GREAT REDOUBT IS ON THE LEFT OF THE MAP SOUTH OF THE RIVER ALMA RIGHT, WE MAY READ THE DETAIL OF THE SCOTS FUSILIER GUARDS LINE AT THE MAIN ACTION ON THE GREAT REDOUBT AS THEY CAME VERY CLOSE TO HANDING THE BATTLE TO THE RUSSIANS. FOR ONCE THE RUSSIAN'S HAD SPLIT THE GUARDS AND HIGHLANDERS ADVANCE, AND THEN SET THEIR CAVALRY LOOSE, ALONG WITH MANY OTHER INFANTRY REGIMENTS AWAITING THIS OPPORTUNITY, THE BATTLE MAY WELL HAVE BEEN LOST FOR THE ALLIES.

It was as well that the other five Battalions of the 1st Division formed into line before advancing onto the approaches to the Great Redoubt. So blocking the advancing Russian columns with Minie rifle fire, as the Russian's counter attacked the leading companies of the SFG with the object of taking them in the centre and then moving around the flanks onto the Battalions moving up the hill from the rear.

DIAGRAM SHOWING POSITION OF COMPANIES OF 1st BATTALION IN THE CRISIS OF THE ALMA

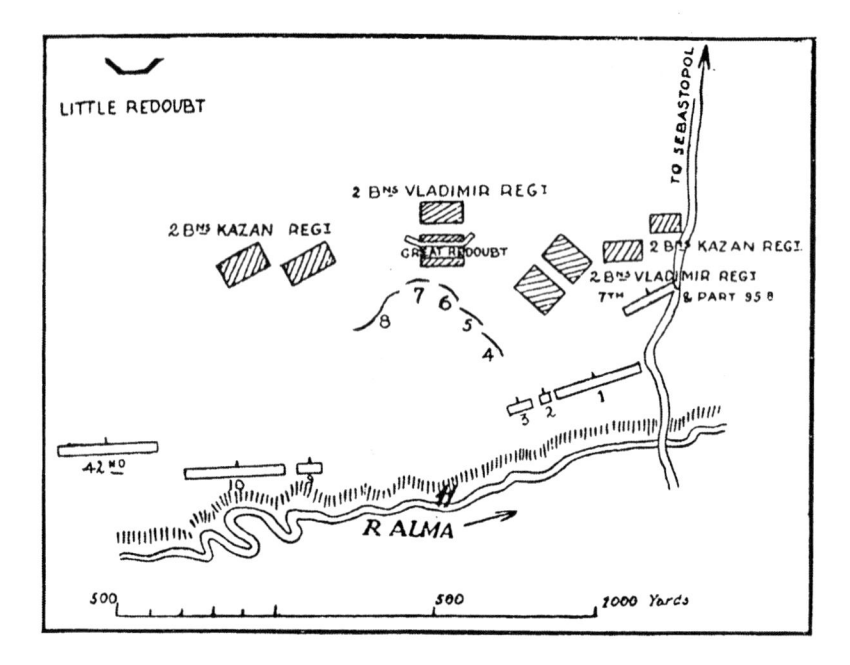

1. Grenadiers.
2. Colours and party of 95th.
3. R.F. Company, Scots Fusilier Guards.
4. No. 1   ,,   ,,   ,,   ,,
5. No. 2   ,,   ,,   ,,   ,,
6. No. 3   ,,   ,,   ,,   ,,
7. Colours and part of No. 4 Company.
8. Part of No. 4, No. 5 and men of the 23rd.
9. L.F. Company.
10. Coldstream.
11. Codrington's brigade and No. 6 Company re-forming.

Alma Battle Positions

This episode which was mainly the fault of the 1st Division Commander HRH the Duke of Cambridge was to lead to a cover up, with the 4 Victoria Crosses awarded, or partly awarded, to the leading and wayward colour party supported by the remainder of the Battalion which had left a company (Left Flank) with the right of the Coldstream Guards who were advancing on the Scots Fusilier Guards left flank. In the diagram we are able to imagine the habble of the Scots

The Battle for the Alma Continues

Fusilier Guards on the Great Redoubt, leaving in no doubt the fact that this ill formed assault could have well turned the battle in the Russian's favour. For further confirmation note the gap between the Grenadiers advancing on the right and the Coldstream Guards on the left. This gap was to produce the main crisis point of the Alma Battle

There now follows an excerpt from the introduction by David McDuff 1986 from Leo Tolstoy's 'The Sevastopol Sketches',

'Like the Engineers, the Russian Artillery was an elite force. Because of the ineffectiveness of the Infantry, who were armed with old fashioned percussion muskets and made their principal contribution in massed, sustained bayonet charges, the Russian army relied heavily on the fire of the Artillery to disorganise the foe and prepare the way for the charge of the Infantry' (JS Curtiss, the Russian Army under Nicholas 1 1825-55)

So now we know for sure the true value of the habble of the Scots (Fusilier) Guards at the Alma!

I shall now be concentrating on the piece of history shown by the Scots Guards regimental painting by Lady Elizabeth Butler depicting a highly 'make over' part of this crucial phase where the battle of the Alma actually came close to being lost as a result of the action shown above,

The painting has been painted to depict the men in front being Lieut. R Lindsay, Sgt. J McKechnie (with the trousers and bearskin showing him to be improperly dressed, a nice touch of poetic license?) Lieut. Thiselthwaite, Pte J Reynolds and Sgt. J Knox. Pte Reynolds and Sgt.Knox were not members of the colour party.

This episode of the battle for the Great Redoubt put into its correct context was the resulting laxity of the Duke of Cambridge failing to give support to the Light Division when it was urgently required. Then followed this act of rash incompetence by the leading companies of the Scots Fusilier Guards, which in the end result was to turn a habble into heroics by way of a very clever piece of deception which the Scots Guards has kept in the picture ever since. Then came a claim to being awarded four Victoria Crosses for this action. There is also the added nicety of the regimental custom at the sounding of the 'Retreat'.

Reg Hist

Battle of the Alma Continues

The 1st Division had deployed with the Guards Brigade on its right, the Highland Brigade on the left. In the Guards Brigade the Grenadiers were on the right, their right being near the main road to Sebastopol; the Scots Fusilier Guards were in the centre and the Coldstream on the left. The left of the Highlanders extended nearly to the village of Tarkhanlar. Thus the 1st division had taken up a considerably wider front than the Light Division and its right overlapped the left of the 2nd Division, a circumstance which, together with the fire in Bourliouk, prevented the 3rd Division, which should have supported the 2nd, from deploying. Thus early was the absence of direction having effect.

When the Guards Brigade came down into the valley and reached the walled enclosures of the gardens and vineyards General Bentinck ordered the Battalions to get through the vineyards and across the river in any way they could do so and reform on the far side. On the right, part of the Grenadiers crossed by the bridge of the Sebastopol road and part waded the river, on the left the Coldstream struck a part of the river where it made an 'S' bend and had to wade it three times, in the centre the Scots Fusilier

Guards moved through the vineyards where they came under heavy fire from the Russian guns. Here lieutenant the Hon. H. Annesley was hit in the mouth by a bullet from the Russian canister which shattered his teeth as he was shouting *'forward, the Guards'*. The Battalion got over the river in a rough line, first of the Brigade, and was in process of forming up in the shelter of the dead ground on the south bank when an urgent call for help came from Codrington to General Bentinck, who then rode up to the Battalion and ordered it to advance at once. The Left-Flank company had not then come up, being delayed by the same causes as had kept back the Coldstream, and it remained with them. On receiving Bentinck's order the Battalion advanced without waiting to complete its formation. The remaining seven companies moved up the slope and as they were about half-way between the river and the Great Redoubt they were met by the retreating mass of Codrington's Brigade, which swept back the 6th and part of the 5th companies on the left and caused some confusion in the others. As some compensation for this a number of the men of the Light Division rallied to the Battalion and advanced with it. The Scots Fusilier Guards got within about thirty yards of the Great Redoubt, where they found themselves unsupported with two strong bodies of Russians (the Kazan Regiment) on either flank. Sir Charles Hamilton ordered the battalion to halt and open fire. Its situation at this time was critical. It was attacked on its left by two Battalions of the Kazan Regiment, and to meet this attack its left was bent back while its right and centre were swept with canister at point blank range by a Russian battery on its right front. Just then someone rode up to Sir Charles Hamilton and shouted 'Fusiliers, retire.' the order was repeated and the right of the battalion began to fall back. Captain (afterwards General) Sir Reginald Gipps, who was near Hamilton at the time, was positive as to the receipt of this order. It was probably meant for the 7th Fusiliers, who were on the right of Codrington's Brigade and with the aid of a wing of the 95th were stoutly holding up two battalions of the Kazan Regiment just west of the Great Redoubt. The gallant stand of the 7th Fusiliers and 95th, played an important part in enabling the right of the Battalion to recover and in aiding the advance of the Grenadiers, who were now approaching. It is probable that Codrington, or someone on his behalf, fearing that the 7th would be isolated when the remainder of the Brigade fell back, told a galloper to order the Fusiliers to retire and the order came to the Scots Fusilier Guards. Fortunately the officers of the right companies, seeing the Grenadiers coming up, stopped the retreat and proceeded to rally their men to the Colours. At this time the five and a half companies with Sir Charles Hamilton were formed in a rough triangle with the Colour party at its apex some fifty yards from the Great Redoubt. The 4th and part of the 5th company, with some men of Codrington's Brigade who had rallied to them, formed the left side of the triangle. The 3rd, 2nd and 1st companies in a ragged line formed the right side. The Colour party consisted of Lieutenant R.J. Lindsay (afterwards Lord Wantage), who carried the Queen's Colour, Lieutenant Thistlethwayte, who had the Regimental Colour, Sergeant J. Mckechnie, Sergeant W. Lane, Sergeant W. Bryce, and Sergeant A. Mcleod. It was for a time almost isolated and surrounded by the enemy, for by this time the head of the Vladimir Regiment had come over the Great Redoubt. The Queen's Colour was found, after the battle, to have twenty-four bullet- holes through it and the pole was shot asunder. Sergeant Lane was killed, McLeod was mortally wounded and Mckechnie slightly. Both the Officers were by some miracle untouched, and inspired by Lindsay's gallant bearing the little party, aided by part of No.4 Company, stood fast long enough to enable the right of the Battalion to rally on it. Captain Viscount Chewton, who commanded the 3rd Company, waving his bearskin, shouted, *'Come on, lads, we'll beat them yet and gain the battle'*, and set an example in bringing the right forward until he fell, his leg shattered by a ball below his knee. He was quickly surrounded by the advancing men of the Vladimir Regiment and badly mauled, and after the battle the only parts of his body found to be without a wound was his left hand and arm. He died in hospital on October 8th. He was gallantly seconded by Captain Haygarth in command of No.2 Company, who fell severely wounded as he attempted to save Chewton, whom he saw being attacked with the bayonet by a Russian. Sergeant Knox and private Reynolds also helped with conspicuous gallantry in rallying the right, which, aided by the advance of the Grenadiers, was able to re-form. Lieut.-Colonel Dalrymple, who commanded the Right-Flank Company, formed it on the left of the Grenadiers as soon as they came in line with him.

On the left of the Battalion the 5th and half the 6th companies were engaged with two Battalions of the Kazan Regiment and were hard pressed when they in turn were relieved by the Coldstream. This Battalion had, as we have seen, been delayed in crossing the river and had been deliberately formed up on its markers in dead ground on the south bank. It now came forward in a splendid line with the Left-Flank company of the Scots Fusilier Guards on its right. The Coldstream drove back the Kazan Regiment in its stately progress. To the Left-Flank company of the Battalion rallied the remainder of the 5th and 6th companies which had been borne back in the retreat of Codrington's Brigade, and the whole line of the Guards was re-formed.

With this the crisis of the battle was over. The Highland Brigade advancing in echelon of Battalions from the right forced the Russians to withdraw their guns from the lesser redoubt, and bringing forward with them the right of Buller's Brigade of the Light Division bore back Menschikoff's right. In the centre the old story of the peninsula was repeated. The Russians fought in column. In their centre were the left column of the Kazan Regiment of two Battalions, shattered by the gallant stand of the 7th Fusilier's and the wing of the 95th, the Vladimir Regiment of four Battalions which had advanced over and on either side of the Great Redoubt against the Scots Fusilier Guards, and the right column of the Kazan Regiment of two Battalions, which had been held in check by the 5th company of the Scots Fusilier Guards and the right of Buller's Brigade. Now with the Grenadiers and the Coldstream up and the Scots Fusilier Guards reformed, the fire of the line of Guards, supported on the right by the 7th and 95th and on the left by the Highlanders, broke the resistance of these eight Battalions.

Update

According to this Scots Fusilier Guards History the Highland Brigade, which we remember was the other half of the 1st Division, and therefore deserved the right of positive mention, moved forward onto the Kourgane Hill, and are shrugged off in the history with hardly a mention? So in the grand finale the Scots Fusilier Guards are awarded four Victoria Crosses for getting it all wrong, and the Highland Brigade and the other two Regiments of the Guard's Brigade are hardly worth any mention for getting it right!?

Reg Hist

The Russians were soon in retreat and the British line sweeping forward gained touch with Canrobert's Division, which had occupied Telegraph Hill. Lord Raglan was eager to pursue with the untouched troops of the two Armies, a business for which the French, who had been but lightly engaged were as well placed, as had been the Prussians at Waterloo, but St. Arnaud, who was a sick man, refused on the pretext that his men had left their packs on the north bank of the river.

The Battle for the Alma Continues

Most of the accounts of the battle do scant justice to the part played by the Scots Fusilier Guards. Hamley, for example, says of the Guards: 'their centre Battalion, the Scots Fusiliers, was disordered and swept down by the retreating troops with a loss of eleven Officers and 170 men. Kinglake's account on which no doubt Hamley's was to some extent based, is, for an able and conscientious historian, singularly unhappy. He says, writing of the period after the retreat of Codrington's men had carried back the 6th and a part of the 5th company:-

'Still for some time the maimed battalion pushed forward and when, afterwards, it came to a halt a hard effort was made to hold the ground, but in vain. Either the over whelming weight of the column in its front, or the mishap encountered by the left companies of the English Battalion, or some other cause of evil, had destroyed its principle of cohesion, for their right wing now followed the fate of the left one, got into disorder and fell back. For a time the whole battalion of the Scots Fusilier Guards was in confusion under the bank of the river.'

One is at a loss to know how Kinglake came to dub the Scots Fusilier Guards an English Battalion, though this is the least of his errors. He makes no mention of Lindsay's stand, nor except in the vague reference to *'some other cause of evil'* to the order to retire, and it is quite untrue that the whole Battalion of the Scots Fusilier Guards was in confusion under the river-bank. He says that Lord Chewton was killed, whereas he did not die till October 8th, and is wrong in the number of casualties of the Battalion. Upon representation from Officers of the Battalion, Kinglake in subsequent editions attempted to correct his account in a number of footnotes and in an appendix to volume ii of his fourth edition. But the result is to make the story of the doings of the Battalion contradictory and confused and to leave it some way from the truth. Even Sir Evelyn Wood, whose account is much the most accurate, says:

'As the Scots Fusilier's went down the hill, some of them no doubt faster than others, the Grenadiers and Coldstream were seen advancing and the Officers of the Fusiliers realising the mistake immediately endeavored to halt their men. This they succeeded in doing soon after the Grenadiers and Coldstream passed on as they mounted the hill, for the Officer commanding the former Battalion, which was a little in front of the Coldstream, halted a minute or two to give the Scots Fusilier Guards an opportunity of re-forming and in five minutes all three Battalions went forward in one line.'

This account, otherwise generally correct, also omits all reference to the stand of Lindsay and his Colour Party, which in my judgment marked the turning point of the struggle. As we have seen, the Scots Fusilier Guards were hurried forward, unsupported on their flanks, without being given time to form a correct line. The Battalion got to within thirty yards of the Great Redoubt over which Codrington's Brigade had swarmed. Codrington's centre and left, but not his right, the 7th Fusiliers, were shattered by the fire of the Russian Artillery and borne back upon the left of the Scots Fusilier Guards. The Left-Flank company of the Battalion, had, as we have seen, been delayed with the Coldstream, and the 5th and 6th met the rush of the retreating men of Codrington's Brigade and were borne back, but not all of them, for some quickly rallied to the 4th company and helped it to make its stand against the two Battalions. Then came the order 'Fusiliers, retire' and the right companies began to fall back for a minute or two until Lieut-Colonel Haygarth and Lord Chewton seeing the Grenadiers coming up rallied their men to the Colours, before the Grenadiers were up in line. Meantime Lindsay with the Colour Party and a few men of the centre Companies never budged. Lord Wantage always maintained that the men on either side of him never gave way, when a Battalion of the Vladimir Regiment, coming over the Great Redoubt in column, closed with them. But for this stand the four Battalions of the Vladimir Regiment would almost certainly have taken forward with them the two Battalions of the right column of the Kazan Regiment, the remnant of the 7th Fusiliers and 95th would have been overwhelmed and a breach been made in the British front, which would have enabled the Russians to take the advance of the grenadiers and Coldstream in flank. The stand of the Scots Fusilier Guards checked the advance of the Vladimir Regiment just long enough to prevent this and to enable the Guards Brigade to form a complete line. It is true that the Scots Fusilier Guards was aided in re-forming by the action of the Grenadiers in wheeling back their left-flank company and in halting and opening fire as they came up with the right of the Battalion, and by the steady advance of the Coldstream on their left, bringing up with them the two and a half missing companies; but that does not alter the plain fact that the heroic conduct of the Battalion in circumstances of extraordinary difficulty prevented what might well have been a serious disaster. That the front of the battalion was quickly re-formed after the mischance of the order to retire is clearly shown by the Duke of Cambridge report to the Commander in Chief written two days after the battle, in which he says: *'The Scots Fusilier Guards reformed with the greatest alacrity.'* while the Staff Officer who wrote *'letters from Head-Quarters'* and was an eyewitness of the event wrote of the incident: *'After a moment or two they rallied and soon regained their comrades.'* The losses of the Battalion were eleven Officers wounded, forty-three rank and file killed and one hundred and twenty-one wounded, a total of one hundred and seventy-five, and of these only twenty-five occurred in the 6th and Left-Flank companies. Colonel Sir C. Hamilton, Lieut-Colonel Ridley and Captain Drummond all had their horses shot under them. The numbers engaged were twenty-six Officers, fifty-three sergeants, eighteen drummers, and six hundred and ninety-four rank and file. Captain Lord Chewton was, as we have seen, mortally wounded. The other wounded Officers were Lieut-Colonels Berkeley, Dalrymple, Hepburn, and Haygarth; Captains Setley, Bulwer, Buckley, Gipps, and Lieutenants Viscount Ennismore and the Hon. H. Annesley. The total British loss was 2,002 and by far the greater part fell upon the Battalions of the 1st, 2nd and Light Divisions. The casualties in the Artillery were thirty-four, and the Cavalry was not engaged. The French returns of losses are unreliable but they are believed to have been approximately five hundred. The Russians stated their losses as 5,709.

Update

As a matter of interest the French post Alma casualty list may have well included their dead from disease and sickness of that time, thus increasing the numbers to a degree which gave the impression that their part fought in the Alma Battle was greater than it had been?

Reg Hist

After the battle the Duke of Cambridge thanked Lieutenant Lindsay before the Guards Brigade for his gallant stand, and when her Majesty established the Order of the Victoria Cross it was awarded for their gallantry in the stand round the Colours and in rallying men to the Colours to Lieutenant Lindsay, Sergeant Mckechnie, Sergeant J. Knox and Private Reynolds. There is little doubt but that had he lived Lord Chewton would also have received the Victoria Cross. Sergeant Knox received a commission with the Rifle Brigade in April 1855.

This is clear evidence of the importance the authorities who were on the spot attached to the stand round the Colours.

The Battle for the Alma Continues

Lieutenant Thistlerhwayte, who carried the Regimental Colour, was suffering from the effects of dysentery and fever, contracted at Varna, when he went into action, and his health broke down immediately after the battle; he died in hospital at Scutari in January 1855. No doubt had he lived he would have also been awarded the Victoria Cross.

The battle was little creditable to the Generalship on either side. Menschikoff failed to make use of the possibilities of a strong defensive position, St. Arnaud, an ailing man, showed no enterprise and missed a great opportunity, while Lord Raglan, as we have seen, went off when none but his skirmishers had fired a shot and left his Divisional Commanders to shift for themselves. Had there been anyone to direct and control the battle on the side of the Allies it is very probable that the campaign would have been decided on the Alma and Sebastopol have fallen at once.

Only the British infantry had come out of the story of the Alma with credit.

The Russians retreated from the battlefield over the river Katcha, seven miles from the Alma, and after a short halt on that river fell back into Sebastopol. There Menschikoff took two wise measures. On the night of September 22nd he had some ships sunk across the mouth of the harbour, and that done he decided to move the bulk of his Army inland, after reinforcing the garrison of Sebastopol, so as to keep open his communication with Russia. He was allowed to do this at his leisure for the Allies remained two days on the Alma. There were no hospitals and no transport for the wounded, so parties of sailors were landed from the ships with hammocks to serve as stretchers, and they set about collecting the wounded and burying the dead. It is said that over seven hundred bodies, the majority being Russians, were buried about the Great Redoubt. The wounded were brought down to the valley of the Alma and hospitals were established in such houses as were left at Bourliouk. With such primitive medical arrangements it is not surprising to learn that cholera at once broke out amongst the sick and wounded and the other troops. Sir Evelyn Wood, then a midshipman in the fleet, says, that before the Army left the Alma the sailors embarked 1,500 of the British army on account of sickness alone. All this took time and it was not until September 23rd that the Allies moved forward towards Sebastopol.

Reg Hist Continues
Lieut-Colonel F. Haygarth

Account of the Alma Battle from his diary in the possession of the Regiment.
Sept 20th

'Up before daylight. The sun rose bright and glorious. Some time getting under way and then marched about an hour, when we had a long halt. I had a good meal of potted meat. St Arnaud and Lord Raglan rode along the head of our column and were loudly cheered. At last we got the order to advance and after some time loaded and formed line. Russian round shot pitched close to us while we were loading. The Russian position certainly looked formidable, but I never doubted our success. We were ordered to lie down for some time and were exactly in front of a large battery, which was by no means pleasant. The round shot pitched about twenty yards in front of us and bounded high over our heads, so that they did not do much harm, but were unpleasant. Meantime some wounded men were carried through us to the rear as the first line was engaged.

The English Army advanced to attack in two lines, the first line being the 2nd Division on the right and Light Division on the left. We supported the latter. The Rifles were extended in front of all. To see them going up the hill was splendid but it looked perilous in the extreme. At length we got the wished-for order to advance and we marched on, our pace quickening as we reached the river. The Russians had fired a village on our right front. There was a perfect storm of grapeshot as we passed through the vineyards. Annesley was hit here. We forded the river, which was much deeper than I expected, almost up to the men's pouches. There was a steep bank on the opposite side and Chewton pulled me up and we helped up the others. We then found ourselves under the shelter of a steep bank, but were not allowed time to form but hurried on and up the slope under a terrific storm of shot and grape. I was rather excited and kept haranguing my company, which I could not get properly into line. I gave up and went ahead of my company and got up to the entrenchment (the Great Redoubt) The 23rd were in a bad way and upset our fellows. A column of Russians came out upon us as we were thrown into confusion by the 23rd. I was horribly distressed on looking back for my company to find them going down the hill and I rushed after them shouting to them to come back as I had never heard the order to retire given. As I was cutting along I saw Chewton fall and immediately afterwards received a blow in my left thigh from a bullet; which broke my thigh and brought me down. The next thing I saw was Russian about to bayonet Chewton, when another brute came at me and fired his musket at my head. The bullet entered my bearskin, grazed my head and made a most awful wound in my shoulder. I feared that I should bleed to death but could do nothing as I was at the mercy of the Russians. Our fellows however rallied at once and came back again and right glad was I when they marched over me."

(Haygarth fell in a gallant effort to save Chewton. He attacked two Russians who were in the act of bayoneting Chewton. (F. M.))

Reg Hist Continues

Captain R. Gipps. Account of the Alma Battle

(The original account is in possession of the Regiment)

Dear Colonel

You have asked me to write an account of the Battle of the Alma, that is the part the Scots Fusilier Guards took in the fray, had you asked for any other part I should have referred you to Mr Kinglake's book but with regard to our Regiment he is singularly inaccurate.

My idea of the battle is given in a few words. We the Scots Fusilier Guards were deployed into line on the plain on the English side of the burning village and after some delay were ordered to advance to relieve the Light Division. On reaching a stone wall surrounding a vineyard we were ordered by General Bentink to break our ranks and climb over the wall and across the vineyard as best we could. We did so and in disorder crossed the river. On reaching the Russian bank of the river we found ourselves much protected from the enemies fire and then endeavoured and partly succeeded, in getting the men into their places in their companies in line. In another moment we should have completely accomplished this, but General Bentink again rode up and ordered us to advance. "Forward Fusiliers, what are you waiting for" was what he said. After this it was impossible to restrain and up the ascent we went in

Captain R. Gipps. Account of the Alma Battle

imperfect formation and not even our bayonets fixed. (My attention was called to this by the men themselves who asked leave to fix them) We were totally unsupported on either flank. The Coldstream and also I believe our own left company had not crossed the river owing to its being deeper to the left and Colonel Hood had not allowed the Grenadiers to advance until he had reformed their broken ranks. We notwithstanding continued to march up the incline. The Light Division seeing us coming, naturally concluded that the Brigade was entire and fell back to allow us to pass through and were themselves hotly pursued by the Russians. Mr Kinglake is mistaken in saying that we advanced in consequence of an appeal from the troops in our front. It was from an express command of our Brigadier.

Our formation already imperfect was more broken by the rush from the Light Division breaking through our ranks, never less we advanced to within I should say 20 yards of the Russian Redoubt, in our progress bayoneting those Russians who had left the shelter of the Redoubt in pursuit of the Light Division. Up to this moment we had continued to advance but now finding our ranks unsupported and masses of the enemy to the front, we halted and commenced firing, as yet we had not fired a shot, waiting for the Grenadiers and Coldstream to arrive, well knowing their eagerness to be with us, and that a few moments at the most would see them at our side. At this moment some one (alas, who was it?) rode or came to our commanding officer and told him to give the word for us to retire and then and only then did we give way to the overwhelming masses to our front. This order to retire was repeatedly given and retire we did, but almost immediately we observed the Grenadiers advancing up the hill, seeing this the officers at once knew that our orders to retire must have been a mistake and instantly gave orders to advance again, but it must be remembered that from the time we broke our ranks in order to scale the vineyard wall our formation had never been complete, the Light Division had still more broken us and the numbers we had killed and wounded made it impossible for the men at once to gain their places so as to make anything like a front to advance with, consequently the Grenadiers and I believe the Coldstream passed us and a short term elapsed before we had regained our formation to advance to them.

Colonel Hood observing this halted the Grenadiers and gave us time. It is so impossible to judge of time in the excitement of an action and under such fire as we were exposed to, that I hardly dare hazard a guess I should say five minutes. This is the only part of my narrative that I have any doubt of excepting where I speak of the intentions or motives of others or where I have by making use of such words as "I believe" or "I think" implied doubt. The rest of the action is simplicity itself.

The Brigade of Guards now complete advanced in line up the hill, took the Russian Redoubt and the next thing we saw was the enemy in full retreat. At no time was there any gap between the Grenadiers right and the Coldstream left after they had advanced from the river bank that other troops could have filled, because though part of the time we were in confusion still we were there, and in this Mr Kinglake is misinformed.

I forgot to say that we were joined by a few parties from the Light Division who instead of retiring through us, advanced with us, but to what Regiments they belonged I do not know. There is one more error in Mr Kinglake's account of the battle that I am anxious to point out because I think it materially proves the inaccuracy of his information about the Scots Fusilier Guards, and also because I am able more than anybody else to refute that part of his statement from the fact of my being Colonel Berkeley's Subaltern. He says 'Colonel Berkeley had advanced with a company of the Fusiliers which he had succeeded in rallying and placed himself on the left of the Grenadiers' or words to that effect. I have not his book by my side. Now Colonel Berkeley had his leg broken while we were retiring and was carried to the rear, consequently he could never have rallied the company at all, and I succeeded to the command of his company and I never parted from my company any time of the action nor were they at any time on the immediate left of the Grenadiers.

(The company which formed on the left of the Grenadiers was the Right-flank company under Colonel Dalrymple, as was natural. Lieut-Colonel Dalrymple formed it as the Grenadiers came abreast of him F.M.)

My account has become much more lengthy than I intended, please excuse its many faults but its substance is correct

believe me

yours very sincerely (signed) R Gipps

Reg Hist Continues

Lord Wantage's account of the Battle of the Alma

(Lord Wantage, V. C., K. C. B. A memoir, p. 35)

The first regiment to come out from the bed of the river and to form in line and to advance up the heights was the centre regiment of the brigade, the 1st Battalion of the Scots Fusiliers led the way by three or four minutes at least in advance of the Grenadiers and Coldstream. Whether this was owing to undue precipitancy on our part, or to carelessness I cannot say, but such was undoubtedly the fact. As brigades usually advance by the centre I should myself say that the other two battalions ought to have been more in line with the Scots Fusiliers than they were'?

Update

I am presuming that Lindsay makes the comment in all seriousness when the placement of the other battalions of the Guards Brigade was quite clear to him at that phase of the Alma battle. Or is this hind sighted viewpoint part of his cover up, for not only were the other 5 Battalions of the Division, but neither was the Left Flank Companies of the Scots Fusilier Guards yet entirely across the river, so the Scots Fusilier Guards Battalion itself was in no order to advance in line when it was not even complete, and I presume that Lindsay and his colour party would be well aware of this fact, or they should have been!

Lord Wantage's account of the Battle of the Alma

Plus the Bn. Commander, Sir Charles Hamilton, was not too far away and should have given guidance. He probably did, but it has been lost in the overall confusion of the battalion advance up onto the Great Redoubt. Lindsay makes it seem as if his detached remnants of the battalion were the only ones in step, with every other soldier of the 1st Division being at fault for not being in line with his colour party, and the Scots Fusilier Guards companies which went up the hill with the colour party. He perhaps could have well argued after the battle that he was pushed forward by direct orders from senior officers. (he possibly did, but this would not be welcomed by those concerned) But when he obeyed those orders to quickly advance he deliberately put his own life, and those of others at great risk, and then to compound the error by placing the blame for the rash move forward on the inability of the other formations to be up with him ready to form line does no credit to his own character. Nor is there any value in not stating the truth of an action which must now be challenged by historical hindsight, and other factors such as most other British versions of the battle.

Neither was Sir Colin Campbell, who with the Highland Brigade on the Kourgane Hill at this time to be very sympathetic on hearing of the Scots Fusilier Guards peril of the colour party advance, and made the comment that it would be better if every man of the Guards was killed rather than turn their back on the enemy.

Traditionally the line formation may only form up and advance at the pace of the slowest parts, even though the line should be held by the center dressing as the controlling element. It was either Airey, Bentink or Hamilton, acting on the haste that Codrington of the Light Division was bringing to the situation who ordered Lindsay up the slope leading to the Great Redoubt. In all probability the Duke of Cambridge was either with Buller or Campbell trying to make sense of the situation, whilst in the process of information gathering

Lord Wantage's account of the Battle of the Alma

for his next order whilst this advance was being hurried along.

Reg Hist.

The lead of time which the regiment gained at the first was continued throughout the advance, till within one or two hundred yards of the redoubt, when the battalion was tremendously shaken by the Russian fire, especially from grape shot and canister, which came in a regular hurricane, but mostly flying high.

Update

This fire would be coming from the Russian guns on the causeway which were in position directly south of the Alma Bridge and covering that particular arc, But it was not a clear nor direct field of fire onto the advancing 1st Division, as its main intent was to cover the bridge across the main Port road and the Alma River. The lead up to the highest part of the Great Redoubt is also 'concave' in form, so the advance was well protected by the shape of the ground at that point. Thus the reason that the firing of the Russian guns was high.

Reg Hist

The left wing suffered severely and was disorganized. Part of the right wing never yielded; not one yard of the ground that a man had gained did we ever give up during the advance. When a portion of the regiment was disorganized a circumstance occurred which proved fortunate for the remainder of the battalions. The Russians, seeing what they considered a renewed success, sprang out of their earthworks and came forward, hoping to capture the colours.

Update

Certainly the colours may have been an attraction for the Russians, but the main object was to seize the tactical opportunity which the Russians now saw as the 1st Division was split wide open by the premature advance of the Scots Fusilier Guards.

Reg Hist

The desperate fire from the redoubt must then have ceased on account of the risk to their own men, for I remember a lull in the fire at that time. It must not be supposed that the Grenadiers and Coldstream were lagging behind, but two or three minutes in a battle seems a long time, and at a most critical moment in the lives of some of us, we witnessed the Grenadiers on our immediate right advancing in perfect order, coming up, as it might be, in the character of a reserve. The effect of this was evidently conclusive; for those who had come out of their earthworks fell back, and a hasty retreat was begun for the battery itself.

The colours were well protected by a strong escort, four noncommissioned officers and eight or ten privates; one amongst them I especially remember on account of his cheery face and perfect confidence-inspiring, trustworthy demeanour. Sergeant-Major Edwards always afterwards took the credit for having selected Reynolds as one of the escort to the colours, but he chose him on account of his size. I always remained Reynolds' friend, and backed him through many a trouble. When the battalion came home I was fortunately able to place him in an excellent situation, which he held till the day of his death.

When the colours were attacked Reynolds did some execution with the bayonet, and Hughie Drummond, who had scrambled to his legs after his horse was killed, shot three Russians with his revolver. Berkeley was knocked over at this time, and all the non-commissioned officers with the colours excepting one sergeant. The colours I carried were shot through in a dozen places, and the colour staff cut in two. Poor old Thistlewayte had a bullet through his bearskin cap. As is frequently the case with troops in their first engagement, the elevation given to the Russian fire was, fortunately for us, too high for the deadly execution which might have been given to it. In my own case I neither drew my sword nor fired my revolver, my great object being to plant the standard on the Russian redoubt, and my impression is that nobody was into the earthworks before I was.

Update
Battle of the Alma, a Russian Chronicle

The great Totleben now contributes his more than two rubles worth

The Excerpts which follow below take us through the Russian view of the Alma Battle and were taken from the *'Crimea Texts'* located on the Internet.

In my opinion Colonel El Totleben was the real architect and extraordinary Russian military leader who through his engineering skills was able to lead the Herculean efforts made by the defenders to continually hold the Allies outside the City, and the Port of Sevastopol. He was born in Latvia of German parents and when first sent to the Crimea to support Menshikov found himself pushed to the sidelines as Menshikov shunned the very idea that the Allies would invade the Crimea at that time of the coming of winter, and for what reason, after all the war with Russia fought on the River Danube was now over at Silitria?

Menshikov was however proved wrong in his thinking, and so Totleben was then thrust into the forefront of building up the Russian defences. However it is now 1864, and Totleben has written his version of events, to be monitored by a *Times* Newspaper Review. I produce them here for the reader to pay attention, and find interest in, the opposing perspective of the opening battle of the Crimea War.

Note Totleben's mention of the new rifle as playing a major role in the Allies winning the battle.

The Times Review 1864

'We now come to the English Army. We have been looking for some time to ascertain what M.de Totleben has done with them. Here they are at last'

"It was thus that while the right wing of our army was still engaged in a bloody struggle, in which the efforts of the English exhausted themselves against the courage and firmness of our troops, the battle on the left wing was already over. It has been said above that towards 2 o'clock, and at the time when Canrobert had succeeded in deploying on the heights, the English reached the right bank of the Alma. They maintained themselves in that position while making us suffer from the effects of a very brisk fire of precision until the whole of Napoleon's men had crossed the river. Having received news that the Prince had effected his passage, Lord Raglan made an onward movement. The Division Brown advanced towards the gardens and vineyards, and the Division de Lacy Evans partly towards the right and partly towards the left of Bourliouk. The division of the Duke of Cambridge, behind the Division Brown, deployed in columns. The Division de Lacy Evans was followed by the Division England and the Division Cathcart, while the cavalry still on the left, somewhat in the rear, assured the movement of the left wing. In front of the centre marched two batteries. Notwithstanding our fire, which caused sensible loss to the enemy, the English advanced in perfect order. Their artillery hailed grape on our skirmishers ensconced in the vines and houses. When the English had reached the bridge two of our batteries, occupying the heights on two sides of the high road, received them with a violent fire of grape, and the riflemen of the Regiment of Borodino and those of the Regiment of Grand Duke Michael concentrated their fire upon them. Codrington's Brigade, which advanced towards the bridge, received by musketry and a cannonade, experienced considerable losses, confusion seized the ranks, and it retired in great disorder behind Bourliouk. But the enemy's riflemen, concealed behind the walls of the gardens, opened fire, and began to penetrate into the villages on the left bank. The snapshooting of the English riflemen caused our troops terrible losses, and above all did great mischief to the two light batteries placed in front of the Borodino Regiment on the left of the high road. The situation of these batteries became more difficult still when, after some time, two English guns succeeded in crossing the Alma by the fords below Bourliouk, and, after having ascended a rise of the hill, got into position, and took our two batteries in enfilade. A hail of rifle balls committed great ravages among the gunners of the artillery, and among the columns of the Regiment of Borodino, which, with the light battery No. 1, placed in advance of its left wing, was obliged to retire. Meanwhile, the light battery No. 2, more on the right, continued to mow down with its fire the retreating battalions of Codrington's Brigade. The troops of General Kiriakow, after their encounter with the French, near the Telegraph, never halted in their retreat till they reached the Katcha, and they were now followed by the Regiment of Borodino. The light battery No. 2 quitted its position last of all. It was with difficulty they could drag their guns up the hill, in consequence of the loss of horses. The passage of the bridge then became more easy. At last the Division of the Duke of Cambridge and of de Lacy Evans having reached the river set about effecting the passage. England's Division and the reserve of artillery alone remained on the right bank as soon as Cathcart and the cavalry began to gain the left side. Brown's Division, notwithstanding the fire of the Chasseurs of the Grand Duke Michael's Regiment, and of 12 guns behind an epaulement on the right of the high road, passed to the left bank also. Seeing the movement of General Brown, Prince Gortschakoff ordered two battalions of the Grand Duke Michael Regiment, which had suffered less than the others, to attack the enemy with the bayonet. The Regiment of Ouglitch was brought forward from the epaulement, and posted in a ravine near the place previously occupied by the Cossack batteries. The 3d and 4th battalions of the Grand Duke Michael Regiment advanced with the bayonet against the English. By this movement the infantry masked the battery, which was obliged to stop its fire of grape. The enemy, seeing the movement of our troops, fell back towards the river, and having let them approach within a little distance opened against them a most murderous fire. The commander of the regiment, Colonel Selespew, and the two majors were killed. It was then that after sustaining a considerable loss, and seeing the greater part of their senior officers fall, our battalions retired directly towards the epaulement, thus preventing the battery from reopening its fire and covering the retreat of our infantry. On the heels of our retreating troops marched the 23 d Regiment of English infantry. On reaching the epaulement our troops occupied the flanks, and thus unmasked the battery, which immediately recommenced firing. But it was too late! The English were not more than a pistol shot from the battery. Our artillerymen, seeing that the enemy were on the point of rushing into the epaulement, limbered up their guns, and retired along with the battalions of infantry, which had suffered a considerable loss. The two other battalions of the regiment placed on open ground and exposed to fire were also much weakened, and could no longer oppose the English columns. Two pieces of the battery of position No. 1 of the 16th Brigade, of which one had the trail broken and the other its two wheelers killed, could not be carried off, and remained behind the epaulement, which was at once occupied by the English. In a moment on the parapet so lately held by our battery we saw the English banner waving. The 1st and 2d Battalion of the Regiment of Wladimir, sent to support the retreating Chasseurs, rushed to the fight. The charge was executed with great impetuosity. Without troubling themselves about the terrible fire of the English the battalion advanced in a compact mass with the bayonet. The enemy could not resist the shock, and, abandoning the epaulement, retreated before they had time to do more than fire a few shots. The epaulement was occupied by our troops, who, concealing themselves behind the parapet, opened a very brisk fire against the enemy now forced to fly precipitately towards the river. While all this was taking place the French had occupied the Hill of the Telegraph, and their reserves were already massed on the left bank, while the troops of Kiriakow were retreating towards the Katcha. In the meantime, the English, driven out of the epaulement and beyond the reach of our smooth-bores, had only to meet the fire of a handful of riflemen of the Regiment of Wladimir, for the riflemen of the Grand Duke's regiment had no more cartridges. The English halted there about 120 yards from the river, and, having begun to reform, opened fire once more. Lord Raglan caused the Divisions of the Duke of Cambridge and de Lacy Evans, which had already effected their passage, to advance to the aid of the weakened troops of General Brown. A fresh attack of the English was imminent. The Division of the Duke of Cambridge, supported by the Division of Brown, which had succeeded in rallying, and by Pennefather's Brigade, once more advanced towards the epaulement. The situation of our troops was becoming very critical. The perilous contest might have been rendered to some extent less unequal by the support of a battery; but as they had not attached one to the Wladimir Regiment, the enemy was enabled to organize his battalions at his ease. The battery, which had quitted the epaulement, could, with great difficulty, carry off the ten guns which remained to it, in consequence of the enormous loss sustained by it in gunners and horses, and found it absolutely impossible to reoccupy the epaulement and renew the combat. They might have advanced the light battery, which was left almost uselessly near the Souzdal Regiment, but it would have had to make a very difficult movement in the bottom of a ravine, in rear of the regiment, and it could not have arrived in time. Notwithstanding the danger of their position, our troops stood firm. The terrible fire of the clouds of skirmishers deprived our troops in a very short time of the greater part of their officers and chiefs. All those who surrounded Prince Gortschakoff fell, the Prince himself had his horse killed under him, and his coat was pierced with six balls. But Prince Gortschakoff and General Kvizinsky did not recoil from a fresh sacrifice to save the position. They both commanded a bayonet charge, and led in person what remained of the Regiment of Wladimir. Animated by the example of its chiefs, the Regiment of Wladimir, with loud hurrahs, rushed on, part over the epaulement, part by its flanks, and precipitated itself upon the enemy. At the sight of the determined onslaught of ^9 Regiment of Wladimir, the first line of the English regiments lost order in the ranks, wavered, and began to retire towards the bridge. But at this supreme moment our troops were suddenly taken on the flank by the French artillery, and this unforeseen attack determined the success of the action in favour of the English. St Arnaud, in fact, having learnt the obstinate resistance which the English were meeting, had suspended for some moments the movement of his troops, and, after the occupation of the Hill of the Telegraph, had advanced against our right flank two troops of Horse Artillery of the reserve, a mounted battery of the 4th Division, and half an English battery. This artillery, numbering 23 pieces, opened a murderous fire against our flank, and at the same moment the French troops recommenced their onward march. Overwhelmed by this incident, as terrible as unforeseen, the Regiment of Wladimir paused, and the English, emboldened, directed against it a very brisk fire. But the regiment after a momentary halt, with loud hurrahs, once more renewed its bayonet charge! Received by the thundering fire of the infantry, and of the artillery of the French and of the English, having lost nearly all of its officers, and having no supports, it was obliged to abandon the attack, and fall back towards the epaulement which we had not time to reoccupy with artillery. The English pursued the Regiment of Wladimir. Its shattered fragments found a refuge behind the parapet and succeeded in checking by a rolling fire the progress of the enemy for a moment. General Kvizinsky, being exceedingly anxious to carry off the two guns abandoned by the battery of position No. 1 of the 16th Brigade, and wishing to afford a means of retreat to the artillery in the epaulement more to the right, halted stiffly with the regiment to check the enemy. Thus opposed in their march, the enemy replied to the fire of the Wladimir Regiment without relaxing their fusillade.

For 20 minutes the regiment maintained itself behind the epaulement, and at the same time that it made head against nearly a whole English division was taken on flank and rear by the fire of the French battery. While the Regiment Wladimir was falling heroically behind the epaulement the Brigade Colin Campbell threatened to turn its right flank, the Division of Prince Napoleon advancing more to the left hastened to cut off its retreat to Sebastopol, the French battery thundered on its flank, and the Divisions Brown, Evans, and the Duke of Cambridge rained on it a hail of bullets and shell. But the Regiment of Wladimir wavered not. Although it had lost its colonel, 3 majors, 14 captains, 30 officers, and about 1,300 men, it stood firm on its ground. Fearing that they might cut off the retreat on Sebastopol, and seeing that neither at the centre nor on the left wing were there any means of making the chances of the battle more favourable for us, Prince Menschikoff, towards 4 o'clock in the afternoon, at last ordered Prince Gortschakoff to order the troops of our right flank to fall back on the chain of heights. Lieutenant-General Kvizinsky, having strengthened the line of skirmishers, began to retire with the remains of the Wladimir Regiment and of the Regiment of the Grand Duke Michael. In the former there was not one field officer left, and only two captains and seven lieutenants, many of whom, though wounded, would not quit the ranks. At the moment when he gave the order to retreat the General had a horse killed under him and was wounded in the foot. That did not prevent his continuing to fight and to take all the measures the occasion demanded. Soon a rifle ball broke his left wrist and hip, and he fell under his heavy wounds. Our troops retired with regularity and good order, so that the artillery, notwithstanding the losses it had experienced, brought off all its pieces except the two of the battery of position No. 1 of the 16th Brigade, which remained on the field and fell into the hands of the enemy, as they could not be dragged up the heights. The English, having succeeded in carrying several guns to the spot lately occupied by the left wing of the Regiment of Souzdal, opened against the Regiments of Souzdal and of Ouglitch a fire of artillery and rifles which caused a loss of nearly 100 men to the latter before they could gain the top of the ridge. To cover the retreat, Major-General Kischinsky, by the orders of the Commander-in-Chief, caused to be placed on a trifling eminence not far from the old position of the reserve the troop of Horse Artillery No. 12 and the light batteries Nos. 3 and 4 of the 11th Brigade. Behind them and on the left of the road to Sebastopol the Regiment of Vollivnia was stationed, and on the right of the road the Brigade of Hussars was posted, with the Cossacks on its right flank. The English, having occupied the ground of the right wing and the centre of our old position, began to pursue our retreating soldiers. Lord Cardigan's Brigade, together with the Horse Artillery, advanced, resting on the right of Colin Campbell's Brigade, and was sustained by the Brigade of the Guard Bentinck and by a part of the Divisions de Lacy Evans and Cathcart, which marched in the rear. The enemy's artillery opened fire, but our troops were already out of range, and suffered no loss. Having approached our rear within cannon shot the enemy were received by the fire of our artillery, which caused them to halt, and to desist from further pursuit. Thus our rearguard secured to the bulk of our army the possibility of arriving without impediment at the Katcha, which they reached about 9 o'clock. At 7 the enemy, reinforced by Torrens from Old Fort, bivouacked on the very ground occupied by our troops during the battle. The motives which prevented the enemy pushing the pursuit further were:- 1st, that their troops were harassed with fatigue from the heroic opposition of the Russians; 2d, that they had not enough of cavalry; 3d, that they were afraid the Russians might halt behind the Katcha, which presented the same facilities for resistance as the Alma; 4th, the illness of Marshal St Arnaud, which prevented the operations after the action receiving the impress of the necessary activity."

The Times assessment

Summing up; The Times 07.09.1864 p 7

So far we have translated almost literally M de Todleben's account of the Battle of the Alma, at the risk of wearying all and of surprising and irritating many of our readers; but the book is very dear and scarce, and it will probably be some time before it appears in an English form. It will be observed that in the main the Russian General confirms the French accounts as to the progress of the great events of the action, and the manner in which the troops were engaged. He quite ignores Lord Raglan's "scarlet arch on the knoll," and the effect of the white plumes of his staff; but he also omits the advance of the Guards, and does not agree with Mr Kinglake as to the value of Sir Colin Campbell's demonstration on the left. It would trench too largely on our space to analyze his statement, but we may observe that the very story of the fight at the epaulement and the capture of the guns, as well as the disposition of the troops, proves that if the English army was not the first to move, it had the hardest fighting and the hottest part of the struggle. The table of losses furnished by Todleben is conclusive on this point. In killed, wounded, and missing the Russian army lost 5,709 men. Of these the regiments defending the position to the right of the high road to Eupatoria - those of Wladimir, Grand Duke Michael, Souzdal, and Ouglitch - opposed to the English left lost 3,028. Some of the regiments on the left of the road were opposed to the English also, and if we put their loss at 500, which is very low, we shall leave a balance of 2,200 as the share of the work done by our allies. It would be absurd, after the testimony which has been adduced, to which is now added that of Todleben, to deny that the French did their work admirably well. National prejudice, morbid feeling, and personal dislike to the Emperor can no longer assert that *his* soldiers belied the ancient reputation of the French army on the heights of Alma, and we of all people can best afford to concede them the high praise their activity and gallantry deserve.

In accounting for the defeat of the Russians, Todleben assigns a high place to the superior armament of the allies, but he also asserts that the Russians were inferior in manoeuvring. It may be useful to point out to those officers who declaim against the Hythe school for its supposed tendency to make the soldier too independent of his officer that Todleben distinctly assigns as an advantage the greater confidence, skill, and mobility which soldiers left to themselves as skirmishers are sure to acquire. "They will not hesitate," he says, "in action nor will they require the continual direction and surveillance of their immediate officers." The opponents of musketry instruction may say that English soldier nature is different from human nature anywhere else in the world. We do not believe them.

Certainly, the Russian is not fit for freedom of action in the field if an Englishman is not. Todleben praises, also, the sword bayonet exercise, and the pas gymnastique, which serve as the complement to the advantages obtained by the rifled arms. The Russian army, remembering the traditions bequeathed by Suwaroff, preferred the shock of the charge to precision of fire at long range; and, while the soldier of the West was taught to develop his presence of mind and individual quality, the Russians were, above all things, trained to act in masses. No army could equal them in manoeuvres by masses, but on difficult ground, where straight lines and precision of movement were no longer possible, and where presence of mind was required in the face of an enemy, the Russians, who did not yield to any army in the world in bravery and devotion, had to suffer great losses and to forfeit the chance of victory.

At the Alma their infantry, armed with smooth-bores, could not hit anything beyond 300 paces, while the Allies reached them at 1,200 paces and more. When they got near enough to equalize the disadvantages, their battalions were disorganized by the allied fire. The artillery exposed to the fire of riflemen, who were out of range of grape, could only make their fire effective by using shrapnel, of which they had only 15 rounds in each light battery.

Ordinary shells were almost useless. Even when the Allies had become disorganized by the united efforts of artillery and infantry, and when it was only necessary to complete their defeat by a cannonade, it was impossible to act in consequence of the loss in guns and horses caused by rifle fire, and the same cause obliged the artillery to quit its position prematurely at times, for fear of being captured by the Allies. The allied artillery caused the Russians very little loss in comparison with the small arms of precision. But among the most important causes of their defeat was the neglect to fortify their position, though they had both time and means for the purpose. The tardy opposition to Bosquet also contributed to their disaster. Finally, the abandonment of his post by Kiriakow, had a fatal influence on the regiments fighting on the right, as it permitted Napoleon and Canrobert to ascend the heights, and was the cause of the losses to Gortschakoff 's men.

In fact, an ill armed Russian force, placed in a position which was not fortified, ill commanded and manoeuvred, was attacked by an enemy superior in numbers and equipment, and was, as the Americans say, "pretty badly beaten."

* Difense de Sebastopol. Ouvrage ngidi sous la direction de Lieutenant-Gunral E. de Todleben, Aide-de-Camp Guitral de S. M. l'Empereur. Tome I. PremiOre Partie, DeuxiOme Partie. St. Pitersbourg: Imprimerie N. Thiebelin et Cie. 1863.4

Update

I now return to the Scots (Fusilier) Guards own Regimental History as once again we consider present updates in line with the hind sighted knowledge of the events written. I am also fully aware that no Regimental history may cover all events during a period of intense hand to hand combat, such as at the Alma, and it is only with some selective hindsight that we begin to understand the details of mistakes made, or of true Regimental or National interest and progress made since those times. I Therefore believe that this selective update adds to not only our knowledge of past regimental history, but also provides stepping stones intelligence to the present, and on into the future, but only if we take the trouble to look for them. If however the eye is ever taken off of the Regimental History ball then certain aspects and skills may be forgotten for ever. The example here being that this 'sharpshooting' mission given to the Brigade of Guards during the Crimea campaign seemed to be quickly forgotten on return to Britain as the role and programme of public duties was to once again assume the main Guards Brigade priority rating.

This change of priorities would have meant that the rifle shooting capability of the individual soldier was to become secondary to the rifles use as an ancillary piece of the parade item, becoming part of the make up and the recognised uniform of the drill square rather more than for the use it was intended, and at which it had now proved itself more than capable during the Invasion of the Crimea, and whilst being used by the soldiers of the Guards Brigade, who were learning to use the rifle for its true purpose at that time.

We must also remember however that a rifle or any individual weapon is only as good as its user is trained or educated on how to use it, therefore regimental priorities do matter. My conclusion being that I remind the reader that you may play football or Rugby, but not both, for excellence may only come by specialisation and competition. Any other muddling through will take you to where there is a good chance of merging into mediocrity in all things. Being a jack of all trades is fine, but when the country you are there to defend is at risk there should be no compromise, as the end result of safety and security of citizens takes precedence over any ceremonial role. In fact the ceremonial role actually challenges the terrorist and promotes acts and may even increase terrorist options just by being there as prima donna targets. So surely the whole idea of Public Duties being performed by regular and professional soldiers rather than acting for the security forces working with the emergency services becomes an act of Governmental and Military waste, and of full blown stupidity.

Yes, history is important especially when we see progress driven backwards, and the citizen then put at further risk for reasons that are less than noble when the free thinking field craft Guardsmen turn themselves into an item on a ceremonial reenactment programme which in these present times is completely unnecessary and undesirable. Above is fact, not opinion!

Reg Hist

CHAPTER IV
Inkerman and Sebastopol

Just before the battalion set out on its march to Sebastopol, colonel E. F. Walker arrived from England to take command in succession to General Dixon. He found a depleted battalion, for the state of September 23rd shows twenty-six officers and five hundred and ninety-three other ranks present and fit for duty. On that day the Allied armies marched to the Katcha and bivouacked on its south bank, where they were joined by the Scots Greys and the 57th, one of the missing battalions of the 4th Division. During the next two days the British troops had to live on biscuit, but on the 26th Lord Raglan, leaving the 4th Division on the Tchernaya, where it was joined by the French, reached Balaklava. On the previous day our cavalry had bumped into the rear of Menschikoff's column, which was moving out to Simpheropol, and captured some of his transport. He had left in Sebastopol a battalion of engineers, 5,000 militia and the crews of the sunken warships to reinforce the garrison under Admiral Nakimoff.

Balaklava provided for a short time a pleasant change from the downs north of Sebastopol. Surgeon-Major Bostock writing from Balaklava on the 27th said:--

'Yesterday we arrived at this place a snug little harbour on the south side of Sebastopol; the fort fell after a slight defence, and now our heavy siege guns are being landed, to be placed in position on some heights which command

the town and harbour of Sebastopol, and of which we took possession yesterday. Lord Raglan sent a summons this day. If the Governor Prince Menschikoff is prudent, he will accept, if not we shall, I suppose, have to attack the place in a few days. The prevalent opinion here is that the affair is nearly over. We shall see how long the Russians can keep us out. At the present time we are in clover surrounded by delicious grapes, peaches and apples with plenty of Crimean sheep and cattle, and after living on salt pork for a fortnight you may imagine how we enjoy these luxuries.'

The 'snug little harbour' proved to be our undoing. The British Admiral insisted on retaining it, and the French courteously gave way and moved their base to Kamiesh Bay, which in the event provided them with much easier line of communication and an easier approach to the works of Sebastopol. It was not long before the fruit of balaklava was exhausted, the army back on hard tack and the cheery optimism of the end of September gone. The distribution of the bases decided the fronts of attack for the Allies. We took the northern front, opening our first parallel on the Inkerman ridge. The French took the southern front, the Great Ravine being at first the dividing-line between the two armies. East of the Great Ravine were posted the 3rd and 4th Divisions, beyond them extending to the Careenage Creek came the Light Division, on the other side of which was the 2nd Division, with the 1st Division behind and south of it towards Inkerman The allies having decided against an immediate assault had to wait until their batteries were in position, and on October 17 a bombardment was opened both from the shore and from the ships.

Though the prime function of the 1st Division was, in conjunction with Bosquet's division to the south of it, to cover the siege against Menschikoff's enterprises it had also to find parties for the trenches, and from October 10th to November 5th the brigade provided four picquets each of from fifty to seventy men, and working parties for the trenches.

On October 16th the brigade was ordered to form a corps of sharpshooters of one N.C.O. and ten men from each battalion under Captain Goodlake of the Coldstream. The N.C O. of the Scots Fusilier Guards chosen for this duty was Sergeant Donald McBeath, one of the best shots of the battalion. McBeath made a name for himself in this work and, as we shall see, distinguished himself later in the siege. He won the medal for Distinguished Conduct in the Field and on his retirement in 1856 became the Duke of Atholl's deerstalker and sergeant-major of the Atholl Highlanders.

Update

The later versions from books written on the Crimea campaign referring to the number of sharpshooters from the Guards Brigade was to increase the number from 30 to 60, for In all probability that initial number of 30 though first thought appropriate would have been 10 per Battalion, making a sum total of 30 from amongst the 3 Guards Battalions. But when the combined sharpshooters actually begun the duties for which they were intended, and on a 24hour/7day programme along with reserves, administration and support services, such as 'runners' and fatigue duties, etc, it was soon noted that 30 was just not enough. So another 10 junior NCOs and men would have been selected from around the Guards Brigade.

In my opinion there would have been more than a little interest and competition amongst the junior NCOs and privates for these sharp shooting missions, for it would relieve them from routine picquet and trench duties, whilst promising a potential of taking the fight to the Russian enemy.

On another level it also raised the question of 'individual markmanship' and a proven ability to select, aim and shoot at selected enemy targets at the longer ranges whilst under their own self management, for as the Minie Rifle and its possibilities and probabilities were tried and tested against a live enemy in the Crimea, so its further potential would be discussed, and perhaps new ideas introduced which would be in line with the ground and the task. An element of further 'democracy' would have also been introduced as the privates and junior NCOs would have added to the discussion and put forward their own ideas founded on their experiences, and on a 24/7 administration and servicing basis. Thus a well practiced, researched and experience which could have served the Brigade of Guards well in the future, and given its image an uplift in the eyes of the rifle brigade and infantry regiments of the line. But it was not to be, and another opportunity for excellence in the field lost, whilst the Royal sentry boxes continued to win the near stagnant presence of the Guards

Reg Hist

These additional duties bore heavily on the battalions, the strength of which, despite the arrival of parties of recovered invalids from Scutari and Varna, steadily diminished from illness. The morning state of October 25th, the day of the Battle of Balaklava, shows twenty-six officers, and five hundred and twenty-four other ranks present and fit for duty, and of these, after deducting the picquets and working parties, about four hundred of all ranks were available to meet a Russian attack. The battalion received tents on October 7th: the rations issued at this time were salt pork, biscuit, rice, rum, sugar, and raw coffee, but the latter proved to be useless as it was impossible to roast and grind it. Fresh meat was issued normally twice a week, but sometimes only once, and owing to the absence of fresh vegetables scurvy and jaundice made their appearance about the end of October.

On the evening of October 17th, after the bombardment, most British soldiers in the trenches were convinced that we could have carried the Malakov and the Redan, but the French guns had been less successful and General Canrobert, who had succeeded St. Arnaud when the latter's health broke down, asked Lord Raglan to delay the assault for twenty-four hours. By then the Russians, inspired by their great engineer Totleben, had repaired most of the damage and the chance was gone. Meantime Menschikoff had been reinforced by troop froms Bessarabia and had decided to attempt to capture our base at Balaklava. In the affair of October 25 the Guards had no part. The Russian attack was a half-hearted one and all danger was over when a series of blunders sent the Light Brigade on their famous charge, which served no useful purpose and resulted in the destruction of the brigade. Tennyson's poem has made the charge the most popular feat in the history of the British Army, and the charge of the Heavy Brigade led by Scarlett against a vastly superior mass of Russian cavalry, which was as gallant as that of their comrades of the Light Brigade, and was militarily a fine and very serviceable achievement, has been completely forgotten. Balaklava was saved, but the Russians were left in possession of the heights commanding the Woronzoff Road and we were later to feel the effects of being deprived of its use. Another result of the battle was that it exposed the weakness of our defences of Balaklava and the Highland Brigade was moved down to strengthen them, leaving the Guards Brigade alone of the 1st Division on the uplands overlooking the Inkerman valley.

Update

I am surprised that the Scots Fusilier Guards history contains no mention of the battle which later became known as 'Little Inkerman' and was fought on October 26th the day after the Balaclava Battle. The Scots Fusilier Guards history has mentioned the forming of the 'Sharpshooters' comprised of 60 of the best shots from the Guards Brigade to form a defensive screen around the front of the 2nd Division on the Inkerman heights covering the Careenage Ravine, Shell Hill and further around the top of the Inkerman Heights around the Barrier and a further link to Home Ridge, all under the command of Capt. Goodlake and Sgt Ashton of the Coldsream Guards, and yet fails to mention their efforts in the sortie which took place on the 26th October?

The end result being the withdrawal of the Russian force of about 5000 men after they had been repulsed by the British who were servicing that part of the British right of line.

Update continues

The Battle of Inkerman

'The Soldiers Battle'

'WE HAVE NOTHING TO REJOICE OVER, AND ALMOST EVERYTHING TO DEPLORE, IN THE BATTLE OF INKERMAN. WE HAVE DEFEATED THE ENEMY INDEED, BUT HAVE NOT ADVANCED ONE STEP NEARER TOWARD THE CITADEL OF SEBASTOPOL. WE HAVE ABASHED, HUMILIATED, AND UTTERLY ROUTED AN ENEMY STRONG IN NUMBERS, IN FANATICISM, AND IN DOGGED RESOLUTE COURAGE. BUT WE HAVE SUFFERED A FEARFUL LOSS, AND WE ARE NOT IN A POSITION TO PART WITH ONE MAN.

William Howard Russell

TIMES CORRESPONDENT

And from the Russian perspective;

'DANNENBURG'S TERRIBLE ACTION IN WHICH WE ATTACKED AGAIN AND WERE BEATEN AGAIN'; AND CONTINUED; IT WAS A TREACHEROUS, REVOLTING BUSINESS, WE HAD TO RETREAT, BECAUSE HALF OUR TROOPS HAD NO ARTILLERY OWING TO THE ROADS BEING IMPASSABLE, AND GOD KNOWS WHY- THERE WERE NO RIFLE BATTALIONS. TERRIBLE SLAUGHTER! IT WILL WEIGH HEAVY ON THE SOULS OF MANY PEOPLE! LORD FORGIVE THEM.'

Leo Tolstoy. FROM A RUSSIAN PERSPECTIVE

Reg Hist

Whether the Russians knew of this weakening of the northern portion of the British line is uncertain, but their next object was to attempt its capture. They were now in a considerable superiority and had within and without the fortress from 115,000 to 120,000 men against the 65,000 of the Allied armies, including 11,000 Turks, whom neither Lord Raglan nor Canrobert thought fit to employ. The Allied commanders were unconscious of their danger, for they had arranged a meeting for November 5, the day of the Battle of Inkerman, to concert measures for an assault on Sebastopol. On October 26 the Russians had made a sortie from the town against the lines of the 2nd Division, which had been easily repulsed, and that division, its piquets on the alert because of this attack, now held the ground menaced by the Russian plans with some 3,000 men fit for duty. To the west of them on the Victoria Ridge was Codrington's brigade, 1,400 strong, and three-quarters of a mile south of them was encamped the Guards Brigade, 1,331 strong. Against these troops the Russians were planning to bring 35,000 men supported by fifty-four guns of position and eighty-one field guns.

Menschikoff's plan was that in the early morning of November 5 a force of 19,000 infantry and thirty-eight guns under General Soiminoff should issue from the works of Sebastopol near the mouth of the Careenage Ravine and attack the position of the 2nd Division from the west, while at the same time another force of 16,000 men and ninety-six guns under General Pauloff should descend from the Heights of Inkerman, cross the valley and the Tchernaya by the causeway and brigade and attack the same position from the north. The remainder of Menschikoff's troops outside the fortress under Gortschakoff were to prevent the troops occupying the ground chosen for the attack from being reinforced, and the guns of Sebastopol were to cover

The Battle of Inkerman

by their fire the right of Soiminoff's attack. The weaknesses of this plan were the difficulty of combining the operations of the two Russian forces and the lack of space for them on the ridge between the Careenage Ravine and the Tchernaya. The plan in fact made it impossible for the Russians to use the weight of their numbers with effect.

The name Mount Inkerman, taken from the name of the heights on the north bank of the Tchernaya, was given by us to a spur bounded on the west by the Careenage Ravine, on the north by the harbour Sebastopol, and on the west by the valley of the Tchernaya. The slopes downwards from this ridge were steep on all three sides, and on the east, cliff-like. Just south of the crest of the ridge was the camp of the 2nd Division, with the camp of the Guards Brigade about three quarters of a mile farther south. The camp of the Light Division was parallel with that of the Guards on the west side of the Careenage Ravine. About half a mile north-north-west of the crest was an almost circular hill on the ridge, which became known as Shell Hill, being the main position of the Russian artillery in the battle. The garrison of Sebastopol had an easy approach to the Careenage Ravine, and from behind the Heights of Inkerman, where Pauloff's force was assembled. The way to the ridge led over a causeway and bridge near the mouth of the Tchernaya, and from the bridge a track ran up the quarry Ravine to the crest. East of the quarry Ravine two spurs ran out to the valley of the Tchernaya. The more easterly of the two, with which the Guards were to be much concerned, was known as the Kitspur.

Menschikoff has been much criticized for not preparing his position on the Alma for defence, but this criticism applies to us with much more force, for though we had been for two months on the ground, hardly anything had been done to strengthen it to meet an attack by the relieving force. At the point where the track from the bridge comes out of the quarry Ravine the 2nd Division had a piquet and there a rough breastwork of stone called 'the Barrier' had been erected. General Evans, who commanded the 2nd Division, had become anxious as to the possibility of attack from the east and had begun a battery on the Kitspur, known as the Sandbag Battery, but this was far from complete when the battle began. The excuse for this lack of preparation was the weakness of the battalions and the number of men required for piquet and work in the trenches before Sebastopol, but with a little foresight much might have been done to strengthen the covering position before the first parallel was opened and thereafter the 11,000 Turks might well have been used. Sir de Lacy Evans was in hospital in Balaklava when the battle began, he came up during its progress but refused to take the command of the 2nd Division out of the hands of General Pennefather.

The morning of November 5 was foggy and Soiminoff, coming out of the fortress before dawn, crossed the ridge. There he formed up about 6 a.m. and, posting his guns on Shell Hill, began the attack without waiting for Pauloff. The piquets of the 2nd Division were pushed back and Pennefather at once began the reinforce them with detachments from his main body, leaving little besides his guns on the crest, and no one south of it. The Russian guns fired at and over the crest, doubtless with the object of preventing the supports of the 2nd Division coming up. As there were no supports the guns did little damage beyond destroying the camp of the division and killing a number of horses. As Soiminoff's columns came forward they reached the part of the ridge where it narrows between the head of the Quarry Ravine and the Careenage Ravine. There his centre and left were crowded out and only his right came forward, to be met by a crashing volley from a wing of the 49th, which then charged and drove the Russians right back to Shell Hill. Soiminoff then led forward 9, 000 of his men, mainly along the eastern slopes of the Careenage Revine to avoid the fire of Pennefather's guns on the crest, while at the same time a column of Russian sailors from sebastopol crept up the Careenage Ravine beyond our left.

Of the Light Division, Codrington's brigade had taken position near the Lancaster battery and there it was tied covering our left, but the other brigade of the division, Buller's, came up in the nick of time to strengthen Pennefather's left. A party of the 77th, together with a piquet of the Grenadiers, which was on the spot under Prince Edward of Saxe-Weimar, charged and drove back the Russian sailors just as they were emerging in rear of our line. A little before this Buller's leading battalion coming over the crest encountered the weight of Soimonoff's column and was pushed back. Three guns of a battery from the 4th Division, which were following this battalion, fell for a time into the hands of the Russians, but a wing of the 47th and the remainder of the 77th coming into the fight broke up Soiminoff's right, and the Russians' centre and left seeing this fell back, leaving the captured guns in our hands. In this struggle Soiminoff was killed and General Buller was disabled by a cannon-shot which killed his horse.

Just as the crisis of this attack was developing Pauloff's first troops appeared on the scene. Eight of his battalions coming up the Quarry Ravine had picked up a stray battalion from Soiminoff's left, and the whole deployed opposite our right with their left on the Sandbag Battery and the right across the road where it enters the head of the ravine. Pennefather had sent General Adams with seven hundred men of his brigade to this part of the field.

As Pauloff's right was approaching the Barrier a wing of the 30th, barely two hundred strong, sprang over and charged, and in a sharp struggle broke up the two leading Russian battalions, and they in their flight carried back with them the remainder of this part of the Russian force. Almost at the same time Adams with the 41st drove back Pauloff's left near the Sandbag Battery.

It was now about 7.30 a.m. and so far all had gone well. The mist of the morning had served to conceal our weakness from the Russians, much of their artillery fire had been misdirected, and they had found no room on the ridge to deploy their full strength. Their attacks been disjointed and had been broken by the initiative of the regimental officers, who, making the best use of the advantage of ground which we had, had counter-attacked before the enemy's columns were fully deployed. Now a fresh and more serious act of the drama began. General Dannenberg had reached the field about seven o'clock and assumed command of both Soiminoff's and Pauloff's forces. Thus there was now unity of direction on the Russian side and Dannenberg had still at his disposal 19,000 infantry and some ninety guns. Fortunately at the same time reinforcements began to reach Pennefather. Cathcart was coming up with 2,100 men of his division, the batteries of the 1st Division were coming into action, and the Guards, who had turned out at the sound of the guns, were nearing the crest or Home Ridge as it was generally called.

Of these reinforcements the Guards were the first to reach the Home Ridge, and at the time of their arrival the general position on our side was that on our left Codrington's brigade was still in position about the Lancaster Battery. The company of Grenadiers and a part of the 77th, which had driven back the Russian sailors, watched the head of the Well-way and 2nd Division and Buller's brigade had a rough forward line bending from the Barrier to the eastern edge of the Careenage ravine, with a supporting line along the Home and Fore ridges along the Kitspur. Most of our guns were on the Home and Fore Ridges. Pennefathers and Buller's available strength did not at that time exceed

The Battle of Inkerman

2,100 men and against the right and centre of that thin line Dannenburg was preparing to launch 10,000 men. The Guards came up to the Home Ridge under the Duke of Cambridge and General Bentink, the Grenadiers leading, followed by the Scots Fusiliers. The Coldstream camp was farther away so they were a little behind. None of these battalions could turn out the whole of their meagre strength owing to detachments on piquet and in the trenches, and the Coldstream were up at first with only four companies. The 1st battalion led with eighteen officers and three hundred and twenty other ranks, the Right-flank company, which had been all night in the trenches, not arriving till later, whilst almost the whole of nos. 3 and 4 Companies were finding guards and working parties.

About the time when the Grenadiers reached the home ridge, Dannenburg's attack on our right and centre had developed. The 30th, which had stoutly held the barrier, was forced out of it by weight of numbers; fortunately this exit from the quarry was momentary and the ravine was gallantly retaken by detachments of the 21st, 63rd and Rifles and held until near the end of the day. But it is with the struggle around the sandbag battery that we are concerned. This work, useless for defence by the infantry, became the centre of a fierce fight and decided the issue of the battle.

The Sandbag Battery and the ground on either side of it was held by Adams with the 41st and 49th. He was attacked with some of Pauloff's battalions, which fighting with more determination than Soiminofoff's men, forced him back with heavy losses. But he himself fell. Pennyfather at once sent a wing of the 95th from the fore ridge, where he had kept it as an escort for his support of Adam's men, and the Duke of Cambridge coming at this moment sent the Guards Brigade after the 95th. The Grenadiers charged and drove the Russians from the Battery and from the eastern slope of the Kitspur, then the Scots Fusiliers under Colonel Walker, coming up on the left of the Grenadiers, met a column of Russians issuing from the ravine between the Kitspur and the next spur to the west of it, known as Inkerman Tusk. They charged and drove the Russians down the hill and then took up the line of defence on the western side of the Kitspur. The Grenadiers in the Sandbag Battery now found that it was of no value for defence as there was no firing step and the parapet was too high even for Guardsman. So Colonel Reynardson withdrew them up the slope, where their fire would be more effective. The Russians at once swarmed into the work and Colonel Walker, whose horse was just then shot under him, scrambled to his feet and ordered Damer to charge with No 2 company and drove them out. This Damer promptly did and Walker ordered a volley from the remaining six companies against the right flank of the Russian column and then led them in a charge which swept the enemy down the hill. He was following in pursuit when he was stopped by an ADC from the Duke and ordered back to his position on the left of the Guards Brigade. The reason for this order was that there was a dangerous gap between the left of the Scots Fusiliers and the Barrier, and the Duke very rightly did not wish to extend it. Walker who had been hit but not seriously fell back reluctantly and the Russians re-formed in the dead ground.

The Duke rode off to Home Ridge to seek reinforcements to fill this gap and in the meantime the Russians came again and again, Walker, who was again hit, led a charge against them, in which Lieut. Col.- Hunter Blair fell mortally wounded, and Captain Drummond, the Adjutant was shot through the body. This time Walker, without the Duke to restrain him, continued the pursuit far down the slope and then brought back what remained of his battalion back to the left of the Sandbag Battery. On his return Walker went into the Battery, where were a handful of the Grenadiers and 95th, and he then saw why the Grenadiers had withdrawn from it. The parapet was nearly ten foot high and there was no bankquette. As he was returning to the battalion he was hit in the jaw, his third wound that day, and the command of the battalion devolved on Colonel C.F. Seymour.

Yet another column of Russians swarmed up the slope and again the Sandbag Battery was captured. But now the Coldstream were seen coming up on the right of the Grenadiers, who forgetting the work was useless, were determined to drive the Russians from it, before the Coldstream could get at them. The Grenadiers again got possession of the Sandbag Redoubt and the Coldstream came up on their right, and on their left the Scots Fusilier Guards poured a steady fire into the flank of the Russian, the men taking turn and turn about to load and fire so that the effect upon the enemy was continuous. Now, too. arrived the reinforcements that the Duke had gone to seek. When he reached the Home Ridge he found that two of Bosquet's battalions had arrived and this enabled Lord Raglan, who was now in command, to let him have the remaining wing of the 95th and a wing of the Rifles. These troops which the Duke had intended to use to fill the dangerous gap on his left all became involved in the melee on the Kitspur in which Guardsmen and Linesmen were mixed up in a mass which had little semblance of order. During the Duke's absence General Bentink had fallen, hit through the arm, and on his return the Duke took direct command of the brigade.

At this time a fierce struggle was on the northern and eastern slopes of the Kitspur. The bulk of the Russians huddled together on the steeper ground were unable to use their weapons effectively, and General Cathcart, who had with him General Torrens with some four hundred men of his brigade, thought he saw an opportunity of dealing them a decisive blow. He told Torrens to move down the slope south of the Sandbag Battery and attack the left flank of the enemy. This was directly contrary to Lord Raglan's orders, for the Commander in Chief anxious like the Duke of Cambridge, about the gap between Kitspur and the Barrier, wished to use Torrens' men to fill it. Torren's naturally obeyed Cathcart, and his attack, together with the pressure of the Grenadiers and Coldstream, broke up the left and centre of the Russians on the Kitspur. Almost at the same time the wing of the 95th coming up on the left of Scots Fusiliers charged, and this put the finishing touch to the work of the 1st battalion. The right of the Russians on the Kitspur, like their left and centre, broke and the whole mass went tumbling down the hill, followed by the Guards and men of the line. General Torrens fell, as did Cathcart as did his A.A.G. Colonel C. Seymour of the Regiment. Lieut. Col F. Seymour, now in command of the 1st Battalion, was wounded but did not leave the field.

The Guardsmen, shouting exultingly as they pursued the flying Russians into the valley, believed that the day was won. Kinglake very aptly calls this 'the False Victory', and having criticized his accounts of the doings of the battalion on the Alma, I must here pay my tribute to the masterly way in which he has disentangled the intricacies of this battle. The gap was still open, the Russians had still troops in hand, and through the gap there now advanced east of the Barrier three Russian battalions, which threatened to cut off men on the slopes of the Kitspur. Just as the leading Russian battalion was approaching there arrived on the scene the Right-flank company of the Regiment under Lieutenant Lindsay. This brought the numbers of the Regiment actually engaged up to nineteen officers and three hundred and seventy-two other ranks. I take the following account of the doing of this Right-flank company from Lindsay's own story, told in the Memoir of Lord Wantage by his wife:--

'The first company of the Scots Fusiliers--of which Sergeant Gordon was colour-sergeant and my right hand and even more--went into action a few minutes after the main body of the regiment. While on picket a musketry fire on our left front plainly indicated what was taking place, and as we were all on the qui vive for fighting in those days, I put my company to the double and never stopped until we were in the thick of it. Once about halfway, I called a halt, for the men, myself included, were impeded and prevented from doubling as fast as we desired, so I ordered my men to take off their greatcoats and to throw them into a hollow place covered with brushwood. We started again, and all through the battle No. 1 Company was conspicuous through being in red, while the remainder of the battalion wore their grey greatcoats.

The battle of Inkerman has been called a 'Soldier's Battle', but few battles have been fought in which the personal influence of the Company Officers has had so much to do.

During the battle of Inkermen no divisional, brigade, or even regimental order was given. The men, headed by their officers, fought in companies or half companies. My own company, or most of it, held together during the day. An instinctive but undeviating rule guided the tactics, if tactics they could be called; these were, to drive the Russians back down the ravines up which they had come, and when the enemy got more on to the plateau, as they did towards the middle of the day, then to interpose the defending force between the enemy and the British camp, and so to drive the Russians back towards the besieged city.

In the course of the performance of these manoeuvres many a personal adventure took place. Two incidents in which I was concerned are fresh in my mind. Two sections of the 1st Company got lower down in one of the ravines than they probably intended, and found themselves cut off from the English camp by a stray detachment of Russians, who facing about, adopted a position precisely opposite to that *which naturally belonged to that of the opposing forces. A short council of war, in which the colour-sergeant and I took the chief part, decided at once to dislodge the Russian and re-establish our selves on our rightful ground. I and Gordon headed the charge, and swords and bayonets crossed each other in the little ravine as they did in a hundred different places during the battle.*

Another incident has probably been told a hundred times in the Russians camp if the Ruski who was the chief actor in it lived to reach Sebastopol. A Russian of apparently high rank and distinguished appearance wore over his shoulder a strap to which was attached a bag full of money. The officer, who had got in advance of his men, had fallen into the hands of four or five Guardsmen, who, with bayonets down, were making short work of him, evidently for the sake of his money bag, which one of them had laid hold of. If the officer had had no money I should probably have allowed things to take their natural course on a field of battle. But the idea of killing a man for his money struck me as outside the scope of warfare, so, sword in hand, I interposed, and throwing up the muskets of the men I released him his enemies and in less than a moment I was him striding towards Sebastopol, making signs of gratitude as he went'

Some of Lindsay's company followed the Battalion down the hill, as he says, but the bulk of his men were stopped by Captain Higginson of the Grenadiers, who had succeeded Stephenson as Brigade-Major of the Guards Brigade, and fought their way back to a small party which the Duke had collected round the colours of the Grenadiers west of Sandbag Battery. Lindsay's company though the last to arrive had the heaviest losses, losing thirty-eight killed and wounded out of fifty-two engaged. The party round the colours, which consisted mainly of Grenadiers with some of the Coldstream and the Right-flank company of the 1st battalion and a few odd parties of Linesmen, numbering barely two hundred men, was all that remained to prevent the Guards Brigade down the slope of the Kitspur being completely cut off from the main body. Though entirely surrounded by swarms of Russians, this gallant band cut its way through to the Home Ridge. Two more of Bosquet's battalions arrived in the nick of time, and one of these attacking the right of the Russians advancing on the Kitspur drove them back, cleared the spur and recaptured the Sandbag Battery. This practically ended the fighting of the Guards Brigade, now reduced to a mere handful. Slowly parties of men found their way back up the slope of the Kitspur and rejoined the colours of the Grenadier Guards on the Home Ridge. There the men were re-formed and ammunition was issued, but there were barely 300 men left of the 1,331 engaged, half had been killed and wounded and there were still small parties scattered over the Kitspur, which had not found their way back.

While this was happening yet another Russian attack developed. Twelve battalions issued from the quarry Ravine, overwhelmed the men of the 2nd Division, who had gallantly held the Barrier, and pushed their advance against our centre and left on the Home Ridge. The Russian right drove in our line on the edge of the Careenage Ravine and took a few of our guns in that part of the field, while their centre for a brief moment got a footing on the Home Ridge. More French reinforcements came up and these, after a first check, drove back the enemy.

By this time, about eleven o'clock, the arrival of more guns, both British and French, gave us for the first time a superiority in artillery. Bosquet, convinced at last that Gortschakoff's demonstration would not develop into an attack, had appeared himself nearly an hour before with the second party of French reinforcements, and now his reserve of 2,400 men was approaching. The Russians, then abandoning all hope of success, slowly withdrew, the British being too few and too weary to attempt a pursuit, and the French not sufficiently confident of the completeness of the enemy's defeat to pursue alone.

The British loss in the battle was 39 officers, and 558 other ranks killed, 91 officers, and 1,669 other ranks wounded; the French 13 officers and 130 other ranks killed and 36 officer and 760 other ranks wounded, a total Allied loss of 3,286. The Russian losses are stated to have amounted to 12,000. Of the 19 officers and 372 other ranks of the Scots Fusiliers engaged 1 officer, 5 sergeants, and 59 rank and file were killed or died of wounds, 8 officers, 5 sergeants, 2 drummers, and 99 rank and file were wounded. Colonel C. Seymour, who served as A. A. G. to General Cathcart, was also killed. The other officer casualties were Colonel Hunter Blair killed, Colonel Walker and Lieut-Colonel F. Seymour, Captains R. Gipps, Shuckburgh, and Drummond, Lieutenant Blane and Assistant-Surgeon Elkington wounded.

Update

The battle of Inkerman was a most complex and confused affair, and if you have never covered the ground physically you can never understand the movements of the soldiers who were to be directly involved direct from the pages of any writings. Especially when you may also consider that the great majority of writers commentating on the battle have never been there, and this includes F Maurice the writer of the Scots Fusilier Guards history.

I have covered the ground many times during my retiral life served in Sevastopol, and in many differing arrangements and programmes, so to enable myself and the folk I am guiding to expressly serve their own reasons

The Battle of Inkerman

for the research they wish to cover over the rough terrain of the Inkerman heights.

I have even been imprisoned on one occasion by the military garrison, (which has now vacated the military area it once covered up at Inkerman) and appalled on another by the waste that has now been left on this hallowed ground by locally contracted refuge collectors who use the area as a dumping ground now that the military garrison has quit the area. I have reported this sacrilege to the British authorities in their Embassy in Kiev, who do nothing to change the situation. Yet by working with the local Sevastopol authorities I could well facilitate a joint operational clean up of this hallowed ground of shared history if the Embassy would render their support for such a mission.

(On much the same lines as I was to support local organisations for a make over of the British Monument at Cathcart Hill back in 2004 whilst preparing for the 'Scots Guards 'Alma Gathering' that was never to happen)

Neither may I adventure around the heights of Inkerman alone, for it is a lonely and desolate place, and even with the mobile phone and other arrangements in place any recovery from the ground after an accident could well prove extremely difficult over the rough terrain.

We may also remember that the British were to leave the Crimea in 1856 and never return until 1993 and so there have been very few who have actually not only just visited, but actually covered the ground the battle took place over.

It constitutes a most interesting experience, and for any Crimea War buff an agended must do.

Meanwhile, and a return to the update, the Guards and Highlanders were never to join together again as a Division during the remainder of the war, though they were alongside each other as a reserve on occasions.

After Sir William Codrington (Coldstream Guards) was given command of the British contingent after the resignation of Sir James Simpson, Sir Colin Campbel was to leave the war in the Crimea after a disagreement with Sir William Codrington around the question of its command element, which follows on from the quotes given earlier in the thoughts and feelings of the Highland Brigade towards those of the privileged hierarchy of the Guards Brigade, and would therefore seem to confirm the bad feeling between the Guards and the Highlanders..

Sir Colin Campbell was to return to the Crimea to command the newly formed Highland Division for the remainder of the Crimea Campaign.

Update Continues

Florence Nightingale arrives at Scutari

November 4th 1854

The lady with the lamp, or the CEO of the medical services at the Scutari Hospital

The young Florence Nightingale had arrived at the gates of the British Military Hospital, Scutari on the evening of November 4th 1854. This was to be a timely arrival as the young Florence at the age of 34 accompanied by 38 selected nurses, was just in time to begin receiving the casualties from the carnage at Inkerman.

Analytical history now sees Florence Nightingale as something more than the ministering lady with the lamp image that has been promoted by the many books and documents that have been written since the events now under discussion. In these modern times history views Florence more as an able, strong and gifted administrator who was fortunate to be born into wealth and privilege, an asset which enabled her to call upon many resources in order to have access to serve the needs of the soldiers she nursed and administered. Whilst under the steady criticism of the male medical staff at Scutari and other hospitals that served the casualties from the Crimea war zone

And just like the Crimea railway which was to come and serve the soldiers outside Sevastopol and on the Balaclava Plain, so Florence had arrived in Scutari just in time to save the British Army from total moral collapse in the Crimea campaign.

As the young Florence Nightingale developed her radical nursing and Christian beliefs she became convinced that man's knowledge of truth released him from blind acceptance of authority and enabled him to act freely, consciously and intelligently. Florence also rejected the prevalent standards of divine revelation. authority, majority opinion and substituted as her criteria conscience, feeling, sense of justice and experience. She was in the vanguard of the Human Rights Movement. she further believed that man is creative, with inherent right to the pursuit of his own development, interests and goals; she strongly objected to man's being used as a passive pawn driven at the will of another opinion, also that creative man has the ability to alter his lot in life and modify his destiny.

She urged that "a better World ... will not be given to us; let us then begin without delay to make one". Nightingale gave expression to the philosophic credo underlying her reforming nature when she said "We Must Alter the state of Life".

She chose Nursing as a profession in 1844, at the age of 24 years, and through Nursing she believed that she would be able to give her service to God. her family strongly opposed her idea of becoming a Nurse.

Her Education for Nursing was limited to fifteen days at Kaiserswerth at 1850, and a year later in this same place for three months. she found the chance to put into action the things she learned at Kaiserswerth when she opened the Nightingale Training School at St. Thomas Hospital, London, in 1860. in a short time, young capable, earnest graduates from this modern Training School for Nurses replaced the old, disreputable, untrained, poorly paid Nurses in Hospitals.

Florence Nightingale's pro-active character had two facets; constructive reform and obstructive action. her rejection of the concept that illness and disease could be the result of specific micro-organisms, rather than of dampness and dirt is an example of her obstructive action.

She rejected bacteriology, antisepsis and the germ theory of disease while living in the contemporary society of Darwin, Mendil, Huxley, Pasteur, John Stuart Mill, Snow, Lister and others. while she was treating with the help of 38 other nurses wounded British Soldiers in Scutari she made certain recommendations on how to provide most useful care to the patients and it is very interesting to note that compliance with sanitation rules were among her leading Ones. therefore we may say that, while she was rejecting antisepsis and microbe theory she was also accepting the realities.

In Britain, the blame for what happened was ultimately laid at the door of the British Army authorities who had failed to see that the building, loaned to the British by the Sultan for use as a Hospital, was properly managed and supplied, the petty jealousies of doctors who were not willing to let a group of women run the hospital and resisted the nurses presence in the wards as well as alleged reluctance of the then British Ambassador to intervene undoubtedly contributed to the catastrophe.

Florence Nightingale faced tremendous odds, in the mid-19th century nursing was anything but a respected profession. add to this the fact that many British Army Officers regarded the men they led with contempt. but in two eventful years, Florence Nightingale changed the thinking of a Nation, laid the foundations of the nursing profession and was responsible for the beginning of reform in the British Army.

"In the midst of the muddle and the filth, the agony and the defeats,..."writes Florence Nightingale's biographer Cecil Woodham Smith." she had brought about a revolution".

Florence Nightingale's zeal as a reformer originated in her great dissatisfaction with the present and her intense desire for social improvement. As a Victorian age woman she was extremely frustrated with the condition of woman and constantly demanded corrective action. Upon this philosophic basis and through this constructive zeal, the profession of nursing was conceived and born. Florence Nightingale, the reformer, got her greatest opportunity when the British Government asked her to go to Scutari to be responsible for nursing the British Soldiers.

The Military Hospitals run by the British Government lacked elementary supplies, a system of maintaining Hospital records and vital statistics, and a system of providing the soldier with any care approaching humane standards. her strong administrative ability became apparent as she initiated corrective action quickly and directly while never losing sight if wider horizons. Achieving these reforms, she went further and established a laundry, reading rooms and classes for the soldiers, wholesome forms of recreation, a banking system so the soldier could save this pay instead of squandering it on women and drink, a Hospital for the wives, woman and children of soldiers who accompanied them to war and were often neglected by military authorities; and a system of corresponding with the soldier's family back home. In brief, Nightingale was the original Red Cross gray lady, dietitian, banker, laundress, supply clerk, teacher, social service worker occupational therapist, recreational therapist, hospital executive officer, chief nurse, army quartermaster, army sanitarian, military registrar and the soldier's nurse. with her eye on her major purpose of national health and army reform, she communicated all her findings with her recommendation for improvement to her staunch ally, sir Sidney Herbert, Secretary for the War, and to everyone else of influence whom she knew.

When Austria resolved to enter the War on the side of the Allies. Russia agreed to a peace and the War which had resulted in the death of a quarter of a million men of each side and left thousands more disabled at last came to an end in February 1856. Sultan Abdul Mecid presented Florence Nightingale with a valuable bracelet for her work and distributed 1000 gold sovereigns among the nurses.

By the time the war was over, she was a formidable opponent to those who advocated the continuance of the status quo, an unquestionable proponent of Hospital and Military reform, and an irrefutable authority on everything concerning the soldier. In the post-Nightingale era the British Soldier was no longer treated as an insensate brute but was considered one of her Majesty's subjects and, as such, entitled to common decency, adequate rations, suitable provisions, quarters sufficient to support life and health, and appropriate medical treatment when he was ill or wounded.

Through Florence Nightingale's successful demonstration of the efficiency of carefully supervised nursing and her system of training women to be nurses, the public's attitude to nursing was raised from that of a disreputable pastime to a worthy and dignified occupation in which woman of good repute and family might safely seek work.

The major organizational reform initiated by Nightingale was that of pinpointing responsibility. an improved, streamlined Army administration, and Hospital management, Hospital construction following sanitary principles, pinpointing Army Medical responsibility, the initiation of a system of vital statistics for Civil and Military Hospitals, as well as evaluating Army Medical Officers according to competency and not seniority, were some of the organizational changes introduced by Nightingale. through her work, Hospitals were converted from pest houses and hellholes to places where those in need could once again receive hospitable and humane help.

Florence Nightingale died in London at 1910 and was buried according to her will in her family cemetery at East wellow, Hampshire on her grave is written only "F.N..1820 1910".

The world-wide services of this noble nurse started at an age when she was still very young. "God has called me to his service", she said, when she was just 16 years old. Thus we see Florence Nightingale preparing herself from this date on, to the time when history made her an international hero of the Crimean War. But we see her service to humanity in a greater scale after the Crimean War ended. She tried to attract our attention to public health in a period when preventive medicine had not been heard of. She said:

"To prevent people from becoming ill is more important than helping them to get well, follow the people into their homes, there you will see many things."

Florence Nightingale was a great nurse with a great heart. without her revolutionary activities in nursing services and in hospital administration, modern medicine could not be successful. In 1954 the Turkish Nurses association decided to place a marble tablet in the tower of the Selimiye Barracks in Uskudar (Scutari), Istanbul in appreciation of the services of Florence Nightingale during the Crimean War. On 7April 1954, to Keep alive her memory, it was decided to turn that section of the Barracks in the north-western tower used by Florence Nightingale during the war in to a Museum.

Although the Museum does not have the original decoration dating from Florence Nightingale's time, everything possible has been done to decorate the room in its original style and many contemporary pictures and writings have been placed in the Museum. the ground floor room which she had used as an examination room contains some medicine bottles and medical equipment used during the Crimean war, and clothing, desk, chair, lamp, mirror, couch and carpet used by Florence Nightingale. the second floor room was her sitting-room, and here there are photographs and pictures dating from the time when the Barracks was used as a Hospital, an original letter in her handwriting and copies of several others donated by the Nightingale School in London, her table, coffee service, and some photographs of her. We are anxious to acquire more historical material so that the Museum may represent the past more effectively and we always appreciate any kind of assistance to acquire such material. although the Museum is located in Turkey, I believe that it will be a valuable treasury not only for Turkish nurses but for nurses all around the World.

Update contd

I have visited the hospital in Istanbul, and it was to be a remarkable experience in which I learned some more hard lessons about the British Government and its ceaseless acts of negligence towards its own history, and of its disdain for British Interests in this very important part of the World.

I do however write fully of this never to be forgotten experience in my next book;

'What a Way to Carry On Ambassador'

Update Continues
William Howard Russell

The *Times* Change;

There are certain memorable characters that the war in the Crimea displayed, and by the same ruling that no Crimea War library would not be complete without Timothy Gowing's book, Neither would any historian whose interest was primarily that of the Crimea War forget to pay tribute to the 1st War Correspondent, William Howard Russell.

Here we reproduce what Fanny Duberly had to say on one particular aspect of the effects of William Howard Russells public reporting was to achieve at Balaclava.

'I think the thanks of the army,or a handsome national testimonial, ought to be presented to Mr. Russell, the eloquent and truthful correspondent of the Times , as being the mainspringof all this happy change'

William Howard Russell 1820 -1907 was an Irish reporter with *The Times*, and is considered to have been one of the first modern war correspondents, after he spent 22 months covering the Crimean War including the Charge of the Light Brigade

As a young reporter, Russell reported on a brief military conflict between Prussian and Danish troops in Denmark in 1850.

Initially sent by editor John Delane to Malta to cover English support for Russia in 1854, Russell despised the term "war correspondent" - though his coverage of the conflict brought him international renown, and Florence Nightingale later credited her entry into wartime nursing to his reports (and although she was not as famous, the international renown of Mary Seacole was mainly down to Russell). He was described by one of the soldiers on the frontlines thus, "a vulgar low Irishman, [who] sings a good song, drinks anyone's brandy and water and smokes as many cigas as a Jolly Good Fellow. He is just the sort of chap to get information, particularly out of youngsters. This reputation however, led to Russell being blacklisted from some circles, including British commander Lord Raglan who advised his officers to refuse to speak with the reporter.

His dispatches were hugely significant: for the first time the public could read about the reality of warfare. Shocked and outraged, the public's backlash from his reports led the Government to re-evaluate the treatment of troops and led to Florence Nightingale's involvement in revolutionising battlefield treatment.

On September 20, 1854, Russell covered the battle above the Alma River - writing his missive the following day in an account book seized from a Russian corpse. The story, written in the form of a letter to Delane, was supportive of the British troops though paid particular attention to the battlefield surgeons' "humane barbarity", and the lack of ambulance care for wounded troops. He later covered the Siege of Sevastopol where he coined the contemporary phrase "thin red line" in referring to British troops, writing that

"[The Russians] dash on towards that thin red streak topped with a line of steel..."

Following Russell's reports of the appalling conditions suffered by the Allied troops conducting the siege, including an outbreak of cholera, Samuel Morton Peto and his partners built the Grand Crimean Central Railway, which was a major factor leading to the success of the siege.

He spent the month of December 1854 in Constantinople, on holiday, returning in early 1855. He was close to Field Marshal Raglan, who he would avoid criticising, but was disliked by Codrington, who became commander in 1855. Russell left Crimea in December 1855, to be replaced by the Constantinople correspondent of *The Times*.

Russell was knighted in May 1895.

He died in 1907 and is buried in Brompton Cemetery, London.

Wikimedia Internet

Reg Hist

Inkerman and Sevastopol Continued

The whole army realized that it had escaped a dire peril and though before the battle the weakness of battalions had been urged as a reason for not preparing defences on the covering position, now, despite the heavy losses of the battle, this work was taken in hand seriously. The Guards were moved up into a position overlooking the Tchernaya valley and were set to work to strengthen it. While they were so engaged, on November 14 a fierce storm swept the Crimea. Every camp was swept away and the ground became a sea of mud. Worse still, a great part of the fleet of store ships in Balaklava Harbour was destroyed, twenty-one ships being sunk and eight damaged, amongst them the ships with warm clothing and comforts intended for the winter. The road from Balaklava became almost impassable and few of such stores as remained could be brought to the troops.

The Hon. J. S. Jocelyn in a letter home gave a good description of the effect on the army of this disastrous storm:--

Camp before Sevastopol

November 16th

I am on outpost duty today, and therefore to a certain extent have the day to myself, as I sit by my Bivouack fire, from whence I can see all my sentries, and the enemy in the plain below, so that I can sit and write to you, & at the same time be on the look out against attack. Since I last wrote to you we have suffered much from the inclement weather and cold. The day before yesterday it blew a hurricane with Sleet and Snow; our tents were all blown down and we had no shelter whatever. This lasted 12 hours, and I never knew such misery before. Nor our poor starved men, only half clothed in rags. Would you believed it? Our regiment has even now never got all its officers' baggage, consequently I have no more even now, than what I landed with. 16 ships, transports, went down in the hurricane, and they say up wards of 8,000 souls perished, besides a great quantity of Provisions, & Ammunition, f200,000 in Gold for the Army, and, what was worst of all, all the Winter clothing and comforts for the men. So here we have a rough winter staring us in the face, & our men only half clothed; in short if we could not have taken this place by a "coup de main", as was at first supposed, it ought never to have been attempted so late in the year. We have now fought two pitched Battles, & several Skirmishes, & lost an immense quantity of life, & are not a bit nearer taking Sevastopol than before.'

To continue, Colonel Ridley was on board H. M. S. Retribution during the storm, three out of four ships' cables parted, but by keeping up steam she managed to ride out the storm. Colonel Ridley went home early in 1855 to take over command of the 2nd Battalion. Colonel Sir C. Hamilton had gone home preparatory to retirement before the battle of Inkerman. His retirement was gazetted on December 14, 1854, and he received the C. B. for his services at the Alma. Lieut-Colonel Lord James Murray joined from home shortly before the battle of Inkerman in which he took part, and Lieut-Colonel the Hon. R. Charteris arrived ten days after it was over.

On November 22 the second draft from England joined with Lieut-colonels de Bathe and Fordyce Buchan, Captain

Lord A. Vane Tempest and Lieutenant Farquharson. This draft numbered one hundred and one and for reasons which will be obvious it became known as the 'Dead Draft'. It was composed of inexperienced young soldiers, who landed in the clothes in which they had left England, and they for some time received nothing in addition. Almost every man was attacked by disease in one form or another. Sixty-nine of them died, fifteen were invalided home and eventually seventeen of the hundred and one came back to England with the battalion. The ground on which the battalion was camped a soft loam and this soon became deep mud well over the tops of the men's boots. The only water available, except rainwater, was from springs in the Windmill Ravine, which had been near the old but was a long way from the new camp, and the approach became so deep in mud that it was impossible to fetch water except in daylight, and the only vessels available were the men's canteens. It was not until well on into January that sheepskin coats and caps were issued and rather later long boots were received, By that time most of the ankle boots were worn out and the men had taken to wrapping their feet in biscuit bags. So the number of sick grew and seventy-two men were evacuated to Scutari during December and one hundred and thirty-one in January. The state on January 1, 1855, shows twenty-four sergeants, one drummer, and four hundred and twenty-three rank and file present and fit for duty hard fallen to ninety-nine. Lord Rokeby arrived in January to take command of the brigade and there found its whole strength less than that of a weak battalion. It is not surprising in these circumstances that Surgeon-Major Bostock expressed himself strongly in his letters home.

'I have no except bad news to tell you. The army is half starved and in rags. The people of England, who have so liberally sent out all manner of comforts for the use of the troops, would be appalled were they to know and witness

the misery and destitution that exists in every part of the camp. The sickness is perfectly frightful. I believe the daily loss of the army has for some time been at the rate of 200 or 300 men. Eleven hundred were brought down in one day, a thousand a few days following. The fresh regiments and drafts from England cannot satisfy this fearful drain upon our numbers. All this is owing to the gross mismanagement and wont of fore-thought on the part of the commissariat and the authorities generally. Everyone blames Lord Raglan very much, and I should think, when the real truth becomes known at home, severe censure cannot fail to be passed on those who have by their negligence, caused this heavy loss. The French, who understand military organization perfectly, are comfortable and comparatively healthy. Their army is regularly supplied while we are starving. Provisions are to be bought out here, but you must go to Balaklava for them, through seven miles of mud, and are then charged enormous prices. I give eight shillings for a small pot of jam a few days since, and everything else is at similar extortionate charges. However, as there is no other way of spending one's money here, one does it with less regret. The practical effects of free-trade have not yet reached this place, and the great wants painfully felt here have not yet been supplied from the redundancy of other places.

The siege of Sebastopol makes no progress; we have not fired a shot for many weeks, in fact, most of our batteries are without guns; those with which we began the siege being either dismounted by the enemy, or quite worn out by repeated firing at long range and with a heavy charge. Fresh guns have arrived at Balaklava, but the difficulty of getting them up to the camp, from the state of the roads and want of horses, is so great, that it will, it is said be a fortnight before anything can be done. In the meanwhile the Russians, who are at home, keep up a fire upon us, and make constant and vigorous sorties upon our advanced works, where our men lie covered up in their blankets, so starved and exhausted, that they can be with difficulty roused, or rather kicked up, to defend themselves from attack. Many have actually been bayoneted while asleep. Such indifference to life can only be the result of continued privation and misery.'

Update

Meanwhile back in Britain, and not before time, the news coming back from the Crimea made it plain for all social classes to realise the dire situation of the British forces in the Crimea, and a clamouring for the political and military change that must now happen, and sooner rather than later. I therefore now include the speech made in Parliament by Richard Cobden MP which I have decided to set out before you in full, for it covers the vast amount of detail that was now having to be thought through by the politicians. For those readers with an interest in Richard Cobden's full career there is much information on the subject matter to be found on the Internet, which will be readily available to most of this particular journal's readers.

Update Continues
Richard Cobden MP

Makes his speech in Parliament with very few listening, but rather late than never?

December 22nd 1854.

Profile

Richard Cobden, was born in Heyshott, near Midhurst, Sussex, on 3rd June, 1804. He was one of eleven children born into the family of a poor farmer. The poverty of the family forced the parents to distribute their children to various relatives and Richard was dispatched to an uncle in Yorkshire, who by all accounts, treated him badly.

With little in the way of education, Richard started work at the age of 14 as a clerk in the textile industry. He went on to become a commercial traveler and later he began his own business. This was followed by a partnership with two other young men in a calico printing company. By 1832 Richard Cobden was a wealthy man living in an affluent part of Manchester.

Cobden's wealth allowed him to travel extensively and his observations prompted him to conclude that Britain was facing a difficult economic future because of the inevitable competition from the emerging economic power of America. In 1835 he published a book on the topic and advocated a policy of free trade, low taxation, reduced military spending and an improvement in the British system and processes of education

Now let us read what 'Encarta' says about Richard Cobden

Cobden, Richard (1804-1865), British economist and statesman, known as the Apostle of Free Trade.

Cobden was born in Sussex on June 3, 1804. At the age of 15 he went to work in London for his uncle, a calico merchant, and in 1828 he established an independent calico business with some friends. His philosophy of free trade was first apparent in two pamphlets he wrote, *England, Ireland, and America* (1835) and *Russia* (1836). In 1838 he joined with the British statesman John Bright and five other merchants to found the Anti-Corn Law League. As part of a campaign to decrease the cost of living, the league agitated for repeal of the corn laws. Cobden successfully stood for election to Parliament in 1841 to work for repeal of the corn duties, which was effected in 1846.

In Parliament Cobden favoured a laissez-faire economic philosophy, that is, minimum interference of government in business. He opposed factory reforms and trade unions and objected to the intervention of government in the affairs of foreign nations. His opposition to British foreign policy cost him his seat in Parliament in 1857. He was so respected by his political opponents, however, that Prime Minister Henry Palmerston offered Cobden the post of president of the Board of Trade in his Cabinet in 1859. Cobden rejected the offer, but remained politically active. The following year he negotiated an Anglo-French commercial treaty. His last important political action was to support the Union in the American Civil War, at a time when other British leaders were hesitant. He died in London on April 12, 1865.

The Richard Cobden MP Speech in Parliament, was being listened to by Lord Palmerston, who was another MP in waiting in the wings to take over as Prime Minister, a British Political option that has only ever worked for a limited period of time.

The interesting thing being that the British Parliament perform this changing act every time the Public see Crisis Management, and decide that changing the Prime Minister is the thing to do?

When will the British people wake up to the fact that the change of Prime Minister only provides a temporary cosmetic change, and what is really required is an overall and complete understanding of the real World we have always lived in, not as we would suppose it to be, or how we would like it to be, but as it really is.

Well now we are beginning to find out, and I believe recognise that changing Prime Minister's is not the answer, so what is. Well perhaps a written British Constitution first and foremost. A Constitution that puts Britain into the real World of Globalisation, a World we now have no choice but to live in as it really is.

It is my contention that Richard Cobden MP lived in his real World at the time of his speech which follows below;

Title: RUSSIAN WAR. Speech I.
HOUSE OF COMMONS, DECEMBER 22, 1854.
Author: Cobden, Richard

Publisher: T. Fisher

Location: London

Speeches on Questions of Public Policy by Richard Cobden, M.P.

[On Dec. 12, the Duke of Newcastle (War Secretary), introduced a Bill, the object of which was to raise a force of 15,000 foreigners, who were to be drilled in this country. The Bill was opposed by the Conservative party, as impolitic and dangerous, but was finally carried, with very little alteration, by 38 votes, on Dec. 22 (163 to 135). Little more than a month after this, the Aberdeen Government resigned, in consequence of an adverse vote of the House of Commons on Mr. Roebuck's motion of Jan. 29.]

We now proceed directly to the Richard Cobden MP speech

'If I ask permission to enlarge a little the scope of our discussion, I have, at all events, this excuse, that the subject-matter more technically before the House has been very ably and fully discussed. There is another reason why the question may be viewed in a more general way, as affecting the conduct of the Government in carrying on the war and conducting negotiations, namely, that we have heard several hon. Members publicly declare that they refuse to entertain the matter now before the House on its merits, but persist in voting, in respect to it, contrary to their own opinions, and simply as a question of confidence in the Government.

I must say, among all the evils which I attach to a state of war, not the least considerable is, that it has so demoralising a tendency as this on the representative system. We are called on to give votes contrary to our conscience, and to allow those votes to be recorded where the explanation would not often appear to account for them. It was stated the other night, by the noble Lord (John Russell) the Member for the City of London, that proposals for peace had been made on the part of Russia, through Vienna, upon certain bases, which have been pretty frequently before the world under the term of the 'Four Points.' Now, I wish to draw attention to that subject; but, before I do so, let me premise, that I do not intend to say one word with respect to the origin of this unhappy war. I intend to start from the situation in which we now find ourselves, and I think it behoves this House to express an opinion upon that situation.

I avow myself in favour of peace on the terms announced by Her Majesty's Ministers. At all events, hon. Members will see the absolute necessity, if the war is to go on, and if we are to have a war of invasion by land against Russia, of carrying it on in a different spirit and on a different scale from that in which the operations have hitherto been conducted. I think both sides of the House occupy common ground in this respect; for we shall all recognise the propriety and necessity of discussing this important and critical question.

Before I offer an opinion on the desirability of concluding peace on these four points, it will be necessary to ask, what was the object contemplated by the war? I merely ask this as a matter of fact, and not with a view of arguing the question. It has been one of my difficulties, in arguing this question out of doors with friends or strangers, that I rarely find any intelligible agreement as to the object of the war.

I have met with very respectable and well-educated men, who have told me that the object of the war was to open the Black Sea to all merchant-vessels. That, certainly, could not be the object, for the Black Sea was already as free to all merchant-vessels as the Baltic. I have met with officers who said that the object was to open the Danube, and to allow the ships of all nations to go up that river.

The object, certainly, could not be that, for the traffic in the Danube has, during the last twenty years, multiplied nearly tenfold, and the ships of all nations have free access there. I have heard it stated and applauded at public meetings, that we are at war because we have a treaty with the Sultan, binding us to defend the integrity and independence of his empire. I remember that, at a most excited public meeting at Leicester, the first resolution, moved by a very intelligent gentleman, declared that we were bound by the most solemn treaties with the Sultan to defend the integrity and independence of the Turkish empire.

Now, Lord Aberdeen has even ostentatiously announced in the House of Lords—for the instruction, I suppose, of such gentlemen as I have referred to—that we had no treaty before the present war binding us to defend the Sultan or his dominions. Another and greater cause of the popularity of the war out of doors has been, no doubt, the idea that it is for the freedom and independence of nations.

There has been a strong feeling that Russia has not only absorbed and oppressed certain nationalities, but is the prime agent by which Austria perpetuates her dominion over communities averse to her rule. I should say that this class was fairly represented by my lamented and noble Friend the late Member for Marylebone, from whom I differed entirely in reference to his views on the question of interference with foreign countries, but for whose private virtues and disinterested conduct and boundless generosity I have always entertained the greatest veneration and respect. The late Lord Dudley Stuart for twenty years fairly represented the popular feeling out of doors, which was directed especially against the Emperor of Russia, and the popular sympathies, which were centred mainly on those territories which lie contiguous to the Russian empire. I used sometimes to tell that noble Lord, jocularly, that his sympathies were geographical—that they extended to all countries, from the Baltic to the Black Sea, bordering on Russia—that if the Poles, Hungarians, Moldavians, or Wallachians were in trouble or distress, he was sure to be, in this House, the representative of their wrongs; or if any unhappy individuals from those countries were refugees from oppression in this country, they were sure to go instantly to him for relief and protection. Lord Dudley Stuart represented a great amount of public sympathy in this country with respect to nationalities, as it is termed; but I ask, whether the ground on which the public impression is founded—that we are going to war to aid the Poles, Hungarians, Moldavians, or Wallachians—has not been entirely delusive; and whether it may not be ranked with the other notions about opening the Black Sea, or a treaty with the Sultan, and about the Danube not being free to the flags of all nations?

I ask, whether all these grounds have not been equally delusive? The first three grounds never had an existence at all; and, as to setting up oppressed nationalities, the Government certainly never intended to go to war for that object. To set myself right with those hon. Gentlemen who profess to have great regard for liberty everywhere, I beg to state that I yield to no one in sympathy for those who are struggling for freedom in any part of the world; but I will never sanction an interference which shall go to establish this or that nationality by force of arms, because that invades a principle which I wish to carry out in the other direction—the prevention of all foreign interference with nationalities for the sake of putting them down. Therefore, while I respect the motives of those gentlemen, I cannot act with them. This admission, however, I freely make, that, were it likely to advance the cause of liberty, of constitutional freedom, and national independence, it would be a great inducement to me to acquiesce in the war, or, at all events, I should see in it something like a compensation for the multiplied evils which attend a state of war.

And now we come to what is called the statesman's ground for this war: which is, that it is undertaken to defend the Turkish empire against the encroachments of Russia—as a part of the scheme, in fact, for keeping the several

States of Europe within those limits in which they are at present circumscribed. This has been stated as a ground for carrying on the present war with Russia; but, I must say, this view of the case has been very much mixed up with magniloquent phraseology, which has tended greatly to embarrass the question. The noble Lord the Member for the City of London was the first, I think, to commence these magniloquent phrases, in a speech at Greenock about last August twelvemonths, in which he spoke of our duties to mankind, and to the whole world; and he has often talked since of this war as one intended to protect the liberties of all Europe and of the civilised world. I remember, too, the phrases which the noble Lord made use of at a City meeting, where he spoke of our being 'engaged in a just and necessary war, for no immediate advantage, but for the defence of our ancient ally, and for the maintenance of the independence of Europe.'

Well, I have a word to say to the noble Lord on that subject. Now, we are placed to the extreme west of a continent, numbering some 200,000,000 inhabitants; and the theory is, that there is great danger from a growing eastern Power, which threatens to overrun the Continent, to inflict upon it another deluge like that of the Goths and Vandals, and to eclipse the light of civilisation in the darkness of barbarism. But, if that theory be correct, does it not behove the people of the Continent to take some part in pushing back that deluge of barbarism? I presume it is not intended that England should be the Anacharsis Clootz of Europe; but that, at all events, if we are to fight for everybody, those, at least, who are in the greatest danger, will join with us in resisting the common enemy. I am convinced, however, that all this declamation about the independence of Europe and the defence of civilisation will by-and-by disappear.

I take it for granted, then, that the statesman's object in this war is to defend Turkey against the encroachments of Russia, and so to set a barrier against the aggressive ambition of that great empire. That is the language of the Queen's Speech. But have we not accomplished that object? I would ask, have we not arrived at that point? Have we not effected all that was proposed in the Queen's Speech? Russia is now no longer within the Turkish territory; she has renounced all idea of invading Turkey; and now, as we are told by the noble Lord, there have been put forward certain proposals from Russia, which are to serve as the bases of peace.

What are those proposals? In the first place, there is to be a joint protectorate over the Christians by the five great Powers; there is to be a joint guarantee for the rights and privileges of the Principalities; there is to be a revision of the rule laid down in 1841 with regard to the entrance of ships-of-war into the Bosphorus, and the Danube is to be free to all nations. These are the propositions that are made for peace, as we are told by the noble Lord; and it is competent for us, I think, as a House of Commons, to offer an opinion as to the desirability of a treaty on those terms.

My first reason for urging that we should entertain those proposals is that we are told that Austria and Prussia have agreed to them. Those two Powers are more interested in this quarrel than England and France can be. Upon that subject I will quote the words of the noble Lord the Member for Tiverton, uttered in February last. The noble Lord said,—

'We know that Austria and Prussia had an interest in the matter more direct and greater than had either France or England. To Austria and Prussia it is a vital matter—a matter of existence—because, if Russia were either to appropriate any large portion of the Turkish territory, or even to reduce Turkey to the condition of a mere dependent State, it must be manifest to any man who casts a glance over the map of Europe, and who looks at the geographical position of these two Powers with regard to Russia and Turkey, that any considerable accession of power on the part of Russia in that quarter must be fatal to the independence of action of both Austria and Prussia.'

I entirely concur with the noble Lord in his view of the interest which Austria and Prussia have in this quarrel, and what I want to ask is this—Why should we seek greater guarantees and stricter engagements from Russia than those with which Austria and Prussia are content? They lie on the frontier of this great empire, and they have more to fear from its power than we can have; no Russian invasion can touch us until it has passed over them; and is it likely, if we fear, as we say we do, that Western Europe will be overrun by Russian barbarism—is it likely, I say, that since Austria and Prussia will be the first to suffer, they will not be as sensible to that danger as we can be? Ought we not rather to take it as a proof that we have somewhat exaggerated the danger which threatens Western Europe, when we find that Austria and Prussia are not so alarmed at it as we are? They are not greatly concerned about the danger, I think, or else they would join with England and France in a great battle to push it back. If, then, Austria and Prussia are ready to accept these proposals, why should not we be? Do you suppose that, if Russia really meditated an attack upon Germany—that if she had an idea of annexing the smallest portion of German territory, with only 100,000 inhabitants of Teutonic blood, all Germany would not be united as one man to resist her? Is there not a strong national feeling in that Germanic race?—are they not nearly 40,000,000 in number?—are they not the most intelligent, the most instructed, and have they not proved themselves the most patriotic people in Europe? And if they are not dissatisfied, why should we stand out for better conditions, and why should we make greater efforts and greater sacrifices to obtain peace than they? I may be told, that the people and the Government of Germany are not quite in harmony on these points. [Cheers.] Hon. Gentlemen who cheer, ought to be cautious, I think, how they assume that Governments do not represent their people. How would you like the United States to accept that doctrine with regard to this country? But I venture to question the grounds upon which that opinion is formed. I have taken some little pains to ascertain the feeling of the people in Germany on this war, and I believe that if you were to poll the population of Prussia—which is the brain of Germany—whilst nineteen-twentieths would say that in this quarrel England is right and Russia wrong; nay, whilst they would say they wished success to England as against Russia, yet, on the contrary, if you were to poll the same population as to whether they would join England with an army to fight against Russia, I believe, from all I have heard, that nineteen-twentieths would support their King in his present pacific policy.

But I want to know what is the advantage of having the vote of a people like that in your favour, if they are not inclined to join you in action? There is, indeed, a wide distinction between the existence of a certain opinion in the minds of a people and a determination to go to war in support of that opinion. I think we were rather too precipitate in transferring our opinion into acts; that we rushed to arms with too much rapidity; and that if we had abstained from war, continuing to occupy the same ground as Austria and Prussia, the result would have been, that Russia would have left the Principalities, and have crossed the Pruth; and that, without a single shot being fired, you would have accomplished the object for which you have gone to war. But what are the grounds on which we are to continue this war, when the Germans have acquiesced in the proposals of peace which have been made? Is it that war is a luxury? Is it that we are fighting—to use a cant phrase of Mr. Pitt's time—to secure indemnity for the past, and security for the future? Are we to be the Don Quixotes of Europe, to go about fighting for every cause where we find that some one has been wronged? In most quarrels there is generally a little wrong on both sides; and, if we make up our minds always to interfere when any one is being wronged, I do not see always how we are to choose between the two sides. It will not do always to assume that the weaker party is in the right, for little States, like little individuals, are often very quarrelsome, presuming on their weakness, and not unfrequently abusing the forbearance which their weakness procures them. But the question is, on what ground of honour or interest are we to continue to carry on this war, when we may have peace upon conditions which are satisfactory to the great countries of Europe who are near neighbours of this formidable Power?

There is neither honour nor interest forfeited, I think, in accepting these terms, because we have already accomplished the object for which it was said this war was begun.

The questions which have since arisen, with regard to Sebastopol, for instance, are mere points of detail, not to be bound up with the original quarrel. I hear many people say, 'We will take Sebastopol, and then we will treat for peace.' I am not going to say that you cannot take Sebastopol—I am not going to argue against the power of England and France. I might admit, for the sake of argument, that you can take Sebastopol. You may occupy ten miles of territory in the Crimea for any time; you may build there a town; you may carry provisions and reinforcements there, for you have the command of the sea; but while you do all this, you will have no peace with Russia. Nobody who knows the history of Russia can think for a moment that you are going permanently to occupy any portion of her territory, and, at the same time, to be at peace with that empire.

But admitting your power to do all this, is the object which you seek to accomplish worth the sacrifice which it will cost you? Can anybody doubt that the capture of Sebastopol will cost you a prodigious sacrifice of valuable lives; and, I ask you, is the object to be gained worth that sacrifice? The loss of treasure I will leave out of the question, for that may be replaced, but we can never restore to this country those valuable men who may be sacrificed in fighting the battles of their country—perhaps the most energetic, the bravest, the most devoted body of men that ever left these islands. You may sacrifice them, if you like, but you are bound to consider whether the object will compensate you for that sacrifice.

I will assume that you take Sebastopol; but for what purpose is it that you will take it, for you cannot permanently occupy the Crimea without being in a perpetual state of war with Russia? It is, then, I presume, as a point of honour, that you insist upon taking it, because you have once commenced the siege. The noble Lord, speaking of this fortress, said:—'If Sebastopol, that great stronghold of Russian power, were destroyed, its fall would go far to give that security to Turkey which was the object of the war.' But I utterly deny that Sebastopol is the stronghold of Russian power. It is simply an outward and visible sign of the power of Russia; but, by destroying Sebastopol, you do not by any means destroy that power. You do not destroy or touch Russian power, unless you can permanently occupy some portion of its territory, disorder its industry, or disturb its Government. If you can strike at its capital, if you can deprive it of some of its immense fertile plains, or take possession of those vast rivers which empty themselves into the Black Sea, then, indeed, you strike at Russian power; but, suppose you take Sebastopol, and make peace to-morrow; in ten years, I tell you, the Russian Government will come to London for a loan to build it up again stronger than before. And as for destroying those old green fir ships, you only do the Emperor a service, by giving him an opportunity for building fresh ones.

Is not the celebrated case of Dunkirk exactly in point? In 1713, at the treaty of Utrecht, the French King, under sore necessity, consented to destroy Dunkirk. It had been built under the direction of Vauban, who had exhausted his genius and the coffers of the State, in making it as strong as science and money could make it. The French King bound himself to demolish it, and the English sent over two Commissioners to see the fortress thrown to the ground, the jetties demolished and cast into the harbour, and a mole or bank built across the channel leading into the port; and you would have thought Dunkirk was destroyed once and for ever. There was a treaty binding the King not to rebuild it, and which on two successive occasions was renewed. Some few years afterwards a storm came and swept away the mole or bank which blocked up the channel, by which accident ingress and egress were restored; and shortly afterwards, a war breaking out between England and Spain, the French Government took advantage of our being engaged elsewhere, and rebuilt the fortifications on the seaside, as the historian tells us, much stronger than before. The fact is recorded, that in the Seven Years' War, about forty years afterwards, Dunkirk, for all purposes of aggression by sea, was more formidable than ever. We had in that case a much stronger motive for destroying Dunkirk than we can ever have in the case of Sebastopol; for in the war which ended in the peace of Utrecht, there were 1,600 English merchant-vessels, valued at 1,250,000*l.*, taken by privateers which came out of Dunkirk.

Then, again, in the middle of the last century, we destroyed Cherbourg, and during the last war we held possession of Toulon; but did we thereby destroy the power of France? If we could have got hold of some of her fertile provinces—if we could have taken possession of her capital, or struck at her vitals, we might have permanently impoverished and diminished her power and resources; but we could not do it by the simple demolition of this or that fortress. So it would be in this case—we might take Sebastopol, and then make peace; but there would be the rankling wound—there would be a venom in the treaty which would determine Russia to take the first opportunity of reconstructing this fortress. There would be storms, too, there, which would destroy whatever mole we might build across the harbour of Sebastopol, for storms in the Black Sea are more frequent, as we know, than in the Channel; but even if Sebastopol were utterly destroyed, there are many places on the coast of the Crimea which might be occupied for a similar purpose.

But then comes the question, Will the destruction of Sebastopol give security to the Turks? The Turkish Empire will only be safe when its internal condition is secure, and you are not securing the internal condition of Turkey while you are at war; on the contrary, I believe you are now doing more to demoralise the Turks and destroy their Government than you could possibly have done in time of peace. If you wish to secure Turkey, you must reform its Government, purify its administration, unite its people, and draw out its resources; and then it will not present the spectacle of misery and poverty that it does now. Why, you yourselves have recognised the existing state of Turkey to be so bad, that you intend to make a treaty which shall bind the Five Powers to a guarantee for the better treatment of the Christians. But have you considered well the extent of the principle in which you are embarking? You contemplate making a treaty by which the Five Powers are to do that together which Russia has hitherto claimed to do herself. What sort of conclusion do you think disinterested and impartial critics—people in the United States, for instance—will draw from such a policy? They must come to the conclusion that we have been rather wrong in our dealings with Russia, if we have gone to war with her to prevent her doing that very thing which we ourselves propose to do, in conjunction with the other Powers. If so much mischief has sprung from the protectorate of one Power, Heaven help the Turks when the protectorate of the Five Powers is inaugurated! But, at this very moment, I understand that a mixed Commission is sitting at Vienna, to serve as a court of appeal for the Danubian Principalities; in fact, that Moldavia and Wallachia are virtually governed by a Commission representing Austria, England, France, and Turkey.

Now, this is the very principle of interference against which I wish to protest. From this I derive a recognition of the exceptional internal condition of Turkey, which, I say, will be your great difficulty upon the restoration of peace. Well, then, would it not be more statesmanlike in the Government, instead of appealing, with clap-trap arguments, to heedless passions out of doors, and telling the people that Turkey has made more progress in the career of regeneration during the last twenty years than any other country under the sun, at once to address themselves to the task before them—the reconstruction of the internal system of that empire? Be sure this is what you will have to do, make peace when you may; for everybody knows that, once you withdraw your support and your agency from her, Turkey must immediately collapse, and sink into a state of anarchy.

The fall of Sebastopol would only make the condition of Turkey the worse; and, I repeat, that your real and most serious difficulty will begin when you have to undertake the management of that country's affairs, after you withdraw from it, and when you will have to re-establish her as an independent State. I would not have said a word about the condition of Turkey, but for the statement twice so jauntily made about her social progress by the noble Lord the Member for Tiverton. Why, what says the latest traveller in that country on this head? Lord Carlisle, in his recent work, makes the following remarks on the state of the Mahometan population, after describing the improving condition of the Porte's Christian subjects:—

'But when you leave the partial splendours of the capital and the great State establishments, what is it you find over the broad surface of a land which nature and climate have favoured beyond all others, once the home of all art and all civilisation? Look yourself—ask those who live there—deserted villages, uncultivated plains, banditti-haunted mountains, torpid laws, a corrupt administration, a disappearing people.'

Why, the testimony borne by every traveller, from Lamartine downwards, is, that the Mahometan population is perishing—is dying out from its vices, and those vices of a nameless character. In fact, we do not know the true social state of Turkey, because it is indescribable; and Lord Carlisle, in his work, says that he is constrained to avoid referring to it. The other day, Dr. Hadly, who had lately returned from Turkey, where he had a near relation, who had been physician to the Embassy for about thirty-five years, stated in Manchester that his relative told him that the population of Constantinople, into which there is a large influx from the provinces, has considerably diminished during the last twenty years,—a circumstance which he attributes to the indescribable social vices of the Turks. Now, I ask, are you doing anything to promote habits of self-reliance or self-respect among this people by going to war in their behalf? On the contrary, the moment your troops landed at Gallipoli, the activity and energy of the French killed a poor pacha there, who took to his bed, and died from pure distraction of mind; and from that time to this you have done nothing but humiliate and demoralise the Turkish character more than ever. I have here a letter from a friend, describing the conflagration which took place at Varna, in which he says, it was curious to see how our sailors, when they landed to extinguish the fire in the Turkish houses, thrust the poor Turks aside, exactly as if they had been so many infant-school children in England. Another private letter, which I recently received from an officer of high rank in the Crimea, states:—

'We are degrading the Turk as fast as we can; he is now the scavenger of the two armies as far as he can be made so. He won't fight, and his will to work is little better; he won't be trusted again to try the former, and now the latter is all he is allowed to do. When there are entrenchments to be made, or dead to be buried, the Turks do it. They do it as slowly and lazily as they can, but do it they must. This is one way of raising the Turk; it is propping him up on one side, to send him headlong down a deeper precipice on the other.

That is what you are doing by the process that is now going on in Turkey. I dare say you are obliged to take the whole command into your own hands, because you find no native power—no administrative authority in that country; and you cannot rely on the Turks for anything, If they send an army to the Crimea, the sick are abandoned to the plague or the cholera, and having no commissariat, their soldiers are obliged to beg a crust at the tents of our men. Why, Sir, what an illustration you have in the facts relating to our sick and wounded at Constantinople of the helpless supineness of the Turks! I mention these things, as the whole gist of the Eastern Question lies in the difficulty arising from the prostrate condition of this race. Your troops would not be in this quarter at all, but for the anarchy and barbarism that reign in Turkey'.

Well, you have a hospital at Scutari, where there are some thousands of your wounded. They are wounded Englishmen, brought there from the Crimea, where they have gone 3,000 miles from their own home, to fight the battles of the Turks. Would you not naturally expect, that when these miserable and helpless sufferers were brought to the Turkish capital, containing 700,000 souls, those in whose cause they have shed their blood would at once have a friendly and generous care taken of them? Supposing the case had been that these wounded men had been fighting for the cause of Prussia, and that they had been sent from the frontiers of that country to Berlin, which has only half the population of Constantinople, would the ladies of the former capital, do you think, have allowed these poor creatures to have suffered from the want of lint or of nurses? Does not the very fact that you have to send out everything for your wounded, prove either that the Turks despise and detest, and would spit upon you, or that they are so feeble and incompetent as not to have the power of helping you in the hour of your greatest necessity? The people of England have been grossly misled regarding the state of Turkey. I am bound to consider that the noble Lord the Member for Tiverton expressed his honest convictions on this point; but certainly the unfortunate ignorance of one in his high position has had a most mischievous effect on the public opinion of this country, for it undoubtedly has been the prevalent impression out of doors, that the Turks are thoroughly capable of regeneration and self-government—that the Mahometan population are fit to be restored to independence, and that we have only to fight their battle against their external enemies in order to enable them to exercise the functions of a great Power. A greater delusion than this, however, I believe, never existed in any civilised State.

Well, if, as I say is the case, the unanimous testimony of every traveller, German, French, English, and American, for the last twenty years, attests the decay and helplessness of the Turks, are you not wasting your treasure and your men's precious lives before Sebastopol, in an enterprise that cannot in the least aid the solution of your real difficulty? If you mean to take the Emperor of Russia eventually into your counsels—for this is the drift of my argument—if you contemplate entering into a quintuple alliance, to which he will be one of the parties, in order to manipulate the shattered remains of Turkey, to reconstitute or revise her internal polity, and maintain her independence, what folly it is to continue fighting against the Power that you are going into partnership with; and how absurd in the extreme it is to continue the siege of Sebastopol, which will never solve the difficulty, but must envelomp the State with which you are to share the protectorate, and which is also the nearest neighbour of the Power for which you interpose, and your efforts to reorganise which, even if there be a chance of your accomplishing that object, she has the greatest means of thwarting! Would it not be far better for you to allow this question to be settled by peace, than leave it to the arbitrement of war, which cannot advance its adjustment one inch?

I have already adduced an illustration from the history of this country, as an inducement for your returning to peace. I will mention another. We all remember the war with America, into which we entered in 1812, on the question of the right of search, and other cognate questions relating to the rights of neutrals. Seven years before that war was declared, public opinion and the statesmen of the two countries had been incessantly disputing upon the questions at issue, but nothing could be amicably settled respecting them, and war broke out. After two years of hostilities, however, the negotiators on both sides met again, and fairly arranged the terms of peace. But how did they do this? Why, they agreed in their treaty of peace not to allude to what had been the subject-matter of the dispute which gave rise to the war, and the question of the right of search was never once touched on in that treaty. The peace then made between

England and America has now lasted for forty years; and what has been the result? In the mean time, America has grown stronger, and we, perhaps, have grown wiser, though I am not quite so sure of that. We have now gone to war again with a European Power, but we have abandoned those belligerent rights about which we took up the sword in 1812. Peace solved that difficulty, and did more for you than war ever could have done; for, had you insisted at Ghent on the American people recognising your right to search their ships, take their seamen, and seize their goods, they would have been at war with you till this hour, before they would have surrendered these points, and the most frightful calamities might have been entailed on both countries by a protracted struggle.

Now, apply this lesson to the Eastern question. Supposing you agree to terms of peace with Russia, you will have your hands full in attempting to ameliorate the social and political system of Turkey. But who knows what may happen with regard to Russia herself in the way of extricating you from your difficulty? That difficulty, as respects Russia, is no doubt very much of a personal nature. You have to deal with a man of great, but, as I think, misguided energy, whose strong will and indomitable resolution cannot easily be controlled. But the life of a man has its limits; and certainly, the Emperor of Russia, if he survive as many years from this time as the duration of the peace between England and America, will be a most extraordinary phenomenon. You can hardly suppose that you will have a great many years to wait before, in the course of nature, that which constitutes your chief difficulty in the present war may have passed away. It is because you do not sufficiently trust to the influence of the course of events in smoothing down difficulties, but will rush headlong to a resort to arms, which never can solve them, that you involve yourselves in long and ruinous wars. I never was of opinion that you had any reason to dread the aggressions of Russia upon any other State. If you have a weak and disordered empire like Turkey, as it were, next door to another that is more powerful, no doubt that tends to invite encroachments; but you have two chances in your favour—you may either have a feeble or differently-disposed successor acceding to the throne of the present Czar of Russia, or you may be able to establish some kind of authority in Turkey that will be more stable than its present rule. At all events, if you effect a quintuple alliance between yourselves and the other great Powers, you will certainly bind Austria, Prussia, and France to support you in holding Russia to the faithful fulfilment of the proposed treaty relating to the internal condition of Turkey. Why not, then, embrace that alternative, instead of continuing the present war? because, recollect that you have accomplished the object which Her Majesty in her gracious Speech last session stated that she had in view in engaging in this contest.

Russia is no longer invading the Turkish territory; you are now rather invading Russia's own dominions, and attacking one of her strongholds at the extremity of her empire, but, as I contend, not assailing the real source of her power. Now, I say you may withdraw from Sebastopol without at all compromising your honour.

By-the-by, I do not understand what is meant, when you say that your honour is staked on your success in any enterprise of this kind. Your honour may be involved in your successfully rescuing Turkey from Russian aggression; but, if you have accomplished that task, you may withdraw your forces from before Sebastopol without being liable to reproach for the sacrifice of your national honour.

I have another ground for trusting that peace would not be again broken, if you terminate hostilities now. I believe that all parties concerned have received such a lesson, that they are not likely soon to rush into war again. I believe that the Emperor of Russia has learnt, from the courage and self-relying force displayed by our troops, that an enlightened, free, and self-governed people is a far more formidable antagonist than he had reckoned upon, and that he will not so confidently advance his semi-barbarous hordes to cope with the active energy and inexhaustible resources of the representatives of Western civilisation. England also has been taught that it is not so easy to carry on war upon land against a State like Russia, and will weigh the matter well in future before she embarks in any such conflict.

I verily believe that all parties want to get out of this war—I believe that this is the feeling of all the Governments concerned; and I consider that you have now the means, if you please, of escaping from your embarrassment, notwithstanding that some Members of our Cabinet, by a most unstatesmanlike proceeding, have succeeded in evoking a spirit of excitement in the country which it will not be very easy to allay. The noble Lord the Member for London, and the noble Lord the Member for Tiverton, have, in my opinion, ministered to this excited feeling, and held out expectations which it will be extremely difficult to satisfy.

Now, what do you intend to do if your operations before Sebastopol should fail? The Secretary-at-War tells us that 'Sebastopol must be taken this campaign, or it will not be taken at all.' If you are going to stake all upon this one throw of the dice, I say that it is more than the people of England themselves had calculated upon. But if you have made up your minds that you will have only one campaign against Sebastopol, and that, if it is not taken then, you will abandon it, in that case, surely, there is little that stands between you and the proposals for peace on the terms I have indicated.

I think you will do well to take counsel from the hon. Member for Aylesbury (Mr. Layard), than whom—although

I do not always agree with him in opinion—I know nobody on whose authority I would more readily rely in matters of fact relating to the East. That hon. Gentleman tells you that Russia will soon have 200,000 men in the Crimea; and if this be so, and this number is only to be 'the beginning,' I should say, now is the time, of all others, to accept moderate proposals for peace.

Now, mark, I do not say that France and England cannot succeed in what they have undertaken in the Crimea. I do not set any limits to what these two great countries may do, if they persist in fighting this duel with Russia's force of 200,000 men in the Crimea; and, therefore, do not let it be said that I offer any discouragement to my fellow-countrymen; but what I come back to is the question—what are you likely to get that will compensate you for your sacrifice? The hon. Member for Aylesbury also says, that 'the Russians will, next year, overrun Asiatic Turkey, and seize Turkey's richest provinces'—they will probably extend their dominion over Asia Minor down to the sea-coast. The acquisition of these provinces would far more than compensate her for the loss of Sebastopol. I suppose you do not contemplate making war upon the plains in the interior of Russia, but wish to destroy Sebastopol; your success in which I have told you, I believe, will only end in that stronghold being rebuilt, ten years hence or so, from the resources of London capitalists. How, then, will you benefit Turkey—and especially if the prediction is fulfilled regarding Russia's overrunning the greater portion of Asiatic Turkey? I am told, also, that the Turkish army will melt away like snow before another year; and where, then, under all these circumstances, will be the wisdom or advantage in carrying on the war?

I have now, Sir, only one word to add, and that relates to the condition of our army in the Crimea. We are all, I dare say, constantly hearing accounts, from friends out there, of the condition, not only of our own soldiers, but also of the

Turks, as well as of the state of the enemy. What I have said about the condition of the Turks will, I am sure, be made as clear as daylight, when the army's letters are published and our officers return home. But as to the state of our own troops, I have in my hand a private letter from a friend in the Crimea, dated the 2nd of December last, in which the writer says,—

'The people of England will shudder when they read of what this army is suffering—and yet they will hardly know one-half of it. I cannot imagine that either pen or pencil can ever depict it in its fearful reality. The line, from the nature of their duties, are greater sufferers than the artillery, although there is not much to choose between them. I am told, by an officer of the former, not likely to exaggerate, that one stormy, wet night, when the tents were blown down, the sick, the wounded, and the dying of his regiment, were struggling in one fearful mass for warmth and shelter.'

Now, if you consult these brave men, and ask them what their wishes are, their first and paramount desire would be to fulfill their duty. They are sent to capture Sebastopol, and their first object would be to take that strong fortress, or perish in the attempt. But, if you were able to look into the hearts of these men, to ascertain what their longing, anxious hope has been, even in the midst of the bloody struggle at Alma or at Inkerman, I believe you would find it has been, that the conflict in which they were engaged might have the effect of sooner restoring them again to their own hearths and homes. Now, I say that the men who have acted so nobly at the bidding of their country are entitled to that country's sympathy and consideration; and if there be no imperative necessity for further prosecuting the operations of the siege, which must—it will, I am sure, be admitted by all, whatever may be the result—be necessarily attended with an immense sacrifice of precious lives—unless, I say, you can show that some paramount object will be gained by contending for the mastery over those forts and ships, you ought to encourage Her Majesty's Government to look with favour upon the propositions which now proceed from the enemy; and then, if we do make mistakes in accepting moderate terms of peace, we shall, at all events, have this consolation, that we are erring on the side of humanity.

Update continues

I believe that the speech reproduced above could still be made relevant to our most recent invasions of Iraq and Afganistan, and therefore neither the British Parliament nor the British people have learned nothing nor forgotten anything since that time of the Cobden speech, nor the Crimea War, as we all still suffer from a form of governance that contrives, and continues living in the dangerous past.

Amen

Reg Hist

Outside Sebastopol
December 1854

Towards the end of December a third draft of one hundred and fifty-four men with Colonels Meyrick and Holder and Lieutenant Lambton arrived. This was nicknamed the 'Sealskin Draft' as the men wore sealskin caps and gloves, but though they were better equipped than their predecessors they merely served to fill the hospitals. In January bad weather set in and the temperature being frequently below 20, frostbite was added to the miseries of the men. An eyewitness thus describes their appearance at this time;-

Their appearance was as wretched as their clothes were bad. Their clothes were ragged and worn out and were of necessity very dirty. Their bodies were infested with vermin. It was rarely possible for men to wash their bodies and never their clothes, as they had no other articles than those actually in wear.'

If such was the state of our men during this miserable winter that of the Russians outside the fortress was even worse. The roads in the Crimea became almost impassable and Menschikoff's men were reduced to the verge of starvation and died like flies. Inside the fortress the state of affairs was different. There good shelter was to be had in plenty, and Todleben used the respite which the weather gave him to make the works really formidable, so that the besiegers by the spring of 1855 were in a worse position than they had been in the previous November. If the British army had been steadily dwindling the French army had been as steadily increasing and, with a shorter and better line of communication and an organization at home capable of dealing with the realities of war, it suffered comparatively little during the winter. At the end of January Canrobert took over the right sector of the British front, which included the ground occupied by the Guards, who at the end of February were moved down into huts on the north side of the harbour of Balaklava.

Update

Lord Rokeby had arrived in January 1855, to take over the Guards Brigade. It was also at about this time that Sir Colin Campbell was given command of the reinforced Highland Brigade which added troops had manifested into Divisional strength. Lord Rokeby was left with the depleted Guards Brigade. The Guards Brigade and part of the Highland Division were then made available as a protective screen for Balaclava, and also as a reserve for the investment of Sevastopol. But Sir Colin Campbell was the officer in command.

Reg Hist

The worst was now over. The letters of 'Billy' Russell, afterwards Sir W. Russell the correspondent of *The Times,* describing the state of the troops during the winter aroused great indignation at home. Supplies and stores of all kinds arrived.

Florence Nightingale reached Scutari to reorganize the hospitals, and as spring began a road was made from Balaklava and early in April a railway was working from the harbour.

Update

In one sentence to be read directly from the last entry the historian and regimental author F Maurice quickly dispenses with two of the most important improvements made in the conducting of the investment of Sevastopol, with the arrival at Scutari of Florence Nightingale on November 4th having arrived on the eve of the Battle of Inkerman. Florence was aged 34 years, and with 38 nurses in tow, it could have well been 39 nurses but Mary Seacole had been refused, (well she was black, and thereby hangs another tale from Sevastopol!?) and then there was the construction of the Balaclava Railway?

In this present age we are now aware that without that railway the concluding of the siege and the eventual withdrawal of the Russians from South Sevastopol may never have happened, and the war would have dragged on and on.

William Howard Russell was to be the first of many journalists who have served alongside British Forces since that war. However the compromise between the two conflicting self interests of military and political security and keeping the public in touch with events, is still a finely stepped line, and may only be worked at from positions of compromise, truth, and plain good old fashioned commonsense. A professional and cordial relationship between those on all sides agreeing on a very piecemeal basis, but therein surely lies the rub, for this process of perfect communication between the various sides of self interests is slow, and so eats into both media and military programme expectations and immediate service deliveries.

It has however also now been registered that by keeping the public in the dark only leads to later recrimination, and normally stems from a conflict of interests anyway, showing just how important clear cut communication and agreement must be reached at all times by all concerned and as quickly as humanly possible. Hence another sideline reason for this amended version of the Scots Guards history covering the Crimea War, for it matters not how long a record may be before it is changed, the fact that it has been changed is important in itself, and for those it reaches out to.

Reg Hist

The health of the men steadily improved and the sick began to return from hospital. On May 2 the fourth draft of four officers and three hundred and nine men arrived, and the state of May 19 shows thirty officers, thirty-four sergeants, sixteen drummers, and six hundred and twenty rank and file present and fit for duty. On June 16 the brigade returned to the lines before Sebastopol and took up a position on the Woronzoff Road, near the centre of the Allied attack.

A great change had now taken place in the nature of the siege during the stay of the Guards at Balaklava. As we have seen, Todleben had been active during the winter. He had improved the two keyworks, the Malakoff and the Redan. He had pushed out in front of the Malakoff and seized and fortified a conical hill called the Mamelon and had constructed a whole serious of rifle-pits in front of the main works, in which the Russian snipers were busy. Mining and counter-mining became a regular feature of the siege. On March 22 the Russians had made a sortie and had broken into the French lines opposite the Malakoff and the British line opposite the Redan, and did a good deal of damage before they were repulsed. On the other hand, the number and power of the British and French guns had been much increased and the supply of ammunition was now adequate.

Update
Building the Balaclava Railway

The railway that ran on time, just in time!

Without any doubt the building of the Crimea Railway in early 1855 saved the British forces in front of Sevastopol and on the Balaclava Plain from further deprivation and starvation, and so the army were able to continue the investment of Sevastopol on a much improved basis.

The 39 mile long railway was built and running to all parts of the front in the incredible time of 60 days from the first order being given in Britain!

At the end of the war it was sold to Turkey, lock, stock and steam engines.

This group of specialist managers and men who thought they could help were Thomas Brassey, Morton Peto MP. and his brother in law Edward Betts who were trading as Peto, Brassey and Betts of Canada Works, plus being confident in the faith and experience that they had invested in their workforce.

On the 30th November, 1854 Morton Peto told the Government that Peto, Brassey and Betts would overcome the supply problem by building a thirty-nine mile long railway from Balaclava to all parts of the front and to cut delay to the minimum They would do this at no profit, would provide men and materials and would run the line when it was finished. News had reached the Government a little earlier that the plight of the Army was desperate. On the

14th November there had been a dreadful blizzard, the troops before Sevastopol only had thin clothing, no tents and no fuel. The icy winds had blown the blankets off the wounded and many froze to death. There was little food for the men or fodder for the horses and soon there were 8000 men in hospital and the replacements from England often died before they reached the front.

Although many doubted if it would be possible to build a railway quickly enough to save the situation in the depth of a Russian winter, the Government were absolutely desperate and they gratefully accepted the offer. Thomas Brassey then set his superb organisation to work, and demonstrated the difference between the criminal incompetence of the Government employees and those of the Birkenhead firm.

On the 30th November, 1854 when Brassey's offer was made the rails and sleepers did not exist, but as soon as Brassey gave the order his men spent the first day drawing up a list of the materials they would need and where they could be produced. To save time they chartered, or brought, vessels near to the location of the materials they were to carry. For example some of the rails were to be produced at Walker-On-Tyne so they brought the screw steamer *'Hesperus'* which was just being completed by Messrs Mitchell in the next yard on the Tyne, and the rails were loaded warm from the furnaces into the hold of the *'Hesperus'*

In three days Peto, Brassey and Betts had brought, or chartered, a fleet of ships, all on verbal order and without any security. All the ship owners and shipyards worked night and day to convert their ships to their new use, and cabins and bunks for Brassey's engineers and navvies were built in a few days.

The first ship brought by Canada Works was the clipper *Wildfire*. She was brought from Tonge, Curry & Co. of Liverpool for 4500sterling and was sailed over to the great Great float, Birkenhead, for conversion and loading. Needless to say she was the first vessel ready to sail, but she was closely followed by others and the Fleet comprised;

WILDFIRE	CLIPPER SAILING SHIP	457 Tons
MOHAWK	CLIPPER SAILING SHIP	800 Tons
LADY ALICE LAMBERTON	CLIPPER SAILING SHIP	511 Tons 90-HP
GREAT NORTHERN	CLIPPER SAILING SHIP	578 Tons 90-HP
EARL OF DURHAM	SCREW STEAMER	554 Tons 90-HP
BARON VON HUMBOLDT	SCREW STEAMER	420 Tons 60-HP
HESPERUS	SCREW STEAMER	800 Tons 150-HP
PRINCE OF WALES	SCREW STEAMER	627 Tons 120-HP
LEVANT	SCREW STEAMER	678 Tons 140-HP

The *'Prince of Wales'* was the same vessel that had suffered the fortuitous accident at Millwall that had given Robert Stevenson the idea of the tubular bridges at Conway and Menai. In three days verbal orders were placed for vast quantities of material and where there was not sufficient time to make the large items of plant or rolling stock they were found and bought. For example, the steam machinery was at work on the Victoria Docks, London which Brassey had built, and as it was needed for the Crimea it was quickly purchased.

The loading of the ships was so organised and the material so distributed that if one vessel was delayed, or lost, then it would not endanger the whole operation. An initial labour force of 500 navvies and engineers was also smartly arranged, many of whom had worked on the Victoria

Bridge and Grand Trunk Railway in Canada and were used to working in extremely low temperatures.

On Wednesday 13th December, only four days after the order was given, the first party of 54 navvies left Euston Station, London, bound for Bikenhead, to embark on the '*Wildfire*' and by Friday 15th December she was ready to sail loaded with equipment built by Canada Works. She was unable to sail however because fierce gales that raged in the Mersey for the next six days.

Thomas Brassey's navvies were the elite, they were paid 2pound-10shillings a week, plus clothing, food and tobacco, which was a very high wage indeed for the day. Before they sailed they all signed allotment papers signing over a weekly sum to be paid to their families and this averaged 1pound a man.

Unlike the Government, Harrison, Heap and Alexander saw to it that Brassey's men were properly clothed, housed and fed and each man was issued with 26 items of clothing, many of which were duplicated so that a change of clothes was readily available when required. His personal bag was to contain his kit plus three days rations, and to facilitate storage no boxes-nor lumber, were allowed. For those working in water there were one hundred pair of hip boots available.

To house the men, they provided ten portable, weatherproof huts, which were made such that they would not easily catch fire and each hut had a stove for heating together with vast quantities of coal, coke and firewood. Each hut was large enough to accommodate forty men and after they saw how successful the huts were, the Government later provided a number for the Army.

There was a plentiful supply of food and one of the new field kitchens was provided for every ten men, these were portable, but were very efficient and could boil, bake or fry, in the open air.

On Thursday 19th December, 'Wildfire' moored by Canada Works and still held up by the weather remained in port. So George Harrison, William Heap and Andrew Alexander gave a dinner at Gougth's Hotel, Woodside Ferry to take leave of one of their colleagues, Mr Shaw who was to be in charge of the first party.

The men who had traveled up from London were accommodated in various inns in Birkenhead and one of them wrote to the editor of the 'Liverpool Mercury' just before he sailed in 'Wildfire'

"You would greatly oblige the thirty miners engaged by Messrs Brassey, Peto and Betts to proceed to the Crimea, and now staying at the Sun Inn, Birkenhead in making known the excellent treatment we have received under the management of our worthy Landlord, Mr Pear, The Sun Inn, Bridge Street, Birkenhead. We have likewise to return our most hearty thanks to our employers and all our supporters for the most gentlemanly manner in which we have been treated, not forgetting Mr Harkdus

I remain your humble servant"

Evelin Flinn

Miner

Birkenhead 20th December 1854"

'On Thursday 21st, four days before Christmas, the winds dropped enough for embarkation to start. Mr Shaw, Mr George Arkle, a relative of William Heap's future partner T. W. Arkle, and a party of miners and navvies left the Sun Inn and walked down Bridge Street to the docks. The pavements were crowded and every window had a crowd of spectators all cheering Brassey's men on their way.

So at 11am on Thursday 21st December, only only twelve days after the order had been given, the first of the fleet, the Clipper '*Wildfire*', Captain Downward in command, set sail and by the 30th December, the other ships had left, or were about to leave Birkenhead, Liverpool, Hull, Sunderland and London loaded with;

50 Horses
1,800 tons of rails and fastenings
6000 sleepers
600 loads of timber for bridges etc
3000 tons of machinery
Fixed engines
Cranes
Pile Drivers
Trucks
Wagons
Barrows
Blocks
Chainfalls
Wire rope
Picks
Bars
Capstans
Crabs
Plant and Tools
Sawing machines
Forges
Carpenters tools
100 railway tarpaulins
A number of Dean and Adam's revolvers

Each ship carried a surgeon and a clerk to attend to the victualling and care for the stores.

The labour force comprised;
One chief engineer
500 navvies-eventually raised to 900
3 Assistant engineers
1 Chief Agent
3 Assistants
I Accountant and clerk
Foreman and bookkeepers
30 Miners
1 Chief Surgeon
4 Assistant Surgeons
4 Nurses from London's leading hospital
Medical stocks and stores
Borehole sinkers
2 Railway missionaries
A selection of books

On arrival one ship was to become a hospital and stores ship and the others to be used as expedient.

This outstanding event was not reported in the Liverpool papers but *"The Illustrated London News"* wrote on 30th December 1854;

'The immense resources of Peto, Brassey and Betts have enabled them with very little exertion to collect, organise and ship off in an almost incredibly short space of time this important expedition for which the order was only given on 9th December'.

At that time the rails were not rolled, the sleepers were uncut and the steam machinery was performing its daily function at the Victoria Docks and several of the ships were not finished

The revolvers that were taken raised some doubts because it was felt that they might endanger Brassey's navvies and again the *"Illustrated London News"* wrote;

Building the Balaclava Railway

"It has been stated that the Crimean navvies are to be armed-this is a mistake-they are too valuable and expensive to be put in the way of shot if it can be avoided".

A few arms have been sent for special cases and a few of the candidates enquired if they might have a shot at the Russians"

The ships made calls at Gibraltar and Malta and the navvies went ashore, becoming fighting drunk and then showing the locals what they were going to do with the Russians.

Eventually the fleet arrived off Balaclava early in February 1855 and their first task was to erect their huts to protect them from the icy, howling blizzards. This was done and in no time, and they then had at their disposal heated, weatherproof accommodation. Compare this with the thin tents the poor soldiers had to live in at Balaclava.

The men named the huts "Peto Terrace", "Preston Hall", "Napoleon", "Victoria", "Blackwall", "Suffolk", and "Lancashire".

The man in charge of building the line was Mr Beattie, a colleague of William Heap who had worked on the 'Grand Trunk', He split the labour force into two, half working by day leveling the ground, laying the sleepers and lines, and the other half worked by night, banking up and filling in between the sleepers with stones and earth. Within the first two weeks of landing they had built their encampment, several bridges and seven miles of line!

As an example of their speed of working one correspondent of the *'Illustrated Evening News'* noted that the line had to cross a small, but very marshy stream that ran into the harbour. A pile driver was landed one evening and carried piecemeal to where it was to sink piles for the bridge. The machine was erected early next morning and all the piles were driven, the machine removed, a stout wooden bridge was constructed and the rails were laid across the bridge and one hundred yards before evening! The same publication carried a story of a 'wild dog hunt' that the Army organised near the front line in a similiar fashion to a fox hunt. Facing them were the Cossacks and when they saw all the activity in the British lines they became very agitated assuming reasonably enough, that the British were about to attack. After a while however it dawned on their incredulous Cossack minds, what was going on, and they watched with with bewildered fascination the progress of the hunt.

A little while after the British noticed two riders from the Cossack lines galloping towards them, so they detained them and found they were two deserters who had tired of fighting. The British Officers found out that the two horses did not belong to the deserters so they took them back towards the Russian lines and pointing them towards the Cossacks, gave them a smack on their rump and sent them back. Gentlemen did not steal horses.

We do not know what Brassey's navvies thought of the soldiers but a Captain Henry Gifford, later Major General Sir Henry Clifford, commented that the navvies looked "Unutterable things, but did more work in a day than a Regiment did in a week". Not surprising since Beattie had not included 'wild dog' hunting in the programme.

In just over six weeks the railway was built and by the 7th April 1855 there were seventeen engines busy pulling the desperately needed supplies to the front, but from the very start of building the railway it was in use shortening the lines of supply that enabled the Army to survive that terrible winter. By the end of March they had carried over 1,000 tons of shot and shell, 3,600tons of clothing, blankets, medical supplies and other goods.

In September 1855 Sevastopol fell and the great Russian Navy base was destroyed by the victorious British Army still being supplied by the men of Peto, Brasssey and Betts running the Crimean Railway.

Beattie, the engineer, had hardly any sleep for the three weeks before the convoy arrived, because he had to survey the route and do the prior planning and he worked continuously throughout the building of the railway. When it was finished he was completely exhausted and worn out and although he was sent back to England he died shortly after his return. He gave his own life but he saved the lives of thousands of his fellow countrymen.

A correspondent wrote that the railway was expected to be finished by the end of April but was completed by mid-March and commented,

"The skill of the men entrusted with the building of the railway appears to have overcome all obstacles in a manner which few could have anticipated, even though accustomed to the celerity of workmanship in England and which to our soldiers in the Crimea, worn out by the failure of so many fine schemes appeared an idle dream. It has once more proved that the men who have made England great by their skill and enterprise and powers of organisation, are of a far different calibre from the officials whom Government employs. While months have been spent in getting warm clothing and the barest necessities for hospital practice a few weeks only has been required for the conception and execution of a novel and most difficult enterprise".

Such was the power and skills of the Birkenhead firm of Peto, Brassey and Betts. Thomas Brassey and his men become National heroes and received acclaim in the press and the Government heaped praise on them in the House of Commons, but like so many others who did good work for the well being of those most in need they have now been forgotten, even in Birkenhead'

With special thanks to Bridget Geoghegan for the above.

It has always surprised me that the only option available for the story of the Crimea Railway to become public knowledge was for the Company to publish it themselves, whilst the many writers of the books published on the Crimea War have been printed for financial profit whilst just researching one from another, and so the railway vanishes from the pages of the Crimea war as an also ran, rather than main line?

Reg Hist

The Spring Offensive

Hope springs eternal for the British soldier

On April 8 they began a great bombardment which lasted ten days and did much damage, but the moral effect of this disappeared when no assault followed. Outside the fortress the Russian field army had been inactive. The strength of the covering works did not now invite and attempt to repeat Inkerman, and, besides the increase in the French army, the Turkish contingent had grown considerable, while in April Sardinia had joined the Allies, and on May 8, 15,000 Sardinian troops under General de la Marmora had begun to disembark at Balaklava. Ere this had happened the Russians had withdrawn from the position they had gained in the battle of Balaklava to the north of the Tchernaya, which gave us again control of the Woronzoff Road.

In the middle of May, Canrobert, partly because of differences of opinion with the Emperor, who following a family tradition was endeavouring to conduct the campaign from Paris, and partly because of his dislike of siege operations and of his want of confidence in himself in their conduct, resigned the command and was succeeded by Pelissier. The new French Commander-in-Chief sent off an expedition to Kertch on the Sea of Azoff, which served as a base for the Russian field army.

The place and all that it contained was destroyed and in the third week of May, Canrobert, who had taken over command of the covering force, crossed the Tchernaya and destroyed the Russian camp at Tchorgoun, while the

The Spring Offensive

Sardinians took up a position on the right towards Baidar and the Turks occupied the hills north-east of Balaklava. Such was the general situation in the first week of June 6 the Allies began another bombardment which lasted thirty-six hours, and at 6.30 p.m. the French assaulted the Mamelon and its adjacent works and storming parties of the 2nd and Light Divisions attacked the quarries; both attacks were successful. Encouraged by this success, Pelissier determined to attack the Malakoff and the Redan, but the preparations were made somewhat light-heartedly and on June 18 the French attack on the Malakoff was beaten off, and though the British attack on the Raden was to be contingent on the success of the French, Lord Raglan proceeded with it and failed even more signally. The result of this was that the 1st Division, in which Highlanders and Guards were once more united, relieved the attacking divisions in the trenches and from June 19 to the end of the siege the Guards were constantly in the line. Depressed by the failure of June 18, Lord Raglan fell a victim to cholera and he died ten days later, to be succeeded by Sir James Simpson.

As a further result of this check the Allies decided to proceed by the slow process or methodical bombardment, sap and approach. This was continued throughout July and August and gradually worn down the defence, but at a price. During August, Lieut-Colonel F.Seymour, still in command, was severely wounded, and Captain Drummond, his Adjutant, was killed. Captains the Hon. W. Coke, F. Baring, and Farquharson and Lieutenant A. C. Campbell were wounded. During this period of the siege nineteen other ranks were killed and ninety-three wounded, while the state of September 1 shows two hundred and twenty-five sick. Captain Lindsay became Adjutant in the place of Drummond. Inside the fortress the losses of the Russians under the constant cannonade mounted at an alarming rate, and the relentless if slow advance of the work of the besiegers had an effect which was the more depressing as

Todleben, who had been the life and soul of the defenders, was severely wounded and left Sebastopol never to return. Early in August the Russian commanders at a council of war decided to make a last attempt to relieve the place, and in consequence they on August 15 attacked the Allied covering force on the line of the Tchernaya, which, as we have seen, consisted of Sardinian, Turkish and French troops under Canrobert. The Russians were beaten off with heavy loss and their defeat decided the fate of Sebastopol.

Update
The Final Battle of the Tchernaya, Retchka

With no more famous British cavalry charges

The conflict of the Tchernaya, Retchka (Black River August 16th 1855)) touched on above was possibly the most decisive battle of the complete campaign as fought outside Sevastopol. It was the last great effort by the Russians to breakthrough the Allied lines and push the Allies back to the sea. It was to fail dismally. Yet the general run of the British writers give it but a cursory mention when in effect it was to be reckoned amongst the most decisive of the Crimea set piece battles, and certainly the last battle in the field.

We might also note that the British forces were not to be invited to participate in the battle by the French, nor the Sardinians, excepting for some elements of the British Cavalry which were camped just two miles distant. However they were not required, nor called upon to perform any more of their famous charges by the French, nor the Sardinians.

Perhaps this battle will confirm beliefs that in reality it was the French who were in charge of the overall proceedings, and the British contingent were to be just hangers on, which in fact proved to be the actual state of affairs throughout the campaign?

Battle of the Black River, 16th August 1855

The Light Cavalry Brigade in the Crimea Extracts from the Letters and Journal of General Lord George Paget (John Murray, 1881).

We had received a special notice on the previous evening of a probable attack in the morning, and the last regiment was just forming on parade on the morning of August 16, when the action commenced by the outposts of the Sardinians being driven in, beyond the Tchernaya, about 3.30 a.m.; the real fight commencing about 5, and lasting till 8. The Cavalry Division advanced about 4 in close column (masses of brigades) across our plain and on to the Causeway heights. Here we halted for a short time and were then disposed as follows:

The Hussar Brigade was sent under General Parlby to our left, to remain in reserve, to somewhere near the spot where on the 25th October the Light Cavalry commenced its advance, and to watch the Inkermann flank, and we saw no more of them the rest of the morning. General Scarlett at the same time ordered me to advance with my brigade as a first line, and occupy the neck of the valley leading down to the ford of the Tchernaya, in the direction of Tchorgun. The Heavy Brigade were ordered to remain in support of us at the foot of the hill, on the higher ground of which stands the village of Kamara.

After I had been formed up a short time in my new position, an aide-de-camp came from General Scarlett (who had ridden to the high ground on our right which formed the position of the Sardinian army on this day), desiring that I would detach a regiment to support Major Barker's battery to the position, from which it performed such essential service to the Sardinians. I sent the Carabineers under. Colonel Jones on this duty.

Here we remained during the whole of the battle (with the exception of a short episode which I will narrate hereafter) in the valley which separated the two armies, the French to our left, the Sardinians to our right. We were under the full range of the enemy's guns on the heights in front of us, which, however, were so fully occupied with more important antagonists, that except a horse or two of some Sardinian cavalry close to us, we did not suffer at all from the enemy's fire. We could see all that was going on on our right with the Sardinians, but could see little or nothing to our left, towards the Tractir Bridge, where the thickest of the fight was raging, the Fedioukine hills interposing between us and that part of the theatre of the contest', but the heavy firing told us of the importance of the affair, of which, indeed, we had visible proofs in the knots of Russian prisoners, wending their way from time to time across the plain to Balaclava.

About 7 o'clock an aide-de-camp came from General Scarlett to inform me that an advance of the cavalry across the river was intended — a somewhat startling announcement, in truth, and one which, had it been carried out, would in every sense have completed the affair of October 25; for not only would the results have been as disastrous (as I will show later), but, oddly enough, we should have commenced this advance from the very point from whence we were driven back on that day. The instructions that I received were as follows:

The Chasseurs d'Afrique were formed up in two lines, in the plain to our left rear, some, 400 or 500 yards from us. They were to advance, and I was to support their movements. I was to give an opportunity to their second line to support their first line, and not to move myself in support of the first line till I was satisfied of no indications of their second line moving in support, but that if their second line showed such a disposition I was to give them " the pas," and then move in their support. The Heavy Brigade had at the same time got the order to advance to our support when they saw us move, but on no account to cross the river after us.

We waited in this disposition for perhaps twenty minutes or half an hour, when I saw the, little greys once again (as at Inkermann) break into open column and trot by us. Watching their second line till I had given them full opportunity to support if they so intended, but seeing no indications of their doing so, I moved off the 12th Lancers (which formed my first line) in open column; and if ever troops were doomed to certain destruction, here was a case in point; but the poor cavalry (who are always doomed to be the victims of mistakes) were saved this time. About three or four troops of the 12th Lancers had broken into open column and were advancing at a trot, when a French staff-officer galloped up to me, ventre à terre, and, holding up his hand begged that I would halt at once, as "On a changé d'intention," General Pelissier having ordered that the movement should be given up.

The Chasseurs in our front were at the same time halted and went threes about. We all then made a movement to the rear, and in half an hour the battle was over, won by the gallantry of our brave allies of both nations some time previously. I soon after crossed the ford and rode with General Scarlett and others as far as Tchorgun, which was by this time abandoned. The gallantry of the Sardinians was conspicuous, and no troops could have behaved better.

It put us in great spirits, for we had, of course, no means before of judging of their mettle, though their appearance had been everything in their favour and it was a pretty sight to see those picturesque Bersagliari scrambling up the opposite hills and driving the enemy before them. The Turks on their right did good service also, I believe, aided as both were by the murderous and well-directed fire of our heavy battery (Grey's).

The Final Battle of the Tchernaya, Retchka

A ride over the field of battle soon after it was over, as far as, and some 300 or 400 yards beyond — that is, to the left of — the Tractir Bridge enabled one to judge of what had been going on for the last three hours, to our left, with the French. And a scene of slaughter it was! The river, the aqueduct, and the little dry ditches that intersected the valley between them and the bills, were positively choked up with dead and dying Russians, and in the most extraordinary attitudes; and strewed all over the ground were little ready-made bridges (so-called), consisting of unpainted ladders about twelve to fifteen feet long.

The chief effort of the Russians had been made against the position of the Fedioukine height, at the foot of the centre of which stands the Tractir Bridge, the Zouaves as usual having borne the brunt of the fight. Their position was on the top of the chain of hills, with a gradual slope of about eighty yards of low brushwood down to a lower ridge, from which is a steep descent of some fifty yards down to the river. There are, of course, many variations of this along the line, but this is the general character of the position. To the top of this second or higher ridge did the enemy three times advance, without a shot being fired at them, but from it they were each time driven down with great slaughter, the French following them to the river at the point of the bayonet. The Russians had been driven on (as is always the tactics with them) by the masses behind them.

Had a chalked line been drawn, the extent of their advance to the brow of the hills could not have been more clearly defined than it was by the line of dead bodies lying on the ground. I am speaking more particularly of a spot where the thickest of the fight had raged, i.e. to our left of the Tractir Bridge. To make the repulse more complete, a French force had been sent down the road leading to the bridge to take them in flank. The victory was indeed a complete one, and the confusion of the retreating 30,000

The Final Battle of the Tchernaya, Retchka

Russians across the plain, I was told by an eye-witness, could only be conceived by those who saw it.

In the endeavour to explain the circumstances under which the allied cavalry would have had to make the contemplated advance, and in order to show the object — the only object which could have been sought for in such an advance — it will be necessary to give a general outline (in a brief sketch) of the positions of the different armies, and the general features of the battle. The attack of the enemy was somewhat as follows:

The Tractir Bridge may be called the centre of their line of attack. Their chief attack was by their right, which advanced across the plain obliquely from the Mackenzie heights and Inkermann heights (I believe), attacking the Fedioukine heights, occupied by the French. Their left attack was chiefly from a range of hills commanding the Tchernaya and extending towards Tchorgun, and against the Sardinians. The allied cavalry were posted in the valley separating the positions of the French and the Sardinians. Now, at the time when our advance was ordered there could have been no question of the enemy's fire against the Sardinians being so successful as to enable them to cross the river on that flank which was the enemy's left, and therefore our contemplated advance could have had no connection with such a success of the enemy.

Again, our advance could have had no connection with a repulse of the enemy's left, for their retreat would have been among hills inacessible to cavalry, while on their left, and on our right front and right, were two gorges (the one leading to Tchorgun, and the other to the right of the Turkish position), which led only into the mountains. We must seek then elsewhere for a solution of the object in contemplation.

The position of the French, as I have said, was opposed to the right attack of the enemy, from the plain. Now the only ground on which our cavalry could possibly act was on that plain. Therefore it is logical to assume that the intention was, that when the enemy's attack should have completely failed against the French, and that when they were being driven back across the plain, our cavalry should be brought up to pursue and harass them, and complete the victory. But it must be here added that a very large force of the enemy's cavalry — probably the whole of them (for it is difficult to conceive where else any of their cavalry could have been on this day) — were, during the battle, posted in the plain under the "Spur Battery" on the Mackenzie heights.

We must now turn for a moment to the position of the allied cavalry at the time, and the phases through which they must have passed before arriving on the plain. Overlooking and commanding the gorge of the valley (about half-a-mile in width) separating the heights, which formed the Sardinian position to our right and the French position on our left, and in which we were formed up, is a range of heights, which formed the left of the Russians on this day. They can hardly be called the left of the Russian position, inasmuch as their right (and indeed centre) was a plain across which they had to cross to attack; the bills commencing to rise from the plain, opposite the Tractir Bridge, and extending to their extreme left towards Tchorgun. Close under this chain of hills, that is, at some eighty yards from its base, runs the river Tchernaya.

Parallel to the river, and at some 300 yards distance from it, runs a watercourse, some twenty feet wide, known as the Aqueduct, which supplies Sebastopol with water. The position of the Light Brigade was some 300 or 400 yards again from this watercourse. Reversing the picture, we had thus some 300 or 400 yards to advance before arriving at the watercourse, after crossing which we had some 300 yards more before arriving at the river. The position in our front which I have endeavoured to describe was bristling with batteries and the slopes with sharpshooters; the force indeed that opposed the Sardinian army during the battle.

I have said that we were well within range of this position during the whole battle, but were of course left unmolested, while we remained where we were, the enemy having plenty to do with the Sardinians. The only passage across the Aqueduct was over a plank bridge some twelve or fifteen feet wide (directly in our front). The only passage across the Tchernaya was by means of a ford, considerably to the right front of the plank bridge which crossed the Aqueduct.

Had not then the order for our advance been countermanded, at the opportune moment when it was (two more minutes would have been too late), I hold that the following must have inevitably occurred, without the possibility of any other solution. The column of cavalry, consisting firstly of what had been the first line of the Chasseurs, secondly of my brigade, and thirdly of the Chasseurs in support (if they had come on), had but some 300 yards to advance before arriving at the Aqueduct. Arrived at this point, a column of sections of threes must have been formed (the plank bridge being not wide enough for more than three horses abreast). This column of sections must then have defiled over the plank bridge. [The question of whether there was one bridge only, or three or four, is simply one of whether the disaster of which Iam speaking is to be divided by three or four.]

Now, as I have before said, our original position was well within range of the enemy's position, and this plank bridge was some 300 yards nearer to it. Inasmuch as — had we remained in open column, while the troops in our front were defiling across the bridge — our column must have been pierced through and through by the enemy's guns, it would have been absolutely necessary to re-form our lines, before crossing the bridge in succession, and after defiling over the bridge, the column of troops must have been again formed, in view of our further advance.

Now it is logical to assume that although, as I have said, we remained unmolested by the enemy's fire while quiescent in our position, the moment that our movements were sufficiently developed to show them our intention of an advance, at that moment would have been concentrated upon us a great portion of their fire. It would therefore be curious to make a calculation of the time that would have been occupied in this movement.

Firstly, the advance in open column to the Aqueduct.

Secondly, the re-formation prior to crossing the plank bridge.

Thirdly, the crossing in sections of threes.

And fourthly, the re-formation prior to our renewed advance (as many of the enemy's guns as could be spared for us, concentrating their fire on us the whole time).

But our troubles would not have ended here — nay this was but the commencement of them. We should now have had before us the remainder of our advance across the plain to the Tchernaya; an oblique advance, as I have said, the ford being on our right front. Arrived on the banks of the river, and now within short range of the enemy's rifles, bristling on the slopes of the hills 200 yards in our front, such of us as remained must have again formed up, during, the, passage of the ford (a good number probably being immersed in the holes that I have described).

Arrived on the opposite bank, we must then have, continued our advance (now to our direct left) and swept along the flat ground which intervened between the base of the hills and the Tchernaya, the configuration of the ground being such that, while at the point from which we should have started from the ford the width of level ground would not probably have admitted more than the frontage of one or two squadrons, we could have gradually increased our front, in consequence of the base of the hills receding from the river until the plain is reached.

Having now, according to the theory which I have already sketched out, arrived with our cavalry on the plain, conjecture can go no further; as the nature of our after-movements must have depended on the position of the retreating masses of the enemy, though it must be borne in mind, as I have said, that a very large force of Russian cavalry, far superior in, numbers to ours, was formed up on the plain, and ready to act against us. The foregoing facts speak for themselves.

Had the result of the morning's conflict been a general advance of the French and Sardinian armies in pursuit of the retiring enemy (concerning the policy of which movement there were many opinions after the battle), the policy of our advance would doubtless have been a sound one; but as to the practicability of sending us alone on this errand, while the battle was raging, and before the enemy's fire from the opposite heights had been silenced, there could be but one opinion.

I carefully rode over the around often afterwards, and the more I saw of it, and the more I reflected on the subject, the more inconceivable was it to me that such an advance was ever contemplated, and but for the fact that no other possible solution of the movement existed than that at which I arrived, I should hesitate to believe in my own senses. I explained all this at the time to many English generals who, having heard of our intended advance being abandoned, questioned me on the subject, and all were equally convinced of the madness of such an advance. I believe the facts of the case to be somewhat as follows:

Firstly, that the position of General Scarlett on this day was not very clearly defined, with regard to the Sardinian and French armies, further than that he was to co-operate with the allies in the best manner that he could. Secondly, that on General de la Marinora would have rested the responsibility of the, advance, had it taken place. And thirdly, that it was unknown to General Pelissier, who first heard of it only when he arrived on the field of battle, some time after its commencement, and that the moment he heard of it he at once countermanded it, his exclamation on hearing of it having been "Ma foi, c'est un très jeune Général."

I have gone at greater length into this episode of the, battle of the Tchernaya than perhaps the occasion deserves, because as usual, after the battle, it was said that the cavalry were slow, and did not take advantage of an opening that presented itself.

Notes

(1) I have the following from Colonel Jones's own lips: In the middle of the engagement, a Sardinian staff-officer rode up to him, and desired him to descend into the plain, and advance against the Russians. He answered by inquiring whose order was this. The reply was, "General de la Marmora;" to which Colonel Jones replied, that he was sent to protect the battery by me, and he should stay with it till he received an order from me or General Scarlett to leave it.

(2) It is remarkable bow exactly the orders I received on this occasion corresponded with those I received at Inkermann — i.e. to move off on each occasion in support of the Chasseurs d'Afrique, when I saw them move to the front, the Chasseurs on each occasion being in position to our left rear, and having to pass us, before we were to move.

Happy was it for every one concerned that the similarity ended where it did!

(3) I visited their camp in the afternoon, and they told me that they had been taken completely by surprise, which is difficult to account for, as we in Balaclava had had intelligence the night before of a certain attack in the morning. However this may be, they certainly permitted the Russians to cross the river, and get up the hill before they opened fire on them, which however, as this was permitted twice again, was probably the result of design rather than of surprise.

(4) I was afterwards told that there had been constructed, immediately before the battle, two or three of these bridges. I can only say that, in riding over the ground afterwards, I could never find them, or any traces of them.

(5) This ford was very deep (up to a horse's belly), and was full of large holes, that would have immersed a horse and his rider, the navigation of which (if I may use such a term) is so intricate, that a mounted Dragoon was always in after-times placed sentry over it, to point out to equestrians the course they should take in crossing it.

(6) It must be borne in mind that it was the Chasseurs d'Afrique that had been ordered to lead the attack, and therefore that it was the advance of those troops that General Pelissier countermanded, my brigade being only a supporting one; and who ordered the advance of the herein lies some difficulty, as to Chasseurs, but I certainly always understood that, it was General de la Marmora.

Update

The summary of the British Cavalries part not to play in the battle ends at that point.

Which is probably just as well?

Reg Hist

The Final Hours

At Last!

On the Regiment's last day in the trenches, September 7, Captain D. F. Buckley was on duty on the advanced sap before the Redan. He was killed while visiting the sentries in front of our works. Two of the sentries, Privates Allen and Sankey, were wounded at the same time. Sergeant James Craig and Drummer Smith then volunteered to go out and bring in Captain Buckley, who was believed to be wounded. Buckley was found to be dead, but Craig and Smith brought in his body under a murderous fire, and for this act of gallantry each received the Victoria Cross.

Update

There is no mention of a Victoria Cross awarded to Drummer Smith for this act of valour, so again we must take it for granted that the Scots Guards RHQ have again re-written historical facts incorrectly. However, perhaps the mention below shows where the mistaken identity arises from?

Only the Scots Guards RHQ may confirm the fact one way or another?

SMITH, Philip. (reg No. 1166).
Corporal. 17th Regiment. *
London Gazetted on 24th February 1857.
VC Medal's Custodian is the Royal Leicestershire Regiment Museum, Leicester .

Born in 1825 at Lurgan, County Armagh, Ireland.
Died on 16th January 1906 at Harold's Cross, Dublin.
Memorial on grave * at Glasnevin Cemetery, Dublin, Ireland.
Digest of Citation reads:
On 18th June, 1855, in the Crimea, Corporal Smith repeatedly went out, after the column had retired from the assault, in front of the advanced trenches against the Great Redan, to bring in wounded comrades, all of the time under an extremely heavy fire from the enemy.
* Leicestershire Regiment.
* Headstone bears the name Scully.

If it was a mistake made by the information rendered to the author by RHQ then it was one of mammoth proportions, and actually gives an indication of the very casual approach given to the writing of this important journal by senior officers at RHQ, and who is to say that the casual approach to regimental history is not changed since those times?

Reg Hist

Sergeant McBeath was in charge of the section on this night and after assisting Craig in the search for Buckley's body he went off to look for Private Sankey, whom he found and brought in on his back. McBeath bore a charmed life, for at Inkerman he had fourteen bullet-holes in his clothes but was untouched, and on this occasion his jacket was shot through but he got back unscathed. As we have seen, he was awarded the medal for distinguished conduct in the field. Craig was given a commission in the 10th Foot, of which he later became Adjutant.

Update

Craig's later story of his life and death in Cape Province, South Africa holds yet another tale of mystery.

Reg Hist

On September 8th the Regiment was relieved in the trenches by the troops of the Light and 2nd Division and told off to attack the Redan. This attack failed, as did the French attacks on the Little Redan and the Central Bastion, but their assault on the Malakoff was successful and as this great Bastion commanded all the other in its vicinity the Russians decided that further resistance was hopeless. During the night the garrison crossed to the north side of the Tchernay by a floating bridge near the mouth of the river after blowing up most of the works and the more important buildings in the town.

The Russian field army remained in position north of the Tchernaya and Pelissier wisely decided to leave it to them to attack if they wished to recover Sebastopol. So for months there was a deadlock on the field while negotiations for peace dragged on. Happily the winter of' 1855-'56 was a very different experience from its predecessor. Our army was now amply provided and reasonably well sheltered. The Brigade remained on the upland and was employed in road-making, drills and musketry practice, while in October there was a race meeting. A marquee was converted into a Crimean Guards Club and provided with newspapers and magazines. Before the winter huts and barracks were erected and so the time passed not unpleasantly. On October 16, 1855, a general order was issued authorizing the Regiment to add the honours 'Alma', 'Inkerman' and 'Sebastopol' on its colours, and these were first added to the colours of the 1st Battalion on December 28.

On November 11 Sir James Simpson resigned his command and was succeeded by Sir William Codrington, and towards the end of the month the Duke of Cambridge was invalided home and his place in command of the 1st Division was taken by Lord Rokeby. A fifth draft of two hundred and twenty-four men joined the battalion on October 8 and the sixth and last draft of two hundred and twenty-four arrived on March 8, 1856. The state of March 15 shows forty-one officers, forty-nine sergeants, nineteen drummers, nine hundred and sixty-three other ranks doing duty, and a total including those on command, in staff employ and sick of 1,048.

Update

HRH Duke of Cambridge had deserted his command of the 1st Division in November 1854, Lord Rokeby came out to the scene of operations in January 1855, but only took over command of the Guards Brigade at this time. He was not to take command of the reformed 1st Division until 13th August 1855, in time to bring the command home.

Reg Hist

On April 2 1856, the news arrived that peace had been concluded on March 30. By its terms the Black Sea was neutralized, no warships were to enter its waters and no dockyards or naval bases were to be erected on its shores, and ships of war were prohibited from entering either the Bosphorus or the Dardanelles. These terms Russia repudiated in 1871 during the Franco-Russian War so that our efforts and sacrifices in the Crimea did not produce any lasting result.

Reg Hist. now continues with the final butchers bill.

The 1st Battalion left England on February 28, 1854, 29 officers and 935 other ranks strong; it received altogether 50 officers and 1,157 men while in the near

The Final Hours

East, making a total of 79 officers and 2,092 men It embarked for England on June 11 with 39 officers, 54 sergeants, 19 drummers, and 1,031 other ranks; so that its losses in killed and wounded and invalided during the campaign were approximately equal to the numbers with which it came home. Five officers were killed or died of wounds, 1 officer died of disease; 23 officers were wounded. Eighty-four other ranks were killed, 47 died of wounds, 315 were wounded and 536 died of disease.

The Battalion landed at Portsmouth on July 4 and went to Aldershot, not long established as a military camp. There the Crimean Guards Brigade met on July 9 and went by train to London for a review by queen Victoria in Hyde Park, where the four home Battalions were awaiting them. The Crimean Battalions marched from Nine Elms station under Lord Rokeby and on arriving at the Park found the home Battalions drawn up in line of quarter columns, with intervals left for them. The completed Regiments were then handed over to their Colonels and the Duke of Cambridge took command of the whole, and the seven Battalions marched past Her Majesty to the tune 'see the Conquering Hero comes'. After the parade the 1st Battalion went to Portmen Street and St. George's barracks and the 2nd Battalion to Aldershot. Soon after its arrival there it transferred two companies to the 1st Battalion.

During the war the establishment of the home Battalion had been increased to twelve companies for the better training of draft for the Crimea. Now the establishment of the two Battalions was equalized and each one had ten companies.

Update

The British War Medal was awarded to 58 officers 1,513 other ranks. of these 22 officers and 571 other ranks gained all four clasps for the campaign.

The medal was not awarded to those who were killed in action, died of disease or died of wounds

Update
The Warriors Final Parade

Victoria Cross & Crimea War Medal

The Crimea War was over. But there was one further Royal event still to take place. In January 1856 Queen Victoria personally approved the design and inscription for a new medal, to be given to all ranks of the Royal Navy and Army 'for Valour'. It was to be cast in bronze from metal taken most from Russian guns captured in the Crimea, with a dark blue ribbon for the Royal Navy and a dark red one for the Army

On 24th February 1857, the official *London Gazette* announced the award of the Victoria Cross for the first time to 58 soldiers, 24 sailors and 3 marines, all for acts of heroism during the Crimean War. The *Gazette's* announcements were repeated in *the Times* and other newspapers.

On 26 June, in Hyde Park, Queen Victoria herself presented the first Victoria Crosses to sixty two of these men.

The parade in Hyde Park showed a characteristically Victorian attitude towards class and status. The men stood together without regard for rank during the ceremony, and the open nature of the award was emphasized by the fact that brevet Major Sir Charles Russell (Bart) and private Anthony Palmer, both of the Grenadier Guards, received the cross for the same action in the Sandbag Battery on 5thh November 1854.

Command of the parade was given to Colonel the Honourable Henry Percy of the Grenadier Guards, who had also won his Victoria Cross in the Sandbag Battery, during the battle of Inkerman on 5th November. A further 26 Victoria Crosses were later awarded, all to soldiers, for deeds committed during the Crimean War, making 111 recipients in all.

Six Victoria Crosses were won at the Alma, no fewer than 19 at the Battle of Inkerman, 5 of them by members of the Naval Brigade, and the same number in the unsuccessful attacks on the Redan during June 1855.

For the second assault on the Redan on 8th September, twelve Crosses were awarded, including one to Lieutenant Colonel Frederick Maude of the 3rd Regiment of foot (The Buffs) Even Maudes heroism in the Redan, however, was outdone by that of Brevet Major Charles Lumley of the The Earl of Ulsters, 97th Regiment of Foot;

Perhaps the hardest won Victoria Cross of the War went to John Simpson Knox, he was a formidable and conspicuous figure, known to all members of the Army in the Crimea, including Lord Raglan by the end of the campaign.

He landed at Calamity Bay on 14th September 1854 as a Sergeant in the Scots Fusilier Guards, was promoted to Colour Sergeant four days later, and fought at the Alma where he played an important role in reforming his Regiments line during a crisis in the Battle.

In March 1855 he was commissioned into the Rifle Brigade, promoted to Lieutenant in April, and performed the second deed which won him his Victoria Cross on June 18th, when he volunteered to lead the ladder party in the first attack on the Redan. Knox continued to advance until his left arm was first broken by a Russian bullet and then nearly torn off by grapeshot.

At the award ceremony in Hyde Park he acted as Adjutant for the Parade, rising to the rank of Major before retiring from the Army in 1872.

The above article was taken from

The War Correspondents

Andrew Lambert & Stephen Badsey 1994

Update

Reference the number of Victoria Crosses awarded for the action at the Alma.

The initial awards of the Victoria Cross during the Crimea Campaign were on occasions, made for several actions, that of Lieut. Robert Lindsay, and Sergeant John Knox for example, where the Scots Guards now proudly add these two Victoria Crosses as having been won at the Alma?

But it seems that the main incident, or acts of courage maybe later graded by the historic recorders, or Regimental chroniclers using poetic licence, and so making their own choice as to where a Victoria Cross has been most deserved, or where it suits what they are recording, or the point they are making in rewriting their own version of that little bit of history to suit either themselves, or perhaps Regimental folk-lore?

An instance being, from the Scots (Fusilier) Guards and the Alma, where the citation for Lieut. Lindsay also makes mention of his actions at Inkerman, and Lieut. Knox commissioned into the Rifle Brigade and again mentioned for his actions at the Great Redan as part of his Victoria Cross citation.

The Crimean War Medal was sanctioned on the 15th December 1854 by order of QueenVictoria.

Two clasps were also authorised at this time, for the battles of Alma (20th September 1854) and Inkermann (5th November 1854). The clasp for the battle of Balaklava (which took place before that of Inkermann, on 25th October 1854) was not authorised until 23rd February 1855. The clasp for the fall of Sebastopol (9th September 1855) was granted on 13th October 1855. A clasp was also awarded to the Royal Navy and Royal Marines for actions in the Sea of Azoff (25th May - 22nd September 1855), being announced in the "London Gazette" of 2nd May 1856. The clasps are worn in date order, with the clasp for Alma being closest to the medal.

The medal itself is a 36mm disc of sterling silver, bearing the diademed head of Queen Victoria on the obverse, together with the legend "VICTORIA REGINA" and the date "1854"; the reverse shows a Roman legionary (carrying a gladius and circular shield) being crowned with a laurel wreath by a winged figure of Victory; to the left is the legend "CRIMEA," which is written vertically. The suspension is an ornate floriated swivelling suspender unique to the Crimea Medal; the clasps are also unique, being in the form of an oak leaf with an acorn at each extremity. The ribbon is 27mm wide, pale blue with yellow edges.

275,000 un-named Crimea medals were awarded (at the time, the largest distribution ever made) to all those in the British Army, Royal Navy and Royal Marines who took part in the campaign in the Crimean peninsula, or in related service afloat. Those who took part in the Baltic campaign or the actions in the Pacific were not entitled: the former received the Baltic Medal; the latter, nothing. Some civilians, most notably the reporter for "The Times," William

Howard Russell, also received the medal. Medals could be returned to the Mint for naming (in a style known as "officially impressed"), but many were crudely stamped with names by recipients who were presented with their medals in the Crimea ("Depot impressed"), or were privately engraved by jewellers in England.

(C) Copyright 1997 - Michael Hargreave Mawson
(C) Print copyright Clive Farmer 1996, prints are available from the author.

Update

Perhaps it is right that some of the final words of this book should belong to the Crimea War Research Society who are always there to give guidance on any questions relating to the Crimea War.

However they still have questions to answer around the issue of the neglect of the British Monument at Cathcart Hill, and the full episode of Mr Ken Horton, the CWRS representative for the 1998 renovations to the monument. Ken Horton was cruelly deported by the local Russian authorities, and the British Embassy and the CWRS stood by and did nothing, and the renovations at Cathcart Hill again remained unfinished?

Thus I conclude on a sad note, for during my long crusade in Sevastopol researching for this book I have met with much aggravation, hypocrisy, and many other failings from those of the British 'Great and Good' who still need to be stood up and counted for their final parade of an episode of British history that still leaves many questions unanswered.

However the tour companies, and the author's of the many British books written still make their financial profit whilst the British Monument at Cathcart Hill continues to crumble, and the waste disposal on the heights of Inkerman continues to grow.

'Laid to Waste at Inkerman' **is how I term the sacrilege**

The above mentioned in not so honourable dispatches also includes the ex-military Colonel (Retd) Patrick Mercer OBE MP also making money from the extra curricular tours he guides around the Crimea War sites whilst tuning a blind eye in the direction of the British Monument at Cathcart Hill.

Cathcart Hill Graphic From Sunday Post

Update

The British Scandal at Cathcart Hill

The official British Monument atop Cathcart Hill, now lying neglected and denied by the British government Establishment was raised to remember those British men and women who made the supreme sacrifice during the Invasion of the Crimea 1854-1856. The Monument was opened uncompleted, in September 1993, by the newly convened British Ambassador to Ukraine. Nor was it fully paid for by the British fund raisers.

Now in Autumn 2009, at the time of this publication, the British Foreign and Commonwealth Office are attempting to deny this history and instead acknowledge the 'Kuchma' reconciliation and 'anniversary' monument as the official British Monument. This is a new monument which was opened as one of four memorials and just part of the 150th commemorations in 2004. Therefore there is no way in which this 2004 monument maybe justified in being titled as the official British Monument.

This proposition is entirely false and one only has to examine the British Embassy Report on the state of the monument by Major Jonathan Dart of 2007 to understand this fact. So what now happens to the official monument at Cathcart Hill?

The monument has been for sale by the incumbent deputy Mayor of Sevastopol, V Kasaren, for some years now. He has also stated that the monument is in 'private' hands thus ensuring that the British officials may never again gain admittance to carry out any of the options stated in the Major J Dart report.

This ploy of the Sevastopol local authority, which in itself is false, is but another act of acrimony between Sevastopol and the British authorities to so continue the dilemma of the British Monument that has now waged between the two governments of Britain and Sevastopol for the many years since the monuments erection.

My personal campaign will continue however, for I now live in Sevastopol and this is my retirement home. I therefore have no other option than to bear a part of the burden and responsibility for this neglected and denied monument by the United Kingdom government, for I am also a British citizen, and an ex-Scots Guardsman, personal legacies I take seriously.

But for the genuine, sincere and historical final word, that comes from Mary Seacole as she says goodbye to those left behind at the English cemetery on Cathcart Hill

"We were amongst the last to leave the Crimea. Before going I borrowed a horse, easy enough now, and rode up the old well worn road-now unfamiliar in its loneliness and quiet- to Cathcart's Hill. I wished once more to impress the

scene upon my mind. It was a beautifully clear evening and we could see miles away across the darkening sea.

I spent some time with my companions, pointing out to each other the sites of scenes we all remembered so well.

There were the trenches, already becoming indistinguishable, out of which on the 8th of September we had seen the storming parties tumble in confused and scattered bodies, before they ran up the broken height of the Redan.

There the Malakhoff into which we had seen the luckier French pour in one unbroken seam.

Below lay the crumbling City and the quiet Harbour, with scarce a ripple on its surface, while around stretched away the deserted huts for miles.

It was something like regret that we said to one another that the play was fairly over, that peace had brought the curtain down and that we, humble actors in some of its most stirring scenes must seek engagement elsewhere.

I lingered behind and stooping down, once more gathered little tufts of grass and some simple blossoms from above the graves of some who had been very kind to me. I left behind, in exchange, a few tears which were sincere. A few days later, I stood on board a crowded steamer, taking my last look of the shores of the Crimea"

Mary Seacole 1856

Conclusions, Considerations. and Consequences
to answer the question;
Did the British army win the Crimea War, or did the British government lose it?
Or perhaps some of each?

I will list the final conclusions, considerations and consequences by asking three not so easy questions, and then my final offering of a colonial parable to produce a comparison of another system of government which has simply evolved from the British model.

The three questions are direct from historical hindsight, and all very much part of the Crimea War fought around Sevastopol from September 1854 to September 1855.

A period covering slightly less than one year, in which the casualty rate for the British Army was to be more than 50%.

From this casualty rate we may also take the loose and general statistic of the British forces 23000 casualties sustained during the conflict, 20,000 of these were from disease, and 3000 from battle wounds. You will note from these figures that the original British forces had been replaced by an equal number of reinforcements during the period of the year long siege. Dreadful casualty figures indeed!

So consider the three questions I am about to ask, remembering that these very high casualty rates were sustained even with the use of the three resources which I now question; It might also be worth remembering that it was the French effort at the Malakov that was to finally unlock the gates to South Sevastopol, whilst yet again, and for the 2nd time, the British were to fail at the Great Redan defences.

The 3 questions;

1) If the Duke of Wellington had lived on for another year or two, and remained as Commander in Chief of the British Army, it could be well argued that the Minie Rifle would not have been issued to the British Army in time for its use during the Crimea War. Consider the consequences?

2) If Florence Nightingale had not argued her way to the hospital at Scutari and been supported by her own resources to enable her to do the job of nursing required, how many more British soldiers would have lost their lives as the campaign continued, and would the British army have collapsed in the Crimea as a result?

3) It was fortunate indeed that the Birkenhead railway building company had been available to volunteer its services to the British government at cost price. Otherwise how could the British have improved its poor record of communication and supplies of men and materials from the investment of Sevastopol, and return to the Balaclava Plain and port?

Final comment

My personal answer to the question of who won the Crimea War does not include the British in the final line up. When the British army returned to Britain it was still a military organization that was in working order, which was probably the best the British government could have hoped for.

In fact the real losers were to be once again the British people who suffer in silence as one war just leads to another, and the Cause and Effect syndrome of British 3 estate governance continues on moving from one crisis to the next.

But now it is 1856. I insert the date just in case the reader becomes confused as the present day fighting caused by the 1947 separation and partition of religious beliefs which became part of the independence agreement of the break up of India. But which again is the reason for the present strife in Pakistan, and may well be confused with the Indian mutiny of 1856, caused again by the British by their arrogance of forgetting other peoples' religious sensitivities. Anyway it was 1856, so now off to India for the British army, in time for the next crisis saga of Empire, which the British themselves had managed to manufacture,

Neither should it be forgotten that this is the British armies fourth military adventure into Afghanistan during the last 200 years. A campaign that was to display yet another painting from Lady Eliabeth Butler, as we see Dr. Bryden the last survivor from the British retreat from Karbul as he entered into Jalalabad, in 1842.

For God's sake when will the British government ever learn what history is shouting at them?

A Personal Final Word, and then a conclusive Parable

My 70th year of a good life, but punctuated and badly marred in parts by a British Government that has never really learned how to govern the British people. But has learned how to interfere with other countries and their peoples by putting into place the established historical order of certain self interests all exported from Britain.

And now my long term conclusion for a new model British State, with another form of Government.

I now share this final parable as my personal favourite all time fact of history, and the easy lessons it seeks to tell us, and which the Motherland of Britain could learn from.

The story of the British Evolution of Australia.

Once upon a time, and not so long ago in human evolutionary terms, the vast open plains of Australia coupled with a coast line of very lengthy proportions become prison settlements, and then home, to countless numbers of English criminals all working together in the Penal settlements.

From that point on the political, social, economic environment of Australia developed, with the added fact that Australia was to evolve and prosper from its penal settlements, not from the presence of British Monarchy, nor Nobility, neither the Lords or Westminster Parliament, nor elitist systems and long term processes of honours and awards but from just several generations of Cockney convicts?

A resident governor general however was imposed from London to do the job of the British State in Australia?

Which just goes to prove what normal everyday folk are capable of when left to their own social needs, plus given time and space with a self produced social environment where everybody is encouraged by a natural urge to all subscribe to the same needs;

Education
Employement
Health Care
Housing

If these four essential elements are put into place within a democratic, governmental process supported with a fair tax system, and with a written constitution to support these factors, then the quality and well being of life is assured, and for the long term as the self fulfilling prophesy takes root. And without any monarchs, lords, special honours and awards patronization ethics, and all the other diversifications of false government, then people will all 'live happy ever after, with, and for each other'.

The result being that Australia is now one of the countries in the World to live and settle with some self initiated comfort and security into the foreseeable future.

But first let us return to where it all began

The newly 'discovered' land of Australia was to become another fast growing British Empire colony requiring workers, and where better to find this working population than from the British prisons?

So now off to Australia where the British could exploit the newly discovered resources, and at the same time colonise the developing and expanding country for its own long term benefits. The indigenous native population, the Aborigines, becoming expendable, or for use as a labour force if and when the need arose.

Another little ploy used by the British Judiciary at the time was to sentence a convict to death, and after a few days awaiting their fate being given the option of a sentence to be served in the penal 'settlement' in Botany Bay, (normally of 7 years) which the prisoner would always accept. Thus the 'System' would change the mindset of the prisoner from a very negative one of waiting for the gallows to appear, or for the option of a very positive relationship between the individual and the State leading to one of endeavour in the future, and anyway Australia could be no worst than the London slums, and certainly more of a future than the hangman's noose??

The first transportation of convicts to Australia reached its destination in January 1788. The first 11 ships carried 759 convicts (male and female), 13 children of convicts, 211 marines and officers, 46 wives and children of the marines, and the governor and his staff. They disembarked at Botany Bay on January 18, but relocated and settled at Sydney Cove (now Sydney) eight days later. Transportation to Australia continued for another 65 years, with over 150,000 convicts exiled to various convict settlements in eastern Australia.

Australia was usually portrayed as a remote and unattractive land for European settlement, but for Great Britain it had strategic and, after the loss of the American colonies (1783), socio-economic value. Control of the continent would provide a base for British naval and merchant power in the eastern seas, supporting Great Britain's growing commercial interests in the Pacific and east Asia.

It also offered a solution to the problem of overcrowded domestic prisons. Food shortages, a harsh penal code, and the social upheaval caused by rapid industrialization and

Conclusions, Considerations, and Consequences

urbanization had led to a sharp rise in crime and the prison population.

Great Britain's defeat in the American War of Independence meant that it could no longer relieve the pressure on prisons by shipping convicts to America. In 1786 the British government announced its intention to establish a penal settlement at Botany Bay, on the south-eastern coast of New South Wales. Mindful of British economic interests and keen as always to save public expenditure, the government planned that Botany Bay would become a self-financing colony through the development of its economy by convict labour.

Captain Arthur Phillip of the Royal Navy was made commander of the expedition. He was to take possession of the whole of Australia, including Tasmania and islands off the east coast, east of the 135th meridian, and was given near absolute powers over the territory as governor.

Here endeth the parable of Australia and the lessons learned from a cornerstone of history during the Crimea campaign, and then the quick look at an optional style and form of government, from the people to the people.

I believe that this particular update should make certain things very clear reference the legacy of the ancient form of British Government onto the present generation of British people. A new model of government demonstrating that in these desperate present times radical reform is urgently required to meet the present democratic vision geared for the future which is to be made available to the British people.

We should therefore begin the fresh political dynamic with a written flexible constitution, then hopefully, the practical application which it will enable.

This positivism will support Britain to sustain its place in the new World order which is now emerging.

The Crimea War showed the British form of government as crisis management leading onto incompetence, and only of use as sustaining the defunct establishment status quo from those times to these, and this is what this update history has attempted to make clear.

The time for radical change in the government of Britain is now here!

Norry Hughes   Sevastopol   Summer 2009

Norry.hughes@gmail.com